handbook
for
business
writers

handbook for business writers

DORIS H. WHALEN
College of Marin

HARCOURT BRACE JOVANOVICH, INC.
NEW YORK   SAN DIEGO   CHICAGO   SAN FRANCISCO   ATLANTA

© 1978 by Harcourt Brace Jovanovich, Inc.

All rights reserved. No part of this publication may be reproduced or transmitted in any form or by any means, electronic or mechanical, including photocopy, recording, or any information storage and retrieval system, without permission in writing from the publisher.

ISBN: 0-15-530800-9

Library of Congress Catalog Card Number: 77-93581

Printed in the United States of America

preface

Almost everyone today is a business writer. This is so because—aside from purely social correspondence—any written communication is a form of business writing. Even if you never spend a day of your life working in an office, over the years you will write and receive a wide variety of business communications. Because business writers are made and not born, no special talent is required, but you do need training and practice. This handbook has been designed to give you the training and practice needed for proficiency as a skillful business writer.

All writing should follow the same rules of grammar, spelling, and syntax; and all writing should be readable and understandable. But *business* writing is different—not in quality but in organization. Business writing is relevant and concise; it gets to the point quickly without developing a theme, building to a climax, or contriving a surprise ending. It is factual rather than fanciful, precise rather than random, explicit rather than subtle. Business writing must be devoid of purposeless expressions of ego or emotion; and it has no place for the circumspect reasoning, hidden meaning, or random conjecture of the story-teller. Terms and terminology must be easily understood; information should be accurate, logically organized, and objectively stated. All of these attributes serve the principal purpose of the business writer: to get the reader to react or respond in a specific, concrete way.

Handbook for Business Writers has been designed as a dual-purpose book. On the one hand, it is intended to serve as a textbook and training manual for the student or beginning writer—especially when used in conjunction with the self-checking exercises provided; on the other, it will admirably serve the experienced business writer, both as a ready reference manual of acceptable language skills and business writing form, and as a means of updating previous training. The text avoids any reference to subjective theories of information and usage choices; instead, it presents in concise and accessible form the factual rules and do-it-this-way information needed to develop or improve your skill as a business writer.

Because this is a handbook, ease in finding and using information has been a major concern in the organization of the material. The numbered Table of Contents and comprehensive Index have been organized to help the user locate specific subjects, terms, and items quickly. The numbered marginal sideheads that pinpoint the text are designed to speed the process of locating topics. Throughout the book, many cross-references clarify related topics. The text is replete with examples of both acceptable and unacceptable usage (labeled, respectively, "Use" and "Avoid"), as well as sample forms that illustrate a variety of business writing applications. Rules are stated clearly and concisely so that application becomes a matter of mechanics and not decision-making.

The thirty self-checking exercises at the back of the book review the points of business style, grammar, and word usage discussed in the text. These exercises will be particularly effective in courses where this manual is used as a textbook, but they will also be of value as a means of self-testing and review to the student working independently and to the experienced business writer.

I cannot possibly single out for thanks all those who contributed in so many important ways to the publication of this handbook. I am especially grateful to my students and colleagues at the College of Marin for their encouraging comments and helpful suggestions; to the research librarians who diligently searched stacks and verified references; to the staff members at Harcourt Brace Jovanovich, many of whom became good friends as they created a handsome book from a pile of manuscript; and most of all to my husband, for his remarkable forbearance and unflagging patience.

DORIS H. WHALEN

reference guide

the business letter — 1

good business writing — 2

language choice — 3

beginning and organizing the business letter — 4

business letters for specific purposes — 5

employment writing — 6

business report writing — 7

personal business writing — 8

punctuation — 9

style — 10

appendix

glossary

exercises

key to exercises

index

contents

Preface   v

1 the business letter   1

Section 1   Parts of the Business Letter   3

1•A	Date	3		1•I	Signature	6
1•B	Mailing Notation	3		1•J	Notations after Signature	7
1•C	Inside Address	3			1•J•1 Identification Initials	7
1•D	Attention Line	3			1•J•2 Enclosure 7	
1•E	Salutation	4			1•J•3 Carbon Copy 7	
1•F	Subject Line	5				
1•G	Body or Message	5		1•K	Postscript	7
1•H	Complimentary Close	5		1•L	Envelope	8

2 good business writing   12

Section 2   Parts of the Sentence   12

2•A	Words	13			2•D•2 Complex 15	
	2•A•1 Subject 13				2•D•3 Compound 15	
	2•A•2 Predicate 13				2•D•4 Compound-Complex	16
2•B	Phrases	14		2•E	Syntax	16
2•C	Clauses	14		2•F	Sentence Order	16
2•D	Kinds of Sentences	15		2•G	Sentence Fragment	17
	2•D•1 Simple 15			2•H	Run-on Sentence	17
				2•I	Sentence Length	18

Section 3   Parts of Speech: Verbs   19

3•A	Uses of Verbs	19		3•A•5	Tense 22	
				3•A•6	Active/Passive Voice 23	
	3•A•1 Verb Phrases 19			3•A•7	Mood 25	
	3•A•2 Transitive/			3•A•8	Shifts in Verbs 25	
	Intransitive 19				a. Shift in Tense 25	
	3•A•3 Action/Being 20				b. Shift in Voice 26	
	3•A•4 Forming Principal				c. Shift in Mood 26	
	Parts 21			3•A•9	Verb Order 26	

Section 4 Parts of Speech: Nouns and Pronouns 27

4•A Noun Form Changes 27

    4•A•1 Plurals 27
    4•A•2 Possessives 28
    4•A•3 Warnings 29

4•B Pronoun Form Changes 29

    4•B•1 Case 29
    4•B•2 Person 30
        a. Person Choice 30
        b. I and We 31
    4•B•3 Number 31

4•C Agreement 31

    4•C•1 Pronoun/Antecedent Agreement 31
        a. Relative Pronouns 31
        b. Indefinite Pronouns 32

    4•C•2 Subject/Verb Agreement 33
        a. Collective Nouns 33
        b. Foreign Nouns 33
        c. Recognizing the True Subject 33
        d. Subject as a Part of Something 33
        e. Compound Subjects 34

4•D Indefinite Reference 34
4•E Ellipsis 35
4•F Shifts in Subjects and Person 36

    4•F•1 Shifts in Subjects 36
    4•F•2 Shifts in Person 37

4•G Placement of Subject and Verb 37
4•H Omission of Subject 37

Section 5 Parts of Speech: Modifiers 38

5•A Usage 38
5•B Adjective and Adverb Form Changes 38
5•C Placement of Modifiers in Sentence 39

    5•C•1 Adjectives 39
        a. Predicate Adjectives 39
        b. Adjective Phrases 39
        c. Adjective Clauses 40

    5•C•2 Adverbs 41
        a. One-word Adverbs 41
        b. Adverb Phrases 42
        c. Adverb Clauses 42

5•D Superlatives 42
5•E Double Negatives 43
5•F Compound Adjectives 43

Section 6 Parts of Speech: Connectors 44

6•A Prepositions 44

    6•A•1 Phrasal Prepositions 44
    6•A•2 Nine Most Used Prepositions 45
    6•A•3 Idiomatic Usage of Prepositions 45
    6•A•4 Prepositional Phrases as Modifiers 46
    6•A•5 Ending Sentences with Prepositions 47
    6•A•6 Unnecessary Prepositions 47

6•B Conjunctions 48

    6•B•1 Coordinate 48
    6•B•2 Correlative 48
    6•B•3 Subordinate 49
    6•B•4 Conjunctive Adverbs 49

Section 7 Letter Writing Principles   50

7•A Parallel Construction   50
    7•A•1 Use of Correlative Conjunctions 51
    7•A•2 Use of Articles and Prepositions 51
    7•A•3 Listing Points 52
    7•A•4 Parallelism in Writing Units 52

7•B Reader-Oriented Writing   53

    7•B•1 Address Letters to Persons, Not Titles 53
    7•B•2 Writer Is Unknown 54
    7•B•3 I or We 54
    7•B•4 Be Concise 54
    7•B•5 Get to the Point Immediately 54
    7•B•6 Answer Letters Promptly 55

3 language choice   57

Section 8 Language Usage Problems   57

8•A Nonstandard Usage   58
    8•A•1 Illiterate 59
    8•A•2 Archaic 59
    8•A•3 Obsolete 59
    8•A•4 Rare 59
    8•A•5 Poetic 59
    8•A•6 Technical or Field 59
    8•A•7 Regional or Local 60
    8•A•8 Foreign Language 60
    8•A•9 Slang 60
    8•A•10 Jargon 62
    8•A•11 Other Labels 62

8•B Language to Avoid   62
    8•B•1 Overused and Out-of-Date Expressions 62
    8•B•2 Redundancies, Repetitions, and Gobbledegook 64
    8•B•3 Ambiguous and Equivocal Statements 66
    8•B•4 Euphemisms 66
    8•B•5 Dysphemisms 67
    8•B•6 Insincere Language 67
        a. Gross Flattery 67
        b. Superlatives 68
        c. Overhumility 68
        d. Sweeping Generalities 68
    8•B•7 Inaccuracies and Incorrectly Used Expressions 69
        a. Malaprops (or Malapropisms) 69
        b. Wrong Prefixes 69
        c. Illiterate Usage 69
        d. Made-Up Words 70
        e. Words with Similar Meanings 71

8•C Choosing Words for Preciseness   75
    8•C•1 Homophones 75
    8•C•2 Sound-Alike Words 75
    8•C•3 Idioms 77
    8•C•4 Negative/Positive Terms 78
    8•C•5 Concrete/Abstract Language 79

4 beginning and organizing the business letter · 80

Section 9 Beginning the Business Letter · 80

9·A Answering Letters · 81
    9·A·1 Reading and Marking Letters · 81
    9·A·2 Collecting Background Information · 81
9·B Initiating Letters · 83
9·C Purposes of Letters · 83
    9·C·1 To Get the Receiver to Respond · 83
    9·C·2 To Give Information · 84
    9·C·3 To Build Goodwill · 84

Section 10 Organizing the Business Letter · 84

10·A Introduction · 85
10·B Body · 87
10·C Closing · 87
10·D Postscript · 90

5 business letters for specific purposes · 92

Section 11 Order Letters · 92

11·A Placing Orders · 92
11·B Acknowledging Orders · 94
11·C Placing Orders for Services · 94

Section 12 Request for Information Letters · 96

Section 13 Favors or Assistance Letters · 97

13·A Requesting Favors or Assistance · 97
13·B Answering Requests for Favors · 99

Section 14 Sales Letters · 100

Section 15 Claim or Adjustment Letters · 104

15·A Initiating the Claim or Complaint · 104
15·B Answering Claim or Complaint Letters · 107
    15·B·1 Agreeing to Writer's Request · 107
    15·B·2 Making Adjustment of Writer's Request · 107
    15·B·3 Rejecting Writer's Request · 110
15·C Writing to Prevent Claims or Complaints · 112

		Section 16	**Collecting Overdue Account Letters**			**113**
16·A	First Reminder	113	16·F	Using Special Postal Services		116
16·B	Second Communication	113				
16·C	Third Communication	114	16·G	Form Collection Letters		116
16·D	Fourth Communication	115	16·H	Duplicated Collection Letters		116
16·E	Final Communication	115				

		Section 17	**Credit Letters**			**117**
17·A	Requesting Credit	117	17·C	Replying to Credit Check		119
17·B	Requesting Credit Information	118	17·D	Granting Credit		119
			17·E	Refusing Credit		120

Section 18   Routine Letters   120

Section 19   Goodwill Letters   122

Section 20   Interoffice Memoranda   123

Section 21   Letter-Writing Shortcuts   123

21·A	Telephoning	123	21·D	Multicopy Memorandum Forms		127
21·B	Postal Cards	125				
21·C	Answering on Bottom of Letter	126	21·E	Other Short Forms		127
			21·F	Form Letters		128
			21·G	Printed Forms		129

6 employment writing   130

Section 22   Employment Writing for Employers   130

22·A	Application Forms	130	22·D·1	Recommendation Considerations		133
22·B	Letters to Applicants	131				
22·C	Letters Checking References	132	22·D·2	Positive Letters		134
22·D	Letters of Recommendation	133	22·D·3	Negative Letters		135
			22·E	Evaluations of Employees		135

Section 23 Employment Writing for Applicants and Employees — 136

23·A Data Sheet — 136
    23·A·1 Education Section — 137
    23·A·2 Work Experience Section — 137
    23·A·3 Personal Section — 138
    23·A·4 References Section — 138
    23·A·5 Other Information — 138
23·B Application Letters — 138
23·C Application Blanks — 142
23·D Thank-You Letters — 143
23·E Acceptance Letters — 144
23·F Refusal Letters — 144
23·G Resignation Letters — 145

7 business report writing — 146

Section 24 Preparation for Writing the Report — 148

24·A Recognizing and Defining the Job — 148
24·B Obtaining the Information — 149
24·C Establishing a Schedule — 152
24·D Organizing Material — 152
24·E Analyzing Data — 152

Section 25 Writing the Report — 153

25·A Forms of Reports — 153
    25·A·1 Memorandum — 153
    25·A·2 Letter — 155
    25·A·3 Short Informal Report — 155
    25·A·4 Long Formal Report — 155
25·B Steps in Writing Reports — 164
    25·B·1 Outline — 164
    25·B·2 First Writing — 165
    25·B·3 Second Writing — 165
    25·B·4 Format of Report — 166
    25·B·5 Documentation of Report — 166
        a. Footnotes — 166
        b. Bibliography — 167
    25·B·6 Graphic and Visual Aids for Reports — 169

8 personal business writing — 174

Section 26 Pointers for Personal Business Writing — 175

Section 27 Specific Personal Writing Situations — 176

27·A Direct Mail — 176
27·B Consumer Complaints — 176
27·C Thank-You Notes — 177
27·D Completing Credit Application Forms — 179

9 punctuation — 180

Section 28 End-of-the-Sentence Punctuation — 180

- 28•A Period (.) — 180
  - 28•A•1 At the End of Sentences — 180
  - 28•A•2 Special Uses — 180
  - 28•A•3 Ellipsis — 181
- 28•B Question Mark (?) — 181
- 28•C Exclamation Point (!) — 181
- 28•D Warnings — 181
  - 28•D•1 Double-Ending Punctuation — 181
  - 28•D•2 Courteous Requests — 182

Section 29 Internal Punctuation — 182

- 29•A Comma (,) — 182
  - 29•A•1 Clauses of Compound Sentence — 182
  - 29•A•2 Items in Series — 182
  - 29•A•3 Coordinate Adjectives — 183
  - 29•A•4 Introductory Words, Phrases, and Clauses — 183
  - 29•A•5 Restrictive/Nonrestrictive Modifiers — 184
  - 29•A•6 Explanatory Elements — 185
  - 29•A•7 Miscellaneous Uses — 185
  - 29•A•8 Warnings — 186
- 29•B Semicolon (;) — 186
  - 29•B•1 Clauses of Compound Sentence — 187
  - 29•B•2 Items in Series — 187
  - 29•B•3 Before Explanation or Enumeration — 187
- 29•C Quotation Marks — 188
  - 29•C•1 Quotation Within Quotation — 188
  - 29•C•2 Special Points — 189
  - 29•C•3 With Other Punctuation Marks — 189
  - 29•C•4 Other Uses — 189

Section 30 Other Punctuation — 190

- 30•A Colon — 190
- 30•B Dash — 191
- 30•C Parentheses — 191
- 30•D Brackets — 191
- 30•E Italics — 191

10 style — 193

Section 31 Abbreviations — 193

- 31•A Abbreviations to Use — 193
  - 31•A•1 With Personal Names — 193
  - 31•A•2 Within Firm Names — 193

	31·A·3	With Time Elements 194		31·B·3	Personal Names 195
	31·A·4	Organization Names 194		31·B·4	Calendar Divisions 195
	31·A·5	Compass Points 194		31·B·5	Street Addresses 195
	31·A·6	State and Province Names 194		31·B·6	Foreign Addresses 195
	31·A·7	Latin Terms 194		31·B·7	Weights and Measurements 195
	31·A·8	Number 194	31·C	Special Points 196	
31·B	Abbreviations to Avoid 195			31·C·1	Forming Plurals 196
	31·B·1	Titles 195		31·C·2	In Tabulated Material 196
	31·B·2	Compass Points 195			

Section 32   Capitalization   196

32·A	Capitalization Rules 196			32·A·9	Titles of Literary Works and Art 198
	32·A·1	Proper Nouns and Adjectives 196		32·A·10	I and Exclamations 199
	32·A·2	Organizations 197		32·A·11	Nouns with Numbers or Letters 199
	32·A·3	Religious Terms 197		32·A·12	Abbreviations 199
	32·A·4	Calendar Divisions and Holidays 197		32·A·13	Initial Words 199
	32·A·5	Geographic Localities 197	32·B	Lower Case Rules 200	
	32·A·6	Trade Names 198		32·B·1	Common Names 200
	32·A·7	Personal Titles 198		32·B·2	Job Titles 200
	32·A·8	Course Titles 198		32·B·3	Diseases 200

Section 33   Numerals   200

33·A	Numbers as Words 200		33·B	Numbers as Figures 202	
	33·A·1	Below Ten 201		33·B·1	Over Ten 202
	33·A·2	Beginning a Sentence 201		33·B·2	More than One Number 202
	33·A·3	Round or Indefinite 201		33·B·3	Days of the Month 202
	33·A·4	Fractions 201		33·B·4	House and Street Numbers 202
	33·A·5	Ages 201		33·B·5	Time 203
	33·A·6	Periods of Time 201		33·B·6	Amounts of Money 203
	33·A·7	With O'Clock 201		33·B·7	Weights and Measurements 203
	33·A·8	Centuries and Decades 202			
	33·A·9	Days of Month 202			

appendix — 205

Reference Sources	206
Suggestions for Dictating	209
Proofreaders' Marks	211
Frequently Used Abbreviations	212
United States Postal Abbreviations	213

glossary — 215

exercises — 223

1	Kinds of Sentences	224	18	Overused and Out-of-Date Expressions	239
2	Syntax: Word Order	224	19	Redundant and Repetitious Expressions	239
3	Transitive/Intransitive Verbs	225	20	Words and Terms to Be Avoided	240
4	Action/Be Verbs	226	21	Confused and Incorrectly Used Words	241
5	Active/Passive Voice	227	22	Opening Sentences	242
6	Verb Shifts: Tense, Voice, Mood	228	23	Closing Sentences	243
7	Singular/Plural: Nouns/Pronouns	229	24	Application Letter Writing	243
8	Possessives: Nouns/Pronouns	230	25	Punctuation: End of the Sentence	244
9	Agreement: Relative/Indefinite Pronouns	230	26	Punctuation: Commas	245
10	Agreement: Subject/Verb	231	27	Punctuation: Semicolons, Commas	245
11	Indefinite Reference	231	28	Other Punctuation	246
12	Noun/Pronoun Shifts: Subject/Person	232	29	All Punctuation	247
13	Placement of Modifiers	233	30	Mechanics: Abbreviations, Capitalization, Numbers	247
14	Prepositions	234			
15	Parallel Construction	235			
16	Reader/You Emphasis	236			
17	Getting to the Point Immediately	237			

key to exercises — 249

index — 261

1

the business letter

The appearance of a business letter or any other piece of business writing is important. Because the first thing that you want the recipient to do is to read the letter, you must use every device you can to bring this about. The appearance may be the deciding factor in attracting the reader. A typed letter that consists of one long single-spaced paragraph with strikeovers and crossed-out words does not make the reader want to take the time and effort to understand the message.

What makes a letter pleasing? The letterhead itself is of great importance and should be attractively designed. Is the paper of good quality? The best quality of stationery has a high fiber content and is of heavy weight. Most letterhead stationery is either white or pastel in color. Presently the machines that sort mail in the large post offices cannot "read" envelopes that are dark colored. In addition, deep colors are difficult to correct. The design of the letterhead should be simple; yet it should contain all of the necessary information: address, phone number, cable address, and the complete name of the firm or individual. The address should be quickly visible so that answering the letter is easy. If your company has no art department to design letterheads, work with the printer. Usually printing companies have samples and suggestions.

The placement and typing of the letter also contribute a great deal to its appearance. The letter should be attractively centered on the letterhead, and the letter style (block, modified block, or another style) should complement the letterhead. The typing should be error free; there should be no strikeovers, crossed-out words, or penned corrections. The type of the machine should be dark and sharp.

May 3, 19-- **DATE**

REGISTERED MAIL   **MAILING NOTATION**
CONFIDENTIAL   **OTHER NOTATION**

The Best Corporation   **INSIDE ADDRESS**
2345 Seventh Avenue N.W.
Seattle, WA 98109

Attention Mr. Richard Martin, Personnel Director   **ATTENTION LINE**

Ladies and Gentlemen   **SALUTATION**

Subject: The Business Letter   **SUBJECT LINE**

This letter is an example of modified block style. All of the parts of the letter are included and labeled.

Although this example shows the date to the right, it could be centered as well. The complimentary close and signature **BODY** are also to the right; they could be centered. The dictator's title may be typed on the same line as the name; or if the title is a long one, it may be typed on the line below the dictator's name.

This letter uses open puctuation, which has no colon after the salutation and no comma after the complimentary close.

      Sincerely yours   **COMPLIMENTARY CLOSE**

      David H. Walker

      David H. Walker   **SIGNATURE**
      Sales Manager

DHW:deh   **IDENTIFICATION INITIALS**
Enclosure
cc Mr. Robert Wills   **ENCLOSURE AND CARBON COPY NOTATIONS**

The postscript is now an attention-getting device. Place it a double space below the last line of the letter. You may include or omit "P.S."   **POSTSCRIPT**

757 THIRD AVENUE / NEW YORK, NEW YORK 10017 / (212) 888-3700

Business Letter Labeled to Show All Parts

SECTION 1 Parts of the business letter

Although the letter is made up of many parts, not all of these parts are necessary to every letter. Look at the example on p. 2. This letter shows and labels all of the parts that are described here.

1·A Date

All letters are dated. Because business letters are ordinarily typed on letterhead stationery that contains the name and address of the firm or person writing the letter, the date is the only part of the heading that the typist need supply. The date is easier to read if the month is not abbreviated. Never use the shortcut, 7/15/--.

If you are not using letterhead stationery, then add to the heading the address of the person signing the letter. Place such an address just above the date.

EXAMPLE: 285 N.W. Madison Avenue
Portland, OR 97320
July 15, 19—

1·B Mailing notation

If the letter is being sent by a postal service other than regular first-class mail, such as *special delivery* or *registered mail*, indicate this by typing a notation, usually in all caps, two spaces above the inside address; also type such a notation on the envelope below the stamp position. Placing the notation above the inside address has two purposes: the recipient knows that the letter is important enough to have been sent by a special service and anyone from the writer's firm can tell from the file copy how the letter was sent.

Other notations, such as *Personal, Confidential,* and *Please Forward,* are also typed above the inside address as well as on the envelope. On the envelope these notations are placed either in the upper left corner below the return address or after the name of the addressee.

1·C Inside address

The inside address contains the complete name and address of the recipient of the letter and is a part of every business letter. It includes a courtesy title with the addressee's name—*Mr., Mrs., Miss, Ms.,* or *Dr.,* for example—even if a company title such as *Sales Manager* is also used. The inside address is always single spaced and agrees with the address on the envelope. The inside address is important both for reference and for filing purposes.

1·D Attention line

The attention line is part of the address. It is preferable to address the letter to a person or department within a company rather than to address the letter to a firm and to direct it to the

THE BUSINESS LETTER   4

attention of a person or department; therefore, the attention line is being used less and less. If you do use an attention line, be sure that the salutation agrees with the inside address, not the attention line. This means that the salutation will probably be *Ladies and Gentlemen,* as the letter is usually addressed to a firm for the attention of an individual.

**1·E
Salutation**

The salutation is the greeting of the letter. It agrees with the inside address; that is, if the letter is addressed to a firm, the salutation should be *Ladies and Gentlemen* (or *Gentlemen*); if the letter is addressed to a person, the salutation should be *Dear Mr., Mrs., Ms.,* or *Miss* (not *Dear Sir* or *Dear Madam*).

The choice of salutation is presently a source of difficulty, particularly when the letter is addressed to a firm. Many businesspeople object to the use of the salutation *Gentlemen* when the firm consists of both men and women. The substitution of *Ladies and Gentlemen* (which many business writers consider awkward) seems to be gaining acceptance. Salutations such as *Gentlepersons* and *Dear People* are occasionally used. If a letter is addressed to an individual whose name and sex are unknown or the letter is addressed to a job title such as personnel director, the salutation choice again becomes a problem. A substitute such as *Dear Person* certainly is not satisfactory. One further possibility is the elimination of the salutation from the letter as the Administrative Management Society suggests in its Simplified Letter style. See the example on pp. 10–11.

Along this same line, some business writers think that the *dear* of the salutation should be dropped. Instead of using *Dear Mr. Howard* as the salutation, the name of the reader is worked into the first line. This goes very well, of course, when the addressee's name is known. It is not appropriate when the letter is addressed to a company or to a person whose name and sex are unknown.

EXAMPLES: Thank you, Mr. Howard. . .
    for sending your check so promptly. Your account is now up-to-date.
    Would you help us, Mrs. Taylor. . .
    We need a few facts about the claim you recently filed with us.
    Yes, Mr. Wilson,
    we can fill your order for a new filing cabinet right away.

If you have not seen this form before, you will probably find it strange. However, it does attract attention, and perhaps it does

SECTION 1 PARTS OF THE BUSINESS LETTER   5

seem more personal than the old way. If there is the slightest chance that such an opening would offend the reader, do use the conventional forms.

Here are the more conventional openings, given in order of decreasing formality:

```
Sir
My dear Sir
Dear Sir
My dear Mr. Black
Dear Mr. Black
My dear Paul
Dear Paul
```

When writing a letter that is being duplicated and sent to a number of persons, you will probably use a general salutation such as *Dear Customer* or *Dear Friend*. These salutations are obviously impersonal. Should you or your firm send a large number of form letters, it might be helpful to install a word processing center. Among its other advantages, the center would eliminate the impersonal tone of the form letters by giving the appearance that each letter has been individually typed.

In general, the choice of salutation is a decision that will need to be made within a firm by those who determine letter style and other letter-writing mechanics. In a small office, such things are determined by the employer or the secretary.

**1·F
Subject line**

The subject line tells what the letter is about and is helpful for quick identification without reading the letter and for filing purposes. Because it is part of the message of the letter, it is placed with the body, usually a double space after the salutation.

**1·G
Body or message**

The body of the letter is the message. This is the most important part of the letter, and the writing of it will be discussed in detail in later sections. It is begun a double space below the salutation or, if the letter contains a subject line, a double space below it. Paragraphs are ordinarily single spaced with double spacing between paragraphs.

**1·H
Complimentary close**

The complimentary close is the goodbye of the letter. It is placed a double space below the body of the letter. It agrees with the salutation in degree of formality. If you are dropping *dear* from the salutation, you will probably want a closing that fits the salutation. These informal closings are placed in the

THE BUSINESS LETTER 6

normal complimentary close position and consist of only a few words.

EXAMPLES: As ever, Best wishes, Thanks very much, Many thanks, Good luck on the new job

If you are using the conventional closings, this list gives them in order of decreasing formality:

Yours respectfully	Most sincerely
Very respectfully yours	Very sincerely yours
Respectfully yours	Sincerely yours
Respectfully	Yours sincerely
Yours truly	Sincerely
Very truly yours	Most cordially
Yours very truly	Yours cordially
	Cordially yours
	Cordially

If you are using the Simplified Letter style, you will omit the complimentary close.

1·1 Signature

The signature generally includes the typed name of the person signing the letter and, if that person represents a company, it can include the name of the firm. However, if the letterhead includes the name of the firm (a common practice), it is not necessary to type the name of the firm below the complimentary close. A letter should always be signed by a person, whether it is written by an individual or by someone representing the firm. (An organization cannot sign a letter.) The signature should include the typed name of the person signing the letter (unless the letterhead includes the printed name) because penwritten signatures are so often illegible. Names may not reveal whether they are masculine or feminine. Use titles with feminine names; however, masculine names never have titles. For example, the woman who uses a name such as "B. J. Martin" will most likely be addressed as "Mr." unless she identifies her sex in the signature.

EXAMPLES: Cordially yours   Cordially yours

B. J. Martin   *Miss B. J. Martin*

Miss B. J. Martin   B. J. Martin

SECTION 1   PARTS OF THE BUSINESS LETTER   7

1·J
Notations after signature

There are a number of notations placed after the signature. Most of them are more helpful to the file clerk or secretary than they are to the writer or recipient of the letter.

The notations include:

1·J·1
Identification initials

Identification or reference initials are usually placed after the last signature line of the letter. They tell who dictated the letter and who typed it. Their value is primarily important to the person or firm sending the letter. Usually the dictator's initials are followed by the transcriber's. There are many styles that can be used.

EXAMPLES: DHW/SG   DHW/sg   DHW:SG   SG

1·J·2
Enclosure

An enclosure notation merely indicates that something is being enclosed with the letter in the envelope. The notation may also indicate the number of enclosures or what is being enclosed. Such notations are useful to those sending the mail and to those receiving it. If the letter shows that there is an enclosure, the person folding the letter is reminded to include it and the person opening the letter can easily check to be sure that the enclosure is included.

EXAMPLES: Enclosure   Encs. 3   Enclosure: Order Blank

1·J·3
Carbon copy

The initials *cc* typed below the identification initials mean that a carbon copy of the letter is being sent to the person or persons listed after *cc*. A title such as *Mr.* should precede the name. The surname is usually enough identification for the carbon-copy notation. If it is not, include the complete name. The address may be given if it will assist the typist in sending the carbon copy or if it is necessary for filing information. A colored check mark placed next to the name on the carbon copy indicates that that person was intended to receive the carbon. The check mark can take the place of a letter of transmittal. The initials *bcc*, meaning *blind carbon copy,* are used when the addressee is not aware that copies of the letter are being sent to others. The original does not carry the notation.

EXAMPLES: cc Mr. Taylor   bcc Mr. Doyle
              √ Mrs. Hayes   cc: Mrs. Carla Thayer

1·K
Postscript

The postscript originated as an afterthought placed at the end of the letter. By writing *P.S.* and a short message, the writer was

THE BUSINESS LETTER

saying, in effect: "I forgot this and realized that I had forgotten it when I finished the letter." Today, should someone forget a point, the secretary can either add it to the letter before typing or retype the letter should the omission be discovered afterwards. The postscript now has a different purpose: to add emphasis and to attract attention. Many times the reader of a letter skips the body and goes to the postscript. Therefore, the postscript often contains something that stimulates interest and that makes the reader want to go back and read the entire letter. This is particularly true in sales or promotional letters, where the first thing the writer wants is to get the recipient to read the letter.

A postscript is typed a double space below the last line of the letter, and it is indented or blocked to agree with the style of the letter. The letters *P.S.* need not be included. In fact, they take additional time to type and probably should be omitted.

EXAMPLES: Return the stamped card immediately and you will save $5.
P.S. Don't forget—our guarantee applies for one full year.

1·L Envelope

The envelope must include the full name and the complete address of the addressee, including street address, city, state, and ZIP Code. The address on the envelope should agree with the inside address of the letter. Business stationery ordinarily has the return address printed in the upper left corner of the envelope; if not, type the sender's name and address. Special mailing notations—*Special Delivery, Registered Mail*—are placed a double space below the stamp position. Other notations such as *Hold for Arrival* and *Please Forward* are placed either after the addressee's name or below the return address.

Envelopes are now addressed to conform to Postal Service recommendations so that mail can be machine sorted. These recommendations are that all addresses are single spaced and blocked, nothing is typed in the lower left corner, the two-letter state abbreviations are used, and the last line of the address contains three things—city, state, and ZIP Code.

The two sizes of envelopes most commonly used are the No. 6¾ and the larger No. 10, which is sometimes called legal size. Use the No. 6¾ for letters of one page; use the larger envelopes for two-or-more-page letters and enclosures.

SECTION 1   PARTS OF THE BUSINESS LETTER   9

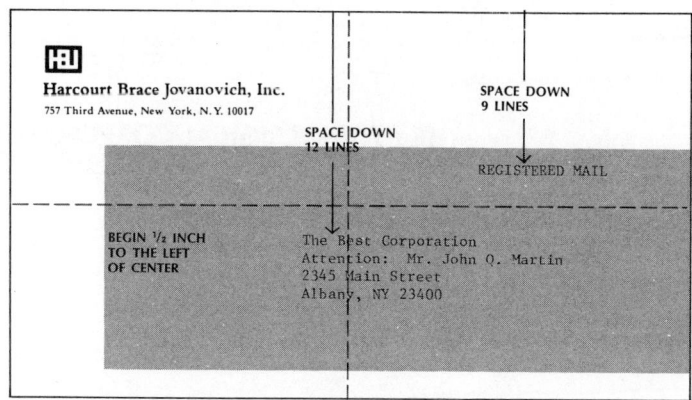

No. 6¾ Envelope with Special Notations

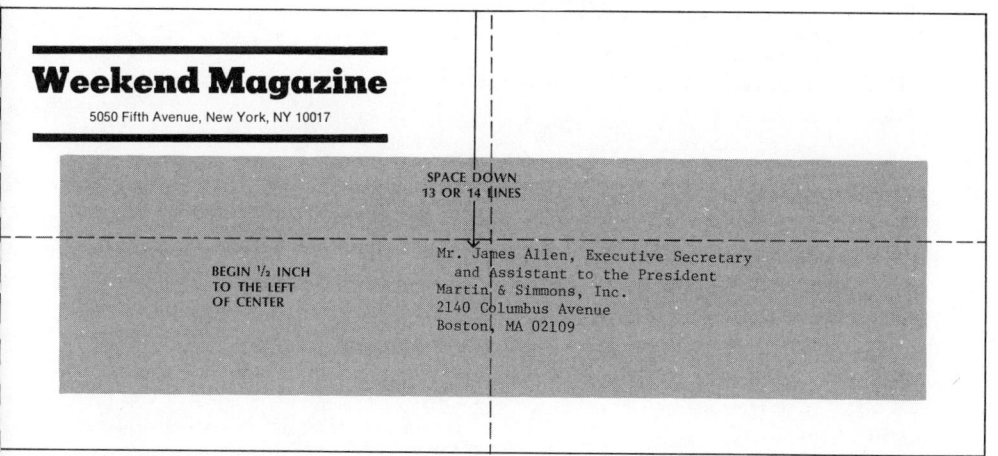

No. 10 Envelope with Read Zone of Postal Scanner Shaded

THE PSYCHOLOGICAL CORPORATION
757 THIRD AVENUE, NEW YORK, N.Y. 10017   (212) 888-4444   CABLE: HARBRACE

May 4, 19--

Ms. Susan R. Johnson
Director of Personnel
Apex Corporation
211 Market Street
Oakland, CA 94300

SIMPLIFIED LETTER STYLE

This is an example, Ms. Johnson, of a letter style adopted by the Administrative Management Society for use in business-letter writing. Because it uses block format and open punctuation and it eliminates certain traditional letter parts, it saves time, cuts costs, and increases the volume of work.

It has these features:

1. All lines are blocked at the left margin.

2. The date is typed six lines below the last line of the letterhead.

3. The inside address is typed at least three blank lines below the date. This letter style is often used with window envelopes so the style of the inside address should agree with the recommendations of the Postal Service for envelope addressing

4. The salutation and the complimentary close are omitted. However, by using the addressee's name in the first paragraph, the letter becomes more personal.

5. The subject line is typed in all capitals a triple space below the inside address. The subject line summarizes the message of the letter. Triple space from the subject line to the body of the letter.

6. Numbered items are blocked at the left margin, but unnumbered items are indented five spaces. All items should be set off by double spacing.

Two-Page Letter, Simplified Style

SECTION 1   PARTS OF THE BUSINESS LETTER

Ms. Johnson
Page 2
May 4, 19--

7. If a second page is needed, carry over at least three lines of the message. The heading of the second page is blocked, and the continuation of the message is a triple space below the heading. Drop down at least an inch to begin the second page.

8. The writer's name and title are typed in all capitals at least five spaces below the body.

9. Identification initials, consisting of the typist's initials only, are typed a double space below the writer's name. Enclosure or carbon-copy notations are typed below the initials.

This letter form saves space and time as well as eliminating the problem of salutation choice.

James T. Stevens

JAMES T. STEVENS - VICE PRESIDENT

dhw
Enclosure

cc Mr. Martin Casey

2
good business writing

What is good business writing? Why is it important? How do you achieve it?

You might answer that good business writing is grammatically correct, the sentences are well written, and the choice of words is precise. In addition, such mechanics as spelling and punctuation are correct; otherwise, the reader's attention can be diverted from the content of the letter by these kinds of errors. However, there are other factors. Good business writing is coherent: The sentences go together; the parts of the sentences are parallel; the message or purpose of the letter is easily understood and cannot possibly be misunderstood. There is a directness to the sentences and to the meanings of the sentences that emphasizes the right points and conveys a clear meaning. The letter or report contains everything the reader needs to know but nothing that he or she does not need or want to know.

The next question that arises is how to achieve good business writing. What are some of the problems and some of the frequent errors? What are some of the writing devices that can be used to convey certain meanings?

The discussions that follow are basic to all writing, not just to letter and other business writing. However, the direction is on writing for business and applying rules to the instances that are most likely to occur in on-the-job situations.

SECTION 2 **Parts of the sentence**

Before beginning the process of putting sentences together, it is essential that you understand what a sentence is. What is a sentence? How do you put the various components together so that the sentence sounds right and conveys the meaning that you want it to have?

SECTION 2 PARTS OF THE SENTENCE

2·A Words

The *word* is the basic unit of any sentence, for sentences are made up of words. There are certain words that every sentence must have or it is not a sentence. These necessary words, or parts, are a *subject* and a *predicate*.

2·A·1 Subject

The subject is the name of something or someone that the sentence is about. It does the action of the verb (or receives the action if the verb is in the passive voice), or the subject is in a state of being if the verb is a linking verb (form of *be*, *feel*, *seem*, and *appear*, for example). It may be a single word (simple subject), made up of two or more nouns or pronouns (compound subject), or a noun or pronoun plus modifiers (complete subject). The subject may also take the form of a phrase or clause.

EXAMPLES: <u>Polly and I</u> left the office early. *compound subject consisting of a noun and a pronoun and doing the action of the verb,* left

<u>One third of the members of the United States Senate</u> are elected every two years. *complete subject consisting of noun plus modifiers and receiving the action of a passive-voice verb*

<u>Whoever applies for the job</u> will be interviewed. *noun clause used as subject*

Usually the subject precedes the verb—this is the natural sentence order. The most frequent exception is beginning a sentence with *there is* (or *are*) or *it is*. When this occurs, the subject comes after the verb and determines whether the verb is singular or plural. Such a construction is called an *anticipatory subject* or *expletive*. It is a weak beginning for a sentence as it takes the emphasis away from the subject.

EXAMPLES: There are no <u>plans</u> for moving the offices from this location. <u>plans</u> *is the subject; therefore, the verb is plural to agree with the subject*

It is difficult <u>to believe the rumor</u>. <u>to believe the rumor</u> *is the subject*

2·A·2 Predicate

The predicate of the sentence is the verb plus the complement or the object and any modifiers. The predicate can be just the verb; usually, though, it contains other words or phrases. The complement is either a noun or pronoun that renames the subject and follows a form of the verb *be* (predicate nominative), or it is an adjective that describes the subject and follows a linking verb (predicate adjective). The direct object follows a transitive verb and receives the action of that verb. It answers *what* or *whom* about the verb.

EXAMPLES: I am she. *predicate includes verb,* am, *and predicate nominative,* she

Mr. Jones is the one to see about the job. *predicate includes predicate nominative,* one, *plus modifying phrase,* to see about the job

The typist left out a sentence from the letter. *predicate includes direct object,* sentence, *and a modifying phrase*

The letter looks attractive. *predicate includes predicate adjective,* attractive

Lois can type and chew gum at the same time. *predicate includes compound verb,* can type and chew gum, *plus modifying phrase*

In addition to words that are used as sentence elements, words are also used as phrases and clauses, which are parts of sentences.

2·B Phrases

A phrase is a group of two or more related words, not having a subject and verb but serving as a part of speech. There are several kinds of phrases: *verb* (main verb and auxiliaries); *verbal* (infinitive, gerund, or participle), used as nouns, adjectives, or adverbs; *prepositional* (preposition and its object), used as adjectives, adverbs, or nouns.

EXAMPLES: Gary should have been studying for the examination. *verb phrase*

To pass the test will require a great deal of studying. *verbal—infinitive—phrase used as a noun—subject*

Standing on the window ledge, the man was able to wash the windows. *verbal—participial—phrase used as an adjective*

George does not like to walk in the rain. *prepositional phrase used as an adjective*

2·C Clauses

A clause is structurally much like a sentence; that is, it has a subject and a predicate. There are two kinds of clauses, *independent* and *dependent* (or *subordinate*). Although any independent clause can be a sentence, no dependent clause can by itself be a sentence. Usually the dependent clause has an extra

SECTION 2   PARTS OF THE SENTENCE   **15**

word at the beginning. This extra word is a *subordinate conjunction*, which is the word connecting the dependent clause to the main clause. It is this subordinate conjunction that makes the clause unable to stand alone.

Dependent clauses are used as three parts of speech: *adjective*, *adverb*, and *noun*. They are discussed with these parts of speech (see pp. 27–44).

EXAMPLES: I cannot buy a new car because I do not have enough money.
    Independent clause: I cannot buy a new car
    Dependent clause: because I do not have enough money.

My uncle, who is seventy years old, jogs five miles every day.
    Independent clause: My uncle jogs five miles every day
    Dependent clause: who is seventy years old

2·D Kinds of sentences

By combining the various sentence elements—words, phrases, and clauses—different kinds of sentences can be formed. These sentences, defined according to structure, are:

2·D·1 Simple

A simple sentence contains one independent clause. It can contain as few as two words, or it can contain many words.

EXAMPLES: Secretaries type. *two words forming a simple sentence*
Secretaries in our company type many reports and take dictation for long periods of time. *simple sentence with compound verb*

2·D·2 Complex

A complex sentence contains one independent clause and one or more dependent clauses.

EXAMPLE: Secretaries <u>who are employed in our company</u> type many reports. *a dependent clause (underscored) and an independent clause*

2·D·3 Compound

A compound sentence has two or more independent clauses.

EXAMPLE: Secretaries type many reports, and they take dictation for long periods of time. *two independent clauses linked by the conjunction,* <u>and</u>

2·D·4
Compound-complex

A compound-complex sentence contains two or more independent clauses plus one or more dependent clauses.

EXAMPLE: Secretaries <u>who work in our company</u> type many reports, but they also take dictation for long periods of time. *a dependent clause (underscored) and two independent clauses*

2·E
Syntax

Syntax is the name given to the arrangement of words, phrases, and clauses into sentences. Correct syntax is arranging words in a logical order to convey a precise meaning. Faulty syntax is, of course, the reverse—words are arranged illogically so that an imprecise, unintelligible, or even erroneous meaning is given.

It is important that the phrase *to convey a precise meaning* be included. A sentence may have all of the needed information and still not convey its intended meaning.

EXAMPLES: Avoid: I have looked everywhere for an instruction book on how to play the concertina without success. *arranged so that it conveys an unintended meaning*

Use: I have looked everywhere, but I have not been successful in finding a book on how to play the concertina.

2·F
Sentence order

The three elements of the sentence—words, phrases, and clauses—have been discussed. There is an infinite variety of ways of putting these elements together to produce sentences. In English the usual sentence order is subject, verb, and object or predicate nominative. Most readers expect that sentences will be in this word order; therefore, any changes in word order can produce varied results. An expected change comes from putting the sentence in question form, when the verb precedes the subject. Other changes may be made. If done deliberately and skillfully, a different or unusual word order can attract attention so that reading will be done more carefully. It may emphasize a clause or phrase by placing that word group at the beginning of the sentence. An unusual word order may provide variety in writing and avoid monotony or dullness. The negative effect of changing the sentence order may be confusion. Because the reader is expecting the usual sentence order, he or she is distracted by the unusual and either does not read what is written or must reread it to get the proper message.

EXAMPLES: Mr. Williams worked hard to overcome the many problems of his job. *usual sentence order*

Let me know when Mr. Williams returns. *normal sentence order with adverb clause after verb*
When Mr. Williams returns, let me know. *adverb clause at the beginning of the sentence for emphasis*

2·G Sentence fragment

What is a sentence fragment? It is a part of a sentence, such as a phrase or a subordinate clause, but it is not a complete sentence; yet it is capitalized and punctuated as if it were a sentence.

Sometimes the opening sentence of a letter is a fragment. Here is an example: *In regard to your inquiry of June 1.* If you wish to tell what the letter is about, use a subject or reference line but don't use a sentence fragment.

EXAMPLES: Avoid: <u>Having worked for the same company for many years.</u> Marie was able to do her work quickly and easily.

Use: Having worked for the same company for many years, Marie was able to do her work quickly and easily.

Avoid: I succeeded in completing the application form. <u>Which was long and rather complicated.</u>

Use: I succeeded in completing the application. It was long and rather complicated.

2·H Run-on sentence

Some sentences are not broken into proper units but contain a number of different thoughts jumbled into one sentence. Such a construction is called a run-on sentence. Often these thoughts are connected by conjunctions and run on for several lines. The reader must sort out the ideas and separate them. This not only is confusing, but it takes time that a busy reader is not willing to give.

EXAMPLES: Avoid: Will you please sign all three copies of the accident report that are enclosed and keep one copy for your files and return two copies to this office so that our agent can release funds for payment of the claim and send the signed copies of the form in the enclosed envelope by certified mail to this office.

Use: Please sign each of the three copies of the enclosed accident report. Keep one copy for your files and return the other two copies by certified mail. When we receive the signed forms, our agent will send you a check in payment of the claim.

2·1 Sentence length

If your writing contains only simple sentences, it can be choppy, uninteresting, or difficult to read. However, if your writing contains only compound-complex sentences, it may also be difficult to read and understand. One of the ways of writing effectively is to get some variety in kinds and lengths of sentences. Sometimes, too, it is a matter of meaning or emphasis; clauses that are not important should be made dependent to the main or important clause. It can also be necessary to use certain clauses in your writing for effective parallel construction.

EXAMPLES: We cannot pay the claim <u>until you supply us with some needed information.</u> *this is a complex sentence: one independent clause plus one dependent adverb clause*

Change the sentence order: Until you supply us with some needed information, we cannot pay the claim.

Where is the emphasis in the first sentence? On the thing that the reader wants to know: when will the claim be paid. Where is the emphasis in the second sentence? It is on supplying information, which may not bring a response from the reader.

A paragraph made up of simple sentences:

Two weeks ago I wrote you about my order. The order was for three T-shirts. I sent the order six weeks ago. I also sent my check for $15.72. I still have not heard from you. I need the T-shirts now. When are you sending my order?

The same paragraph rewritten:

I am writing again about my order for three T-shirts, which I sent you along with my check for $15.72 six weeks ago. I wrote you two weeks ago inquiring about the order, but I still have not heard from you. If you are unable to fill the order, will you please refund the money that I sent you. I should like very much to have an immediate reply.

SECTION 3 Parts of speech: verbs

The parts of speech are the names given to words to show their function or form in sentences. Words have four functions in sentences: to name (nouns and pronouns), to show action or being (verbs), to modify (adjectives and adverbs), and to connect (conjunctions and prepositions). You have learned to recognize the parts of speech of many words by their form (*am* is a verb, for example). However, the function of a word in a sentence is a more important identification, for many words can be used as more than one part of speech. *Run* can be a noun, a verb, or an adjective.

CHART OF PARTS OF SPEECH, PHRASES, AND DEPENDENT CLAUSES

USE	PARTS OF SPEECH (WORDS)	PHRASES	DEPENDENT CLAUSES
Name	noun pronoun *gerund *infinitive	prepositional gerund infinitive	noun
Show action or being	verb	verb	
Modify	adjective adverb *participle *infinitive	prepositional participial infinitive	adjective adverb
Connect	conjunction preposition	**phrasal preposition	

* The verbals—infinitives, gerunds, and participles—are not ordinarily classified as separate parts of speech. Verbals are defined as verb forms used as adjectives, adverbs, or nouns. This chart is a breakdown of these verbals to show their uses in sentences.

** A phrasal preposition is two or more words used as a preposition.
Examples: because of, in spite of, according to

3·A
Uses of verbs

Verbs express action, condition, or state of being. Most people recognize verbs, use them reasonably accurately, and do not consider them to be nearly so confusing as some of the other parts of speech. In order to be able to use verbs effectively in writing, you should pay careful attention to the description of verb characteristics that follows.

3·A·1
Verb phrases

Verbs can be one word or a phrase. If the verb is a phrase, it will consist of a main verb, which expresses the action or being, and one or more auxiliaries. The auxiliaries convey tense (time) and other meanings such as possibility (*may, might*), obligation (*should*), condition (*may*), and emphasis (*do*). The auxiliary will be the first part of the phrase followed by the main verb. Certain verb forms—past or present participles—cannot be used without auxiliaries; therefore, the clause, *I done my work,* is incorrect.

EXAMPLES: should have been studying
have been heard
did understand

3·A·2
Transitive/intransitive

Verbs are either transitive or intransitive, which is a grammatical device that helps in the correct choice of verbs. A transitive verb always has an action that it passes either to the direct object or back to the subject of the sentence. An intransitive verb does not have any action; it describes the subject or expresses a condition or state of being. Any form of the verb *be* is intransitive because it expresses no action, only state of being. Knowing whether a verb is intransitive or transitive is by itself of little value; but in understanding the correct choice of verbs, such information can be very helpful.

3·A·3
Action/being

Verbs can show action or being. The use of action verbs rather than linking verbs generally creates more forceful writing. The linking verbs connect the subject of a sentence with a modifier or a predicate nominative. Some linking verbs are *feel, seem, appear,* and all forms of the verb *be.* The chart on p. 21 gives all of the forms of *be.* Although *is, was,* and *are*—the three most common words in the English language—are convenient for making general statements, they are neither precise nor emphatic. Therefore, if you want your writing to be forceful, to convey precise meanings, and to attract the attention of the reader, use positive action verbs. Such action verbs are also more economical in use of words.

EXAMPLES: Avoid: Our company is the largest producer of fine office equipment in the country.
Use: Our company produces more fine office equipment than any other company in the country.

SECTION 3 PARTS OF SPEECH: VERBS

Avoid: It is my hope that a reasonable settlement can be reached.
Use: I hope that a reasonable settlement can be reached.
Avoid: He is a person who can do a lot of work quickly and efficiently.
Use: He works quickly and efficiently.

You can also convey a positive meaning by the choice of adjective after the linking verb. The sentence, *We believe that you will like our product,* is not so forceful as, *We are sure that you will like our product.* In the second sentence, it is the adjective that makes the statement positive, not the choice of verb.

	BE		
PRESENT		**PRESENT PERFECT**	
I am	We are	I have been	We have been
You are	You are	You have been	You have been
He is	They are	He has been	They have been
PAST		**PAST PERFECT**	
I was	We were	I had been	We had been
You were	You were	You had been	You had been
He was	They were	He had been	They had been
FUTURE		**FUTURE PERFECT**	
I shall (or will) be	We shall (or will) be	I shall (or will) have been	We shall (or will) have been
You will be	You will be	You will have been	You will have been
He will be	They will be	He will have been	They will have been

Be can serve as an auxiliary as well as a main verb. When an auxiliary, *be* will make the tense progressive or the voice passive.

The progressive tenses of *be* are formed by adding *being* (the present participle) to the simple tenses. For example, the present progressive first person singular is *I am being.*

3·A·4
Forming principal parts

Verbs form their principal parts regularly by adding *-d* or *-ed* to the present tense. Irregular verbs—such as *rise, write, do, go,* and *run*—follow no set rules. There are about eighty of these verbs. Usage over a period of time has made some of them regular (for example, *weave*; in the past tense *weaved* is often used instead of *wove*) and some regular verbs, irregular (for example, *dive*; in the past tense *dove* is often used instead of *dived*). If you are unsure of the correct form of the principal parts of any verb, consult a late edition dictionary. Forming principal parts of verbs in itself is not important; but since the principal parts are the framework on which all verbs are formed, it becomes a necessary tool.

3•A•5
Tense

Verbs go through many form changes to convey tense. By definition, tense refers to the form of a verb used to express time distinctions. Although this is a true definition in most instances, there are exceptions. Notice that future meaning is conveyed in the sentence, *I leave tomorrow;* yet the verb form is present tense. In the sentence, *Classes begin at eight o'clock,* the time sense is habitual action occurring over a period of time, not the present time meaning of the verb *begin.*

There are six tense forms for verbs. The primary tenses include the *present, past,* and *future.* The perfect tenses include the *present perfect, past perfect,* and *future perfect.*

The primary tenses indicate the time that their names indicate. However, the present tense, in addition to showing action taking place now, is also used to indicate general or permanent truth or habitual action.

The perfect tenses show action or state of being that is completed. The form is always a verb phrase made by adding a form of *have* to the main verb. The present perfect indicates action begun in the past and completed in the present; it can also indicate habitual or repeated past action. The past perfect tense indicates action begun in the past and completed before a stated time in the past. The future perfect tense indicates action that will be completed before some stated future time.

This chart shows the regular verb *walk* in all six of the tense forms:

WALK			
PRESENT		**PRESENT PERFECT**	
I walk	We walk	I have walked	We have walked
You walk	You walk	You have walked	You have walked
He walks	They walk	He has walked	They have walked
PAST		**PAST PERFECT**	
I walked	We walked	I had walked	We had walked
You walked	You walked	You had walked	You had walked
He walked	They walked	He had walked	They had walked

SECTION 3 PARTS OF SPEECH: VERBS

FUTURE		FUTURE PERFECT	
I shall (or will) walk	We shall (or will) walk	I shall (or will) have walked	We shall (or will) have walked
You will walk	You will walk	You will have walked	You will have walked
He will walk	They will walk	He will have walked	They will have walked

Notice that the third person singular present tense form adds an -s to the verb; this is true of any verb form.

Choice of verb tense can cause trouble; however, it is usually in spoken language rather than in written language that the problem occurs. Sometimes, too, the past tense is used when the present tense is required for an action that is not complete.

EXAMPLES: Avoid: The radio reported that the forecast was for rain. *the forecast is still in effect; therefore, the present tense should be used*

Use: Last week the forecast was for rain, but this week the forecast is for fair weather.

3·A·6 Active/passive voice

Verb forms show active or passive voice. The voice of a verb—active or passive—is an important device to convey meaning. Voice is defined as the characteristic that shows whether the subject is acting or receiving the action.

EXAMPLE: The earthquake destroyed the city. *the subject,* earthquake, *does the acting—active voice*
The city was destroyed by the earthquake. *the subject,* city, *receives the action—passive voice*

There is a simple mechanical way of identifying a passive-voice verb: Such a verb will always be a phrase made up of some form of the verb *be* plus the past participle.

EXAMPLES: was told   should be written
has been seen   could have been read

An intransitive verb cannot be used in the passive voice; therefore, all passive-voice verbs are transitive with the subject receiving the action of the verb.

What is the importance of active/passive voice in business writing? Generally, as a matter of style, you will use active voice. It is more direct, more forceful, and uses fewer words. Passive voice is awkward; the sentences sound unnatural. When you compare two sentences, one active and one passive, all of the reasons for using active voice become obvious. In a simple sentence such as—*Our salesman called on four customers*—try changing to passive voice: *Four customers were called on by our salesman.* Certainly all of the arguments for active voice can be used for writing the first sentence. The second is awkward and unnatural; it uses more words; and it is neither direct nor forceful. And it most definitely is not the way most people write or talk.

When, then, do you use passive voice? If passive voice produces such awkward, unnatural sentences, why is there no rule saying never use passive voice? Simply because there are times when the passive is used, when you wish to convey the meaning or emphasis that only the passive can give. You will certainly use the passive when you want to emphasize what happened without saying who did it. It changes the emphasis from *who* to *what*. It changes the natural subject of the sentence from a doer to a receiver. It is a more objective type of writing, as what was done becomes more important than who did it. For example, in this passive-voice sentence: *Large gains were made in all sales areas,* the emphasis is on *large gains.* Change to active voice: *We made large gains in all sales areas.* Now the emphasis is on *we.* It is a weak beginning for a sentence to start with *we.* It also changes the emphasis from the natural subject, *large gains,* to someone (*we*) not important to the sentence.

The passive voice is probably more valuable in writing reports than in writing letters. In the use of the passive, particularly in report writing, there is the implication that the action is not carried on by individuals but by a group (the firm or company). This is a good use of the passive; for the work and efforts of the company are being emphasized, not the efforts of a few individuals.

The passive is often used in minutes and other formal writing.

EXAMPLE: It was moved and seconded . . . *the emphasis is on the motion, not on the person who made the motion*

Passive voice can also be used when the doer is unknown. In the sentence, *Lies were told about him,* the emphasis is on *lies,* not *who told them.* Perhaps the teller of lies is unknown or only suspected. In any event, you want to emphasize the act, not the doer.

Use of the passive voice should be confined to situations in which you want to emphasize *what,* not *who.* Always use pas-

SECTION 3 PARTS OF SPEECH: VERBS

sive voice for a specific reason and be sure that the emphasis is on the right object. Remember, passive voice emphasizes things, not persons.

3·A·7
Mood

Verbs also change form to indicate mood. Mood is the form of a verb that indicates the manner of action expressed by that verb. There are three moods: indicative, imperative, and subjunctive. Indicative mood is the most common—it indicates a fact or asks a question. Imperative mood gives a command or makes a request. Subjunctive mood expresses doubt or condition.

In English the use of the subjunctive instead of the indicative is a matter of choice. Except in formal language—such as that used in resolutions, demands, and rules, and in certain uses of the verb be to express statements contrary to fact—the subjunctive is being used less and less frequently in American English.

EXAMPLES: Christmas shopping began early this year. *Indicative*

Do your Christmas shopping early this year. *Imperative*

If I were you, I would do my Christmas shopping early this year. *Subjunctive*

The subjunctive or conditional can be a useful device in letters, particularly collection letters. It permits you to say such things as: *If I were in your position . . . Should this amount not be correct . . . Could it be that you have forgotten . . .* Often these expressions are gentler reminders than using the indicative: *If this amount is not correct . . .* or *Have you forgotten . . .*

Here is an example from a warranty for a steam iron: "Should your product not perform properly, service is provided in our company-owned servicenters and in over 150 authorized service stations."

By using the conditional, the company is conveying the idea that, although it is highly unlikely that the product will need service, if this event does occur, service is provided.

3·A·8
Shifts in verbs

Shifted or mixed construction can occur not only in verb forms but in other grammatical constructions as well. These other shifts will be discussed in later sections. Such a shift means that a writer begins with one form and ends with another. Here are three ways that verbs can be shifted:

a. Shift in tense Shifting tenses within a sentence can create problems. If the sentence has more than one verb—and, with the exception of compound verbs, this means more than one clause—the verb tenses should be the same throughout the sentence. Usually the verb in the subordinate clause conforms with the verb in the main clause.

EXAMPLES: Avoid: During my conversation with Ms. Jones, she said that our new electric typewriter is for sale in five foreign countries and that service was also available for the machine. *shift from present to past*
Use: During my conversation with Ms. Jones, she said that our new electric typewriter is for sale in five foreign countries and that service is also available for the machine.

b. Shift in voice Be careful, too, to avoid shifts in voice. This will usually involve a shift in subject as well.

EXAMPLES: Avoid: Joyce typed Mr. Hill's letters, but his dictation was taken by someone else. *shift in both voice and subject*
Use: Joyce typed Mr. Hill's letters, but Ann took his dictation.

c. Shift in mood Avoid shifts in mood just as you avoid shifts in tense and voice.

EXAMPLES: Avoid: First raise your hand to be recognized, and then you may speak to the class. *the verb raise is in the imperative mood; may speak is indicative*
Use: Raise your hand to be recognized and then speak to the class.

3•A•9 Verb order

A syntactical error can be made in the order of verbs. Logically verbs are arranged in the same order in which they occur. Caesar would not have said: "I conquered, I saw, I came," for that was not the order in which the events occurred. Nor would you write: *The order will be delivered and shipped promptly,* since the shipping must take place before the delivery. Violation of this logical order has an imposing name: *hysteron proteron.*

SECTION 4 Parts of speech: nouns and pronouns

You know, of course, that nouns are the names used in writing. They can be in the form of words, phrases, or clauses. They can be compound—either spelled as one word, two words, or hyphenated—as in *business letter, businessperson,* and *self-control.* Nouns can be written with the first letter capitalized (proper nouns) or with no capitals (common nouns).

Any noun must be used accurately; that is, it must be spelled and capitalized correctly; it must be in the correct form (singular, plural, possessive); and it must be correct for whatever it is naming. For instance, is the person to whom you are writing Irene K. Martin or Irene T. Martin; or is the date Friday, December 5, or Friday, December 15? Above all, it must convey the precise meaning intended.

Most spelling problems can be solved by consulting a dictionary. The spellings of personal names, though, can be difficult because personal names have innumerable spelling variations. The feminine name *Catherine* is an example; *Kathryn, Katherine,* and *Cathrine* are only a few of the possibilities. Check previous correspondence and directories for help in spelling personal names.

4·A Noun form changes

Nouns change form to show two things: plurals (number)— *boy/boys; man/men; lady/ladies*—and possessives—*Mary/Mary's; women/women's; child/child's.*

4·A·1 Plurals

Noun form changes that show plurals:

To form the plural of a singular noun, ordinarily add *-s* to the singular form.

EXAMPLES: typewriter/typewriters; student/students; office/offices

EXCEPTIONS:

a. If the singular form of a noun ends in *ch, sh, s, x,* or *z,* add *-es.*

EXAMPLES: miss/misses; tax/taxes; rush/rushes; chintz/chintzes

b. If the singular form of a noun ends in *y* and the *y* is preceded by a consonant, change the *y* to *i* and add *-es.* If the *y* is preceded by a vowel, add *-s.*

EXAMPLES: company/companies; copy/copies; journey/journeys; attorney/attorneys

 c. Many singular nouns form their plurals by changing a vowel or vowels within the word.

EXAMPLES: man/men; woman/women; foot/feet; mouse/mice

 d. Some singular nouns ending in -*o* add -*es*, even though the plural does not form another syllable.

EXAMPLES: veto/vetoes; potato/potatoes

 e. Many singular nouns ending in *f* or *fe* change the *f* or *fe* to *v* and add -*es*.

EXAMPLES: leaf/leaves; wife/wives; half/halves
     But: safe/safes; chief/chiefs; proof/proofs

 f. Hyphenated compound nouns and compound nouns made up of two or more words form their plurals by making the significant word plural. A compound noun written as one word forms its plural at the end of the word.

EXAMPLES: sales manager/sales managers; mother-in-law/mothers-in-law; footnote/footnotes

 g. The plurals of letters, numbers, symbols, signs, and words regarded as words are formed by adding an apostrophe and -*s*. This is the only time that an apostrophe is used to form a plural.

EXAMPLES: 5/5's; F.O.B./F.O.B.'s; $/$'s

4·A·2
Possessives

Noun forms change to show possession (ownership).

This is the basic rule: If the noun that is to become possessive ends in -*s*, add an apostrophe only; if the noun is also singular and consists of one syllable, you may add an apostrophe and -*s*. If the noun does not end in -*s*, add an apostrophe and -*s*.

EXAMPLES: woman/woman's; women/women's; children/children's; ladies/ladies'; boys/boys'; boss/boss' or boss's

EXCEPTIONS:

 a. To form the possessive of a compound noun, add the apostrophe or 's to the end of the word only.

SECTION 4 PARTS OF SPEECH: NOUNS AND PRONOUNS

EXAMPLES: father-in-law's; policyholder's

b. Joint ownership is shown by making the last noun possessive. If each noun is made possessive, it indicates separate ownership of two or more items. If this is the intended meaning, whatever is owned must also be plural.

EXAMPLES: Jack and Bill's car *two persons owning one car*
Jack's and Bill's cars *two persons owning two or more cars*

c. There is an idiomatic use of the possessive in expressions involving time, amounts, or personification.

EXAMPLES: one day's pay; four months' leave; a year's pay; season's greetings; today's weather

4·A·3 Warnings

1. If a proper noun is being made plural, do not vary the original spelling of the singular form.

EXAMPLES: Mary/Marys; Otto/Ottos

2. Spell names of organizations exactly as they are officially spelled. Do not add an apostrophe to a name unless the apostrophe is officially included.

EXAMPLES: Veterans Administration; Childrens Hospital; McDonald's Restaurant

4·B Pronoun form changes

The form changes of pronouns can be more difficult than those of nouns. This is because of the changes that indicate case (nominative, objective, possessive), person (first, second, third), and number (singular, plural).

The following chart gives the various forms of personal pronouns:

CASE	NOMINATIVE		OBJECTIVE		POSSESSIVE	
Person	**Singular**	**Plural**	**Singular**	**Plural**	**Singular**	**Plural**
First	I	we	me	us	my, mine	our, ours
Second	you	you	you	you	your, yours	your, yours
Third	he, she, it	they	him, her, it	them	his, her, hers, its	their, theirs

4·B·1 Case

Notice that pronouns change form to indicate nominative and objective case. Case is the form of a pronoun (or noun) indicating its relationship to other words in the sentence. The case of a pronoun is determined by the use of the pronoun in the sentence. Both nominative and objective cases have many uses and are often confused; possessive case has only one use—to show ownership.

Nominative case is used when the noun or pronoun is:

    a. Subject of a sentence or clause
    b. Predicate nominative
    c. Complement of the infinitive *to be* when that infinitive does not have its own subject
    d. Direct address
    e. Appositive when the noun or pronoun the appositive stands for is in the nominative case

Objective case is used when the pronoun is:

    a. Direct object of a transitive verb
    b. Object of a preposition
    c. Subject or object of any infinitive
    d. Complement of the infinitive *to be* when that infinitive has its own subject
    e. Indirect object
    f. Appositive when the noun or pronoun the appositive stands for is in the objective case

4·B·2 Person

There are three persons in grammar: First person (*I, we*) denotes the speaker(s); second (*you*), the person(s) spoken to; and third (*he, she, it, they*), the person(s) spoken of. Pronouns change form to show all three persons; all nouns are regarded as third person.

a. Person choice Avoid, if possible, referring to yourself or your company in the third person, for it gives a stilted, detached tone to the writing. For example, do not refer to yourself as *this writer* or *the undersigned*; instead, use *I* or *we*. If it is at all possible, of course, change the emphasis to *you*. Avoid, also, the third person indefinite pronoun, *one*; use an appropriate personal pronoun instead.

EXAMPLES: Avoid: Please return the enclosed form to the writer of this letter.
    Use: Please return the enclosed form to me.
    Avoid: Please return the contract to our company.
    Use: Please return the contract to us.
    Avoid: The undersigned is of the opinion . . .
    Use: I think . . .
    Avoid: One should always submit purchase order forms in duplicate.

Use: Please submit purchase order forms in duplicate.
Or: Will you please submit purchase order forms in duplicate.

b. I and we Occasionally business writers have difficulty in choosing between the singular *I* and the plural *we*. Use *I* when you refer to yourself, and use *we* when you refer to the company or to other employees within the company. It is possible to use both *I* and *we* in the same letter.

EXAMPLE: I have been asked to check the order that you recently sent us.

4·B·3 Number

Number means the form changes that nouns and pronouns take to show whether the words are singular or plural. Personal pronouns change forms to indicate whether the pronoun is singular or plural.

4·C Agreement

Agreement in a sentence occurs in two ways: (1) a pronoun must agree with its antecedent (the word for which the pronoun stands) in number, gender, and person; and (2) the subject of a sentence must agree with its verb in person and number.

4·C·1 Pronoun/antecedent agreement

Agreement problems arise when relative and indefinite pronouns are used.

a. Relative pronouns Relative pronouns are those pronouns that join dependent adjective clauses to their antecedents. The three most frequently used relative pronouns are *who* (or a form of it), *which*, and *that*. These pronouns do not by form show whether they are singular or plural; however, they do agree with their antecedents in number, gender, and person. Therefore, it is the antecedent that determines the number of the verb or pronoun that refers to the relative pronoun.

Determining whether a relative pronoun is singular or plural often causes difficulty in sentences such as this: *My friend is one of those persons who are always on time.* The problem, of course, is that the subject of the sentence—*my friend*—is singular; yet the descriptive clause—*who are always on time*—does not describe the subject but describes *persons*, which is plural.

EXAMPLES: My new typewriter, <u>which is described as self-correcting</u>, is excellent.
I have one of those new typewriters, <u>which are described as self-correcting</u>.
All of the books <u>that are used for reference</u> are in the north wing of the library.
It is not I <u>who am requesting a transfer to another department</u>.

b. Indefinite pronouns Indefinite pronouns (sometimes called adjective pronouns) do not name any particular individual or thing. They are such pronouns as *someone, no one, another, everybody, either, each,* and *nobody.* These pronouns are usually considered to be singular; therefore, if these pronouns are used as subjects of sentences or clauses, any verbs or pronouns referring to them must agree. In informal usage, however, this is often violated. You are much more likely to hear, "If anyone calls, tell them I'll return at three," than, "If anyone calls, tell him I'll return at three." These indefinite pronouns can in some instances be treated as collectives; if they are, the pronouns referring to them are plural.

The recent trend is to get away from words considered to be masculine or feminine. Substituting words that are neither and thereby used for both sexes has resulted in great awkwardness, particularly in the area of pronouns. There is no pronoun to indicate either masculine or feminine gender. Formerly *he* was used when the antecedent was an indefinite pronoun. For example: *Somebody parked his car in my driveway.* Now it is expressed more awkwardly: *Somebody parked his or her car in my driveway.* Until a new pronoun that refers to both genders is coined and accepted, perhaps it would be better to use: *There is a strange car parked in my driveway.* Or: *Somebody parked a car in my driveway.* The meanings are not the same, and the constructions are weaker. However, it does avoid *his or her.*

EXAMPLES: Everyone is expected to observe the new parking rules.
No one must leave his or her typewriter uncovered.
Or: All typewriters should be covered.
One of the women left her sweater in the office.
Everyone approved of Mr. Scott's speech, and they applauded vigorously when he concluded. <u>everyone</u> *is considered collective; the persons making up the collective are plural*

4·C·2 Subject/verb agreement

Ordinarily subject and verb agreement causes little trouble. The verb form changes to show number are few: all verb forms add -s or -es to the third person, singular, present tense form—*goes, walks, reaches, has*—and the verb *be* has a number of form changes to show number—*am, is, are, was, were*. The problems come about in deciding whether or not the subject is singular or plural.

Here are the instances when difficulties can arise:

a. Collective nouns If a collective noun is the subject of a sentence or clause, the verb is usually singular because the collective noun primarily acts as a unit. It can be plural if the members of the collective noun act individually.

When certain collective nouns—*number, crowd, group*—are preceded by the article *a* and followed by a prepositional phrase with a plural object, the verb may be plural.

EXAMPLES: The crowd is angry.
A crowd of angry spectators were shouting from the bleachers.
The committee is holding its meeting in Room 400.

b. Foreign nouns The plurals of foreign nouns, since they are not usually formed by adding -s, are often difficult to recognize. Check a dictionary if you do not know whether a noun is singular or plural.

EXAMPLES: The crises in the newly formed government seem unending.
Tracy's one criterion for success is making a lot of money.

c. Recognizing the true subject It is sometimes difficult to recognize the true subject if there is an intervening phrase between the subject and the verb. If the subject follows the verb, recognizing the subject can also be difficult.

EXAMPLES: One of the sales clerks is ill today.
Joan, as well as Meg and Barbara, is on vacation.
On the desk lay the plans for the new building.
There is no method that can solve the problem.

d. Subject as a part of something When the subject of the sentence is a word signifying a part of something, the number of the verb is determined by what the subject is a part of. If it is a part of something that is plural, use a plural verb; if it is a part of something that is singular, use a singular verb.

EXAMPLES: Half of the typed report is lost.
Over a third of the errors are the result of carelessness.

e. Compound subjects If the subject is compound—two nouns or pronouns joined by *and*—it is considered to be plural. If the compound subject is joined by *or* or *nor*, the verb agrees with the part of the compound nearer it.

EXAMPLES: You and I are assigned to the file room.
Either Bill or the boys are waiting for me.
Neither the boys nor Bill is waiting for me.

EXCEPTIONS:

If the subject joined by *and* is considered to be the same person or thing, the subject is singular.

EXAMPLES: The secretary and treasurer is Mr. Shaw. *If there are two persons serving in two positions, the article the is placed before the second position:* The secretary and the treasurer are Mr. Shaw and Mr. Wilson.
Oil and vinegar is the house salad dressing.

If the subject joined by *and* is preceded by *each, every,* or *many a,* it is singular.

EXAMPLES: Every cat and dog in the area is kept under strict control.
Many a student and faculty member has used the library.

4·D Indefinite reference

One of the writing problems involving pronouns has to do with reference. A pronoun is identified or recognized because it refers to some other word in the sentence (the antecedent). If the antecedent is not clear, indefinite reference exists.

EXAMPLES: Avoid: Mrs. Lee and Miss Evans left in her car.
Use: Mrs. Lee and Miss Evans left in Mrs. Lee's car.

Placing nouns that identify pronouns in parentheses to avoid indefinite reference makes an awkward construction.

SECTION 4   PARTS OF SPEECH: NOUNS AND PRONOUNS   35

Unless you are quoting directly and cannot change the sentence, avoid such a construction.

EXAMPLE: Mrs. Lee and Miss Evans left in her (Mrs. Lee's) car.

Confusion and ambiguity can also come about when there is no antecedent to which the pronoun can refer.

EXAMPLES: Avoid: At present he cannot save any money nor can he plan on <u>it</u>.
Use: At present he cannot save any money nor can he plan on saving any.
Avoid: She did not seem to know when her boss was angry, <u>which</u> was probably just as well.
Use: She did not seem to know when her boss was angry. This was probably just as well.

Never write sentences that attribute thoughts or action to the elusive *they*.

EXAMPLES: Avoid: They say that the interest rate will drop next month.
Use: The bankers in our city think that the interest rate will drop next month.
Avoid: They are closing the library for two weeks.
Use: The board of directors of the library is closing the library for two weeks.
Or resort to the passive voice if the doer is not important:
The library will be closed for two weeks.

The antecedent of *any* pronoun in your writing should be easily recognizable. Look for the pronouns; can you easily find the antecedent for each one?

4·E
Ellipsis   A syntactical error is created when a word or words that are necessary to convey the intended meaning or for the correct understanding of the sentence are omitted. The name for such an omission is *faulty ellipsis*.

Not all omissions, though, are faulty. Sometimes, for example, the relative pronoun is omitted from the subordinate clause. For example: *I read the book you recommended.* In this sentence, *that* is omitted from the clause, *you recommended.* The omission of the relative pronoun is permissible if the pronoun is not the subject of the dependent clause and if no confusion or ambiguity results.

> **EXAMPLE:** The book is not a bad one; it is just one that is not very good. *that could not be omitted; the sentence would not make sense*

Another permitted ellipsis is the omission of words that, although they are grammatically necessary, can be easily supplied by the reader without affecting the meaning of the sentence. This sentence contains an omission at the end: *Judy types faster than I.* The meaning is: *Judy types faster than I do.* There is no confusion about the meaning; the missing verb is supplied by anyone hearing or reading the sentence. Be careful, though, that in such comparisons that you do not write or say sentences such as: *Judy types faster than me.*

No one, of course, approves writing that omits words and obscures the meaning. It is merely that in many instances the meaning is understood and the ellipsis is acceptable.

> **EXAMPLES:** If (it is) possible, I shall finish the work.
> Mr. Waite is (at) home today.
> He did not wish to leave early, but he had to (leave early).

To insist that the words enclosed in parentheses be included would add words that could easily be left out.

4·F Shifts in subjects and person

Shifts in verbs were discussed earlier on pp. 25–26. You can also create writing problems by shifting the subjects of clauses in compound sentences and by shifting person within a sentence.

4·F·1 Shifts in subjects

Shifts in subjects:

> **EXAMPLES:** Avoid: My father reads many books each year, but magazines and newspapers are also read by him. *the shift is from the first subject, my father, to the second subject, magazines and newspapers; there is also a shift in the voice of the verbs*
> Use: My father reads many books, as well as magazines and newspapers, each year.

4·F·2
Shifts in person

Shifts in person:

> **EXAMPLES:** Avoid: I am considering changing jobs as one should not stay where promotion is not possible. *the shift is from first person, I, to third person, one.*
> Use: I am considering changing jobs as I do not think that I should stay where promotion is not possible.
> Avoid: All secretaries will like this new typewriter; you can correct without using erasers. *the shift is from third person, all secretaries, to second person, you*
> Use: All secretaries will like this new typewriter; they can correct without using erasers.

4·G
Placement of subject and verb

A further suggestion in placing sentence elements is that subjects should be kept near their verbs.

> **EXAMPLES:** Avoid: The plan that either one of the supervisors or one of the clerks in the mailroom should open all incoming mail regardless of how or to whom it is addressed is impractical. *the subject, the plan, is so far from the verb, is, that undoubtedly the reader would be confused*
> Use: We do not think that it is practical for one of the supervisors or clerks in the mailroom to open all incoming mail regardless of how or to whom it is addressed.

4·H
Omission of subject

Be sure, too, that each sentence has a subject unless the sentence is in the imperative mood. Include subjects, particularly for closing sentences, in any sentence that is in the indicative mood.

> **EXAMPLES:** Follow all directions carefully. *imperative mood, no subject needed*
> Avoid: Hope to see you at our sale.
> Use: We hope to see you at our sale.
> Avoid: Nice to know that you liked our product.
> Use: We are glad that you liked our product.

SECTION 5 Parts of speech: modifiers

Modifiers are those words, phrases, and clauses that in some way change, modify, restrict, or qualify some other element in the sentence. Usually adjectives and adverbs are considered to be the modifiers, but they are not the only sentence elements that can modify. There are a number of other words, phrases, and clauses that are used as adjectives or adverbs. For example, two of the verbals (those verb forms that are not used as verbs but as other parts of speech)—participles and infinitives—modify. Too, most prepositional phrases modify, as do most subordinate clauses.

Modifiers cause two problems: the first is a matter of usage —which modifier do you choose to convey the exact meaning that you want; and, second, where do you place modifiers in the sentence?

5·A Usage

The choice of the most accurate modifier is a matter of semantics. Dictionaries and thesauruses are helpful, but there are other factors as well. For example, if you use the phrase, *inexpensive car*, what reactions do you suppose you would get? The high-school student might think one figure; the highly paid executive, another; an automotive mechanic might not equate the expense with the purchase price but the frequency of repairs; the service-station attendant might determine expense by the amount of gasoline that the car used, and so on. When a car is said to be "the most expensive car I ever owned," further description is needed. When "I had a repair bill for it every month" is added, the description is qualified; the reader understands the meaning in this instance of *expensive*.

Remember, too, that the written word does not convey meaning by facial expression, voice inflection, or gesture. The vague clause, "The chair is about so high," is descriptive when accompanied by a hand motion to show the height that is meant; but if you are writing a size description of a chair, give its measurements in the actual number of inches.

5·B Adjective and adverb form changes

Both adjectives and adverbs change form to show degree of comparison. The adjective or adverb form found in the dictionary is the simple or positive form. It is possible to make changes in this simple form to show a greater or lesser degree of the characteristic than the adjective or adverb expresses. Such changes are called *degrees of comparison*.

The three degrees are *positive*, *comparative*, and *superlative*. The comparative degree is used to compare two items; the superlative, three or more. The superlative can also be used for emphasis. The dictionary will show how each adjective or adverb is compared, sometimes by adding -er or -est; sometimes by changing the word itself; and sometimes by the addition of words such as *more, most, less,* or *least.*

EXAMPLES: big, bigger, biggest
good/well, better, best
nicely, more nicely, most nicely
efficient, less efficient, least efficient

5·C Placement of modifiers in sentence

The greatest problem with modifiers is their placement in sentences. Generally, modifiers are placed near or next to whatever is modified. When modifiers are not correctly placed in sentences, they are said to dangle or to be misplaced. Sentences are also incorrectly written when they contain no element that the adjective or adverb can modify.

5·C·1 Adjectives

Placement of single-word adjectives causes very little trouble. In English the adjective is almost always placed before the noun or pronoun that is modified. The phrases, *red barn, electric typewriter,* and *air-conditioned office,* are written in adjective-noun order and are easily understood.

Be sure that a single modifier is not placed before two or more words when it modifies only one of them.

EXAMPLES: Avoid: Jim bought an air-conditioned house and lot.
Use: Jim bought an air-conditioned house and a lot.

a. Predicate adjectives An adjective can be placed after the verb and modify the subject. These are called predicate adjectives. Predicate adjectives always follow linking verbs.

EXAMPLES: The letter is <u>long</u>.
The refrigerator feels <u>cold</u>.
The lemon tastes <u>sour</u>.

Because these are adjectives, they should not have adverb endings. Do not write: *I feel badly.*

b. Adjective phrases Adjective phrases (participial, infinitive, and prepositional) are placed next to the nouns or pronouns that they modify.

EXAMPLES: The house <u>in the middle of the block</u> is for sale.
prepositional phrase modifying <u>house</u>
<u>Standing in the rain</u>, the package became soggy.
participial phrase modifying <u>package</u>
He made an effort <u>to finish the report</u>. *infinitive phrase modifying* <u>effort</u>

Many adjective phrases contain verbals—participles, infinitives, or gerunds. Verbals are defined as verb forms used as adjectives, adverbs, or nouns. They look like verbs but do the work of other parts of speech. They have no classification as separate parts of speech; yet they do the work of three parts of speech. To use verbal modifiers correctly, just be sure that they are placed next to the words that they modify and that they do not dangle. A verbal modifier is considered to be dangling when it is not placed next to the word it modifies—in most instances it is placed next to a word that it could not possibly modify—or when there is no word in the sentence that the verbal could modify.

Ordinarily the dangling modifiers are either participial phrases or prepositional phrases containing gerunds and used as adjectives. The dangling modifiers are often amusing, usually confusing, and sometimes both.

EXAMPLES (taken from newspaper articles):

Avoid: Sitting in the widening pool of sulphuric acid, State Department of Fish and Game wardens found three drums of cyanide.

Use: State Department of Fish and Game wardens found three drums of cyanide sitting in a widening pool of sulphuric acid.

Avoid: Actress and singer Polly Bergen was there with her husband looking marvelously glamorous in a midnight green dress adorned with large polka dots of banquette rhinestones.

Use: Actress and singer Polly Bergen, looking marvelously glamorous in a midnight green dress adorned with large polka dots of banguette rhinestones, was there with her husband.

c. Adjective clauses Adjective clauses (also called relative clauses) are usually introduced by *who, which,* or *that.* The subordinate conjunctions that introduce these clauses are also considered to be relative pronouns. The antecedents of relative pronouns are always placed right before the relative or adjective clause.

EXAMPLES: Avoid: Ralph Nader spoke of a vast number of chickens with a sort of chicken cancer that are on the market. *the relative clause does not modify* cancer; *it modifies* chickens
Use: Ralph Nader spoke of a vast number of chickens that are on the market and that have a sort of chicken cancer.
Avoid: The boy is lost who is at the police station. *the relative clause describes* boy *and should be placed after it*
Use: The boy who is at the police station is lost.

There is a punctuation problem when using adjective clauses; that is, to determine whether they are restrictive or nonrestrictive. A restrictive clause is necessary for understanding the sentence; a nonrestrictive clause is not necessary but merely adds additional information. If the modifier is restrictive, it is not set off by commas; if the modifier is nonrestrictive, it is set off by commas.

EXAMPLES: Any employee who is ill should remain at home. *if the clause,* who is ill, *is omitted, the sentence is not true:* all employees should not remain at home; *therefore, the clause is restrictive and should not be set off by commas*
My secretary, who has worked for me for ten years, is ill. *the adjective clause,* who has worked for me for ten years, *is not needed for the rest of the sentence to be true and merely gives additional information; therefore, the clause is nonrestrictive and is set off by commas*

5·C·2 Adverbs One-word adverb modifiers, like adjectives, are placed either before or after the word that is modified. However, adverb phrases and clauses can be placed either at the beginning or at the end of sentences or clauses. Too, adverbs modify more parts of speech than do adjectives, for adverbs can modify verbs, adjectives, and other adverbs.

a. One-word adverbs Single adverbs are placed before or after the words that they limit or describe.

EXAMPLE: Mr. Hunter said that he sold used cars.
Place <u>only</u> in this sentence. It can be placed before or after every word in the sentence and by its placement produce a different meaning each time. Here are some examples:
Only Mr. Hunter said that he sold used cars.
Mr. Hunter said that only he sold used cars.
Mr. Hunter said that he sold only used cars.

b. Adverb phrases Prepositional and infinitive phrases can be used as adverbs. When these phrases are used as adverbs, they answer why, when, or where or express condition (if).

EXAMPLES: Jane studies <u>to improve her grades</u>. *infinitive phrase used as an adverb; it modifies studies and tells why* <u>Jane studies</u>
Toni hiked <u>in the national park</u>. *prepositional phrase used as an adverb; it modifies* <u>hiked</u> *and tells where* <u>Toni hiked</u>

If the sentence has more than one verb, placement of adverb modifiers can create an even greater variety of meanings.

EXAMPLE: Kim said that she would buy me a cup of coffee on the way to work.
At the beginning: On the way to work, Kim said that she would buy me a cup of coffee.
Or: Kim said that she would, on the way to work, buy me a cup of coffee.

c. Adverb clauses Adverb clauses, like phrases, answer why, when, or where or express condition. The normal placement of an adverb clause is after the verb. It can also be placed at the beginning of a sentence; this sentence order changes emphasis or gives variety to writing.

EXAMPLES: <u>When you are camping</u>, be very careful with open fires. *adverb clause placed at the beginning of the sentence and out of its natural order*
Be very careful with open fires <u>when you are camping</u>. *adverb clause at the end of the sentence and in natural sentence order*

5·D
Superlatives One usage problem with adjectives and adverbs is choosing words to convey sincerity. Too many superlatives—*best, greatest, most wonderful, largest, latest*—produce a tone of insin-

cerity. Both oral and written advertisements have tended to dull our sensitivity to statements such as:
Prices are at an all-time low.
This is positively your last chance to make tremendous savings.
We are sure (or positive) that you will want to take advantage of this marvelous offer.

Most readers would prefer to be given the facts and to make their own judgments. They would prefer to compare prices over a period of time to prove that they are at an "all-time low" and then make their own decisions. See Superlatives, p. 68.

5·E Double negatives

Two negative statements in the same clause or sentence should not be used to express a single negative.

EXAMPLES: Avoid: I couldn't hardly believe that Mr. Queen was quitting.
Use: I could hardly believe that Mr. Queen was quitting.
Avoid: I didn't find the file nowhere.
Use: I didn't find the file anywhere.

There are times, though, when one negative statement qualifies or modifies another negative statement in the same clause or sentence. This can give a meaning that has a special emphasis.

EXAMPLES: This is not an impossible situation.
This is a possible situation.
What does the first sentence mean? It means that, although it is an extremely difficult situation, it can be worked out. The second sentence, by eliminating the double negative, changes the meaning entirely.
His action is not illegal.
His action is legal.
If the double negative contained in the first sentence is eliminated, obviously the meaning is changed.

Therefore, avoid statements such as, *I don't have no money,* but use double negatives when you wish to convey a certain meaning or a certain emphasis.

5·F Compound adjectives

A compound adjective consists of two or more descriptive words, usually connected by hyphens, and serves as a single adjective. Although a compound adjective is always hyphenated when it precedes the noun that it modifies, it need not be hyphenated when it follows the noun that it modifies (as in the case of predicate adjectives). The tendency is, though, to hyphenate a compound adjective regardless of its position in the sentence.

> **EXAMPLES:** His off-the-cuff remarks were widely quoted.
> I thought his remarks were off-the-cuff.

Compound words are sometimes coined by putting together two or more words that separately would have entirely different meanings. Usually the usage is informal, but often the phrase is quite descriptive. Care in choosing such phrases must be taken—do not use them too often in writing and be sure that they are not trite.

> **EXAMPLES:** know-how how-to
> Johnny-come-lately do-it-yourself

In a series of adjectives modifying the same noun, hyphens followed by a space are used to carry the modifier over to the noun. These are called suspending hyphens.

> **EXAMPLES:** Will the meeting be a two- or three-day conference?
> Do you want the two- or four-door model?

SECTION 6 Parts of speech: connectors

There are two connectors of sentence elements: prepositions and conjunctions. Some words can be either prepositions or conjunctions—*but*, for example. Classification of words as prepositions or conjunctions is determined by the elements that they connect.

6·A Prepositions

Prepositions are those little words that connect nouns or pronouns to the rest of the sentence. These nouns or pronouns become the *objects of the preposition*. The preposition plus its object and any modifiers is a *prepositional phrase*.

> **EXAMPLES:** on Friday
> in the letter
> with great speed

6·A·1 Phrasal prepositions

Another term to know is *phrasal preposition*. A phrasal preposition is one or more words used as a single preposition.

SECTION 6   PARTS OF SPEECH: CONNECTORS

EXAMPLES: because of
in spite of
by means of
in accordance with
in the case of

If possible, avoid these roundabout phrases and use single prepositions.

EXAMPLES:
phrasal prepositions:	replace with:
by means of	with or by
for the purpose of	for
in regard to	about or concerning
in order to	to
in connection with	of, in, or on
in accordance with	with or by
inasmuch as	since
in relation to	toward or to
in the matter of	in
in the amount of	for
in the time of	during
in the case of	in or if
on the part of	for
with reference to	on, about, or concerning
on behalf of	for

Sometimes a phrasal preposition can be omitted with no replacement.

EXAMPLE: Please tell us how many hours are spent (in connection with) checking clerical errors.

6·A·2 Nine most used prepositions

It is helpful in understanding prepositions to learn the nine that are the most frequently used (These nine account for over 90 percent of all prepositions used): *at, by, for, from, in, of, on, to,* and *with.*

6·A·3 Idiomatic usage of prepositions

There are certain prepositions that go with certain verbs to convey specific meanings. This is idiomatic usage. For example, use *free from worry,* not *free of worry.* When you are in doubt about choosing the correct preposition, check the verb in the dictionary. Very often, examples showing the various prepositions used with verbs and the meanings of the combinations will be given.

EXAMPLES: agree to . . . a proposal
agree with . . . a person
agree on . . . a plan
compare to . . . to discover similarities only
compare with . . . to discover likenesses or differences
convenient for . . . a purpose
convenient to . . . a person
die *of* (not *with*) . . . disease
differ from (not *with*) . . . an opinion
differ about (or *over*) . . . a question
free *from* (not *of*)
in search *of* (not *for*)
unequal *to* (not *for*)
unmindful *of* (not *about*)

Prepositions can have a great effect on the meanings of verbs. Consider what happens to the verb *run* when the preposition following it is changed. What are the meanings of the various combinations: *run into, run by, run for, run on, run with, run around, run down, run up, run across, run against?* Try putting these combinations into sentences. The variety of meanings is obvious.

EXAMPLES: I ran into Helene at the library.
I'll run by with the book.
Walt has been running around all day.
He ran up a big bill at the department store.
I ran across a reference to the problem in this magazine article.

Should you try to understand the meaning by defining the words literally, there would be complete confusion. These idiomatic expressions have been developed over a long period of time by people using the language.

6·A·4
Prepositional phrases as modifiers

Prepositional phrases can modify; that is, they can be used as adjectives or adverbs. If used as adjectives, they are ordinarily placed after the nouns that they modify.

EXAMPLE: Turn right at the house on the corner.

Adverb prepositional phrases are usually placed after intransitive verbs or after direct objects of transitive verbs; they may also be placed at the beginnings of sentences. Placement of modifying prepositional phrases is also discussed on p. 42.

EXAMPLES: Turn <u>at the next corner</u>. *phrase used as adverb and placed after intransitive verb*
Make a turn <u>at the next corner</u>. *phrase used as adverb and placed after direct object*
<u>At the next corner,</u> turn right. *phrase used as adverb and placed at the beginning of the sentence*

6·A·5
Ending sentences with prepositions

Whenever prepositions are discussed, the question of ending a sentence with a preposition is usually raised. To say that a sentence should never end with a preposition is a pedantic rule; there are sentences that do end correctly in prepositions. If the sentence becomes awkward by trying to get a sentence order that does not end with a preposition, then by all means end the sentence with a preposition.

EXAMPLES: Try rewording these sentences so that the preposition is not at the end:
She could not imagine what I had been through.
What do you want this for?
Do you know what it is about?
His action is uncalled for.

When the preposition is the important word in the verb-preposition combination, putting the preposition at the end of the sentence will provide emphasis.

6·A·6
Unnecessary prepositions

Be sure that you do not add extra and unnecessary prepositions. For example, <u>The item will be priced at about $25</u>. *At* means a specific point; *about*, approximate. Not only is the preposition extra, but the meaning is impossible. Use: <u>The item will be priced at $25</u> if the price is definitely $25. Use: <u>The item will be priced about $25</u> if the price is approximate.

EXAMPLES: Avoid: Where are you going <u>to</u>?
Use: Where are you going?
Avoid: When are you going to start <u>in on</u> the typing?
Use: When are you going to start typing?

When considering superfluous prepositions, some reference should be made to *up*. This word is added to many, many verbs for no apparent purpose. Here are some of the combinations: *call up, size up, eat up, divide up, drink up, type up, climb up, rest up, wake up, hang up, cut up, mix up.* Perhaps the reason for such extras is that there are certain verbs to which *up* is added for special meanings; for example, *pick up, hurry up, keep up*. In most instances this is informal or spoken usage; certainly it is not something that would be found in anything but the most casual writing.

Up is not the only preposition that is added in this manner. *In* and *out* (often with *of*) are frequently added to verbs, making such combinations as: *listen in, call in, run in, come in, get out, walk out, run out, back out, come out*.

In addition, many verb-preposition combinations become nouns. Again, most of these are used informally.

EXAMPLES: sit-in, walkout, walk-up, breakdown, markup, trade-in, lookout, set-to, showdown, setup, shoot-out, markdown, knockout

Notice that all of these examples are spelled either as one word or are hyphenated. Check dictionary spellings, for some of these same words when used as verbs will be spelled as two words.

6·B Conjunctions

The other connector of sentence elements is the conjunction. Conjunctions are more complex, for they are divided into four kinds according to the sentence elements that are connected. The four kinds of conjunctions are *coordinate, correlative, subordinate,* and the *conjunctive adverb*.

6·B·1 Coordinate

The best-known and most frequently used conjunctions are the coordinate. The six most common ones are *and, or, nor, for, but,* and *yet*. They connect sentence items of equal grammatical rank—nouns to nouns, verbs to verbs, and noun clauses to noun clauses, for example.

EXAMPLES: Karen <u>and</u> Susan missed their eight o'clock class.
coordinate conjunction connecting two nouns
David could not eat <u>or</u> drink after the accident.
coordinate conjunction connecting two verbs
The girl did not say that she had cheated <u>nor</u> that she had not. *coordinate conjunction connecting two noun clauses*

6·B·2 Correlative

Correlative conjunctions, including such pairs as *either/or, neither/nor,* and *not only/but also,* are really parts of coordinate conjunctions, as the second member of the pair is always a coordinate conjunction. Their purpose in sentences is to add emphasis. By putting a word such as *either, neither, not only,*

SECTION 6 PARTS OF SPEECH: CONNECTORS

or *both* before the first member of a series, it becomes more emphatic.

EXAMPLE: Either you will be on time or you will be dismissed.
in this direct order, the either *before the first clause excludes there being any other action*

6·B·3 Subordinate

The subordinate conjunctions (*that, which, who, when, while, if,* for example) are conjunctions that connect dependent adjective, adverb, or noun clauses to independent clauses. If the clauses are adjective or adverb, they must be placed next to the elements modified or—for adverb clauses—at the beginning of a sentence (see pp. 40–42). Aside from correct placement, these conjunctions present few problems.

A usage problem occasionally arises in choosing between coordinate and subordinate conjunctions in connecting clauses. If you choose a coordinate conjunction as a connector, you will join two independent clauses (compound sentence); if you choose a subordinate conjunction, you will be joining a dependent clause to an independent clause (complex sentence). The choice will be determined by one of two things: meaning or style.

EXAMPLES: He stopped walking when I called to him.
I called to him, and he stopped walking.
In the first example, the events are related in that the independent clause, he stopped walking, *was caused by the dependent clause,* when I called to him. *In the second example, the relationship has a different meaning—the two actions are equated.*
She failed the French course, for she did not study.
She failed the French course because she did not study.
There are no differences in meaning between these two examples.

The choice of conjunction in such instances becomes a matter of style. You may decide to use one or the other to vary your writing or to achieve parallel construction. Be sure, though, that there is no difference in meaning and that the meaning is not changed by the choice of conjunction.

6·B·4 Conjunctive adverbs

The conjunctive adverbs are those ponderous words such as *moreover, nevertheless, consequently,* and *likewise.* They connect two independent clauses and show a relationship between the connected clauses. Coordinate conjunctions also connect independent clauses; but they do not, as conjunctive adverbs do, show a relationship between the two connected independent clauses. The conjunctive adverbs are more appropriate to formal writing than to general writing or business letters. Because they give a stilted tone to writing, they should be used very sparingly.

SECTION 7 Letter writing principles

Good business writing involves using the same techniques and principles as are used in any good writing. Mechanics, organization, and emphasis may vary somewhat between business writing and other writing, but effective writing for whatever purpose is based on certain fundamentals. These are adapted for business writing and discussed here.

7·A Parallel construction

One of the basic fundamentals of good writing is parallel or balanced construction. When sentence construction is not parallel, it is called shifted construction. Part of this has already been discussed in the sections on nouns and verbs (see pp. 25–26 and 36–37).

The sentence is, of course, the basic element of all writing; and basic to the writing of sentences is the principle that the components of the sentence be arranged in a parallel manner.

Parallel construction is the arrangement of a series of two or more grammatically equivalent words, phrases, or clauses so that they are balanced. These grammatical elements are connected by coordinate conjunctions. The connected pair—or series—must be so balanced grammatically that not only are words joined to words, phrases joined to phrases, or clauses joined to clauses, but also gerunds are joined to gerunds, prepositional phrases are joined to prepositional phrases, and noun clauses are joined to noun clauses.

Why is this construction so important? It makes writing easier to understand, it adds directness to sentences, and it lets the reader know what to expect. It makes sentences go together more smoothly, creating unity, coherence, and clarity.

EXAMPLES: Avoid: This appliance is both a time-saver and indispensable. *This is not parallel, as the conjunction connects a noun,* time-saver, *to an adjective,* indispensable.

Use: This appliance is both timesaving and indispensable. *The conjunction now*

SECTION 7 LETTER WRITING PRINCIPLES   51

connects two adjectives, timesaving, *and* indispensable.
Avoid: I read in the office *and* while riding on the train. *This is not parallel as the conjunction connects a prepositional phrase and a gerund phrase.*
Use: I read in the office *and* on the train. *The conjunction in this example connects two prepositional phrases.*

Consider these points that are important to parallel construction:

7·A·1
Use of correlative conjunctions

When you are using correlative conjunctions (*either/or; neither/nor,* for example), the connector—which is the conjunction used to connect items of equal grammatical rank—is coordinate. To keep the items parallel when using correlative conjunctions, be sure that each member of the correlative pair is placed immediately before the words that they connect.

EXAMPLES:
Avoid: You will either attend the morning *or* afternoon *session.*
Use: You will attend either the morning *or* afternoon *session.*
Avoid: Mr. Eastman said that he either expected to correspond with Miss Johnson *or* talk to her by telephone.
Use: Mr. Eastman said that he expected either to correspond with Miss Johnson *or* to talk to her by telephone.

7·A·2
Use of articles and prepositions

An article or a preposition coming before members of a series must either be used with only the first item or be repeated before every item. However, repeating a preposition, an article, the *to* of an infinitive, or the introductory words of a phrase or clause can help to make the parallel construction clear. The repetition of the article in a series can also add emphasis.

EXAMPLES:
Avoid: Alan went to the store, bank, and to the gas station.
Use: Alan went to the store, bank, and gas station.
Use: Alan went to the store, to the bank, and to the gas station.
According to the rules of reason, according to the natural course of the malady,

and according to whatever laws govern economics and world politics, we should not survive.

—Edward Teller, *Harpers*

This is an excellent example of repeating the phrasal preposition, according to.

7·A·3
Listing points

If you are listing points, list them in the same form. You can use subject, verb, object, for example, or any other form that is written in the same sentence order.

EXAMPLE: Avoid: Your checking account will be free if:
1. You maintain a balance of $300 at all times.
2. No more than fifteen checks each month are written.
3. Your savings account is with this bank.

Use: Your checking account will be free if:
1. You maintain a balance of $300 at all times.
2. You write no more than fifteen checks each month.
3. You have a savings account with this bank.

7·A·4
Parallelism in writing units

So far the discussion has been concerned with writing that is parallel in mechanics; that is, expressing the grammatical units of a sentence in a balanced order. However, parallelism can be a device used throughout an entire letter or report. Parallel structure should be given to the ideas and concepts that are of equal importance within the writing unit as well as to the grammatical units. If an idea is worth one paragraph, then another idea of equal importance should not be dismissed with one sentence. An outline is an excellent way of assigning importance or weight to various items. The items assigned I, II, etc., should be parallel; those, A, B, etc., parallel.

Parallelism in business writing requires that sentences be similar in structure, pattern, length, and order. This enables the reader to follow the thoughts and organization of the writer. The reader is not thrown off by a change in sentence pattern or by trying to decide the importance given to various points. If the reader has trouble understanding a business letter, chances are that it is poorly organized and the ideas are not parallel. A lack of parallelism in writing is a reflection on the writer; obviously the thinking or ideas have not been organized —the result is muddled writing that is not easily understood.

Not only should the grammatical constructions of the sentences be parallel but the ideas presented in the letter or report should also be parallel; this can be done by practice and planning.

7·B Reader-oriented writing

First of all, when you write any letter, be very aware of the person who will read your letter. The reader is the one who will do or not do what you want or will react favorably or unfavorably to your writing. How do you positively impress this unknown reader? Simply by putting yourself in the place of the reader. This is called empathy. In writing it means that you read the sentences you have just written and ask yourself how you would react to what has been written. The reader understands the letter in relation to individual circumstances and concepts, not in relation to you, and orients the writing to his or her situation. For instance, is the sale offering products that the reader wants? Probably you would not send a sales letter for motorcycles to the residents of a retirement home.

7·B·1 Address letters to persons, not titles

In most business letters, the recipient is completely unknown. Sometimes not even a name is available; the letter is addressed to a title such as a *sales manager*. If it is at all possible, address letters to persons. Try, for example, to get the names of the sales manager or vice president rather than address the mail to titles. Usually, and particularly in large organizations, the mail will get to the proper person more quickly if addressed to a name than if it is addressed to a title and has to be routed through a mail room. Check previous correspondence or directories, make telephone calls, ask questions—try to find the name of the person to whom you are writing. Be sure that the name is correctly spelled. The salutation that reads *Dear Mrs. Lewis* is much more personal than the letter that begins *Dear Madam*. A letter addressed to *Dear Sir and Madam* seems even more offending; *Dear Mr. and Mrs. Lewis* sounds both friendly and personal.

If you know the person to whom you are writing or something about that person, so much the better. Even if you know only the vocation or profession of the reader, this can be helpful; the language and vocabulary that you use will be understood. Many other factors can be helpful: age group, sex, occupation, and education of the recipient are important factors to consider when composing letters.

GOOD BUSINESS WRITING

**7·B·2
Reader is unknown**

As you write the letter, remember that the reader cannot see or hear you. There are no facial expressions, no gestures, no speech emphasis, no tone of voice, or any other aid to convey meaning. The old complaint, "It's not what you say but the way you say it," does not operate in writing. All that the reader has is the typed page to give clues.

**7·B·3
I or we**

Look at a letter that you have just written or received. What is the first word of the letter? Is it *I* or *we*? Look at the beginnings of each paragraph; ask the same question. Count the number of *you*'s, then the number of *I*'s and *we*'s. The ratio should be two or three *you*'s to the *I*'s and *we*'s.

**7·B·4
Be concise**

Another annoyance to the reader of a letter is to have to read more than he wants to know. If you must write a long letter—if there is absolutely no way of leaving out any of the information—then make the letter more readable by using short sentences and short paragraphs. Keep the sentences to no more than twenty words in length; the paragraphs, no more than three or four typed lines. A long letter that is greatly overwritten takes longer to read, covers the important facts with verbiage, and confuses the reader to the point where often the letter is ignored.

**7·B·5
Get to the point immediately**

Another way in which you can be considerate of your reader is to get to the point immediately. Do not say, for example, to the person you are writing that you are answering a letter of the 21st; the reader knows that he or she wrote you and is waiting for an answer. If you avoid telling the reader immediately what he or she wants to know, perhaps the reader won't read far enough to get the message. Not only does getting to the point immediately help the reader, but it also helps you by forcing you to keep to the facts and preventing you from wandering.

Contrast these examples:

```
I have been a charge-account customer at your
store for over fifteen years, and in this time I
have purchased many items from you. They have all
been satisfactory. However, I recently ordered an
Apex Pocket Calculator from you. It was delivered
today, and it is broken and will not operate.
Perhaps it was damaged in shipment as the package
was crushed upon arrival . . .
```

At this point, the reader is probably wondering what the

SECTION 7 LETTER WRITING PRINCIPLES   55

writer wants to say. Skip the past history and say what really happened:

```
The Apex Calculator that I ordered from you was
delivered today, but the package had been crushed
and the case of the calculator is cracked. I should
like the calculator replaced so I am returning it.
Would you please either send me another calculator
or let me know if the calculator is not available
and remove the charge from my statement.
```

Suppose you are enclosing a check. This is happy news for any recipient. Tell the reader right away what you are doing.

EXAMPLES: Avoid: We are refunding the amount of $50 that you overpaid on last month's statement. Our check for this amount is enclosed.

Use: A check for $50 is enclosed. This is the refund for the overpayment that you sent us last month.

Avoid: I am writing to inform you that your name has been proposed for membership as a National Associate of the XYZ Institute. *this is an opening from an actual letter*

Use: Your name has been proposed for membership as a National Associate of the XYZ Institute.

**7·B·6
Answer
letters
promptly**

Another factor that shows consideration is the speed with which letters are answered. When a letter cannot be answered promptly—for example, the information requested cannot be quickly obtained—it should be acknowledged immediately. If the reason for writing the letter has been to get a response and if someone has taken the time and trouble to write, that person wants and deserves an answer. All letters pertaining to company business should be opened and—if the person who ordinarily would handle the matter is unavailable—referred to someone else for either attention or acknowledgment. If the sender of a letter must write a second time, keeping that person as a customer becomes unlikely. Mutual of New York has a policy that all incoming letters are answered within three days; many mail-order companies have similar policies. Even a postcard stating that an order is on its way is reassuring. Answering or acknowledging a letter is particularly important when letters contain complaints. If a person is already angry or annoyed because of dissatisfaction with the product or service, ignoring a letter of complaint will only aggravate the situation.

When you are writing a letter in confirmation of a telephone or personal conversation, write as soon after the conversation as possible. The information will be more accurately remembered, and both you and the recipient of the letter will have a written reminder. Such a letter also keeps the facts straight and builds goodwill.

Letters are written, too, as reminders of deadlines, appointments, or payments that are due. A reminder letter should be written far enough in advance so that the reader has time to respond. No one can keep an appointment for the 25th if the reminder is received on the 26th.

3

language choice

There are many, many terms to describe language usage. We speak of formal and informal, standard and nonstandard, literary and general usage, to mention a few. These are inclusive terms that really do not tell much. In most instances, what you would really like to know is: Is this expression, construction, phrase, or sentence all right to use? If not, why not? Where do you find information concerning correct usage? What can you substitute if you find that a term or phrase is unacceptable? Or are you a Humpty Dumpty, who told Alice (*Through the Looking Glass* by Lewis Carroll), "When I use a word, it means just what I choose it to mean—neither more nor less."

There are some who might argue that there is language for business writing that is different from other language. Although there are terms used principally in certain types of business (they would probably be considered technical terms), business writing has no more freedom in using unacceptable words or expressions than has any other writing. The stereotype of the uneducated and semiliterate businessperson who cannot write anything but a cliche-ridden, incorrect letter is just that—a stereotype.

SECTION 8 Language usage problems

In discussing language usage or choice of words (diction) in this section, mechanical problems such as grammar and spelling are not included. What will be discussed is the correct choice in business writing of expressions, words, and even definitions. There are many books (many of them written by journalists) that tell what usage is acceptable and what is not (see Appendix, p. 208); dictionaries also give you much information on standard usage. In spite of all of the available information, a lot of errors are made every day. Many errors are made in ignorance. The retort to being told that something is wrong is: "What's wrong with that?" Some would no doubt be considered nitpicking, for even authorities do not always agree. Time, too, affects usage in two ways: Some expressions are dropped; other expressions that had not before been approved become acceptable. This ever-changing quality of language usage is one of its fascinations, for it makes language living, exciting, and vivid.

Although language usage is becoming more permissive, there are still many times when you will need help. A good dictionary is probably your first source of information. In most instances this source will be sufficient. If you cannot find the information that you want in a dictionary, you may have to search in one or more of the many usage books, such as Fowler's *Modern English Usage*. The Appendix contains a list of such books.

There are many good desk-sized dictionaries available (see list in Appendix, p. 206). However, choose one that seems easiest for you to read and use; that is, such things as the symbols and pronunciation marks should be easy to understand. Become familiar with your dictionary. Learn what all of the entries about a word mean. Check the date of any dictionary that you intend buying; usually dictionaries are kept up-to-date by frequent revisions. Because language is constantly changing and new words and new ways of using words are being added to the language, it is important that your dictionary be a late edition and that it be replaced as later editions are published.

Dictionaries usually place words into labeled and unlabeled categories. Words in the first category carry labels concerning their usage along with other information—definition, pronunciation, syllabication, and so on. The general division of labels is into categories of standard and nonstandard. The standard words do not carry labels that restrict their usage; nonstandard words are in some way restricted. It is easy to say that any word or expression that is not standard American English is therefore nonstandard; this assumes that there is a standard language spoken and written throughout the United States. Most people, particularly in their spoken language, include nonstandard expressions. However, most people also recognize that there are standards and would be satisfied to let dictionaries settle usage problems.

8·A Nonstandard usage

The labels that follow are considered to be nonstandard usage and should ordinarily be avoided, at least in writing. However, some can be used by the skilled writer for effective writing.

SECTION 8   LANGUAGE USAGE PROBLEMS   59

8·A·1
Illiterate   This includes words that are usually spoken and are corruptions of correct forms.

   EXAMPLES: ain't   his'n   dassant

8·A·2
Archaic   These are old words that are no longer used.

   EXAMPLE: afeard for afraid

8·A·3
Obsolete   These are words that were once used but that have disappeared from the language.

   EXAMPLE: <u>instance</u> when it has the meaning of impelling motive

8·A·4
Rare   These are words that were never commonly used and for which there are better synonyms.

   EXAMPLE: <u>cadent</u>, meaning having a white-hot glow, incandescent.

8·A·5
Poetic   These are shortenings of words, such as *e'er* and *o'er*, which are common to poetry but not to other writing.

8·A·6
Technical or field   These are specialized words having to do with technical, industrial, professional, or scientific areas. Often they are labeled in dictionaries with the field or area in which they are found, such as *Chem.* or *Bot.*

There are instances when technical terms or ordinary words having special meanings in a particular area can and should be used. If an engineer is writing to someone with an engineering background—or a lawyer is communicating with someone with a knowledge of law—the language may be such that it could not easily be understood by the ordinary reader. Unless you know, though, that your reader is knowledgeable in a technical area, confine your writing to generally understood language. However, be careful not to use an inexact or wordy expression instead of a needed technical term merely because you are afraid that such an expression could not be understood. If necessary, define such terms. For example, it might be necessary to write about a life insurance policy based on *actuarial principles*. If you do, explain that actuarial principles are based on statistical computations having to do, in this instance, with life expectancy. Avoid an explanation that simply quotes a dictionary definition, for often dictionary definitions are limited to general meanings.

LANGUAGE CHOICE

8·A·7 Regional or local

These are words used frequently in one area or region of the country rather than throughout the country. They can also be common words that are used to convey special or different meanings in a region or area. There are, in addition, differences of usage among the English-speaking countries—*elevator* is labeled *U.S.* and *lift, Brit.*, for example.

> **EXAMPLE:** a backyard <u>barbeque</u> on the West Coast would be called a <u>cook-out</u> on the East Coast.

Regional words should not be confused with dialect, which, although it is often regional, involves pronunciation, speech patterns, and grammar as well.

Regional or local expressions in the United States are disappearing as people increasingly travel from one region to another and come in contact with more and more people from other areas. Television, in addition to the wide circulation of newspapers and magazines, has contributed to communicating on a national basis. Even language peculiar to those in certain age or ethnic groups is understood nationally by persons in similar groups. Informal or colloquial language, as well as slang, is more likely to be regional than is standard usage language.

8·A·8 Foreign language

These are words that are taken from another language.

More and more the tendency is to use English-language words and expressions rather than resorting to foreign-language terms. The Latin abbreviations, *id est, exemplia gratia, et cetera, et alii,* and *ibidem,* for example, are being replaced by their English equivalents. If you use foreign terms (often French) to display superior knowledge, you are, as Fowler (*Modern English Usage,* H. W. Fowler) writes, "inconsiderate and rude" and such use is a "vulgarity." There are, of course, certain words of foreign origin that are a part of the English language—*chauffeur, baton, ballet, junta,* for example. The sciences rely heavily on Latin terms, but these are often technical terms that are unknown to the average person. Certainly business writers need to use language that can be quickly and unmistakably understood and that can be found in American dictionaries.

8·A·9 Slang

The American Heritage Dictionary definition of slang is: "Nonstandard vocabulary of a given culture or subculture, consisting typically of arbitrary and often ephemeral coinages and figures of speech characterized by spontaneity and raciness."

SECTION 8 LANGUAGE USAGE PROBLEMS

There are times when slang can be effective, when it is colorful and descriptive; unfortunately, often it is tasteless and inexact. Too, it is often temporary, staying in current usage only briefly, although occasionally it survives for centuries. Sometimes it is vulgar, obscene, crude, or profane; it can be funny, entertaining, imaginative, and precise. It may be regional or universal, or it may be used by one age group, nationality, or race. It may be peculiar to an occupation, the military, or a group such as jazz musicians or actors. Historic events and current happenings may produce their own slang, or it may appear spontaneously from no known source.

There is only one warning: Use slang in business writing sparingly and cautiously. While it is often difficult to distinguish between current, colorful language and slang, it is not so much the words that are used as the skill with which such language is employed. Remember, too, that written slang has no gestures, tone of voice, or facial expressions to help convey meaning.

If you use slang in business writing, be sure that it is appropriate and not overdone. Because of its informality, slang is used most often in letters in which an informal conversational tone is wanted; sales letters, for example. Too, slang has limited usage—one age group, region of the country, nationality, or profession, for example. Be certain, therefore, that it is appropriate to your reader. Not all slang is universal or is generally understood; what may be well-known to you or your contemporaries may not be understood by others and may actually be offensive.

This example (which is an actual letter) has a limited appeal. It probably would not be understood by anyone over twenty-five.

```
Hi....

Are your present wheels a little shaky?

ENTERPRISE 70 is the 'in' way to solve your blues.
Its purpose is elementary, yet quite signifi-
cant.....to provide swinging transportation, new or
used, foreign or domestic, at prices and interest
rates lower than are available at any auto dealer-
ship. In other words, what's happening is....we
of ENTERPRISE 70 are here to fill a need. ENTERPRISE
70 exists due to a growing need for people of
limited budgets to own an 'out of sight' set of
```

wheels at 'insight' prices. Check us out before your present wheels space you out with a monster repair bill.

see ya................
Joe Hart   Jean Stevens   Bill Craig

8·A·10 Jargon

Jargon is language that is peculiar to a trade, profession, or industry. It is not technical language nor is it slang, but rather something in-between. For example, a relatively new aspect of secretarial work is an area called word processing, which is a term for the whole area that uses automatic typewriters in dictation and transcription. The name itself is probably unfamiliar to most persons. However, it has introduced a vocabulary or jargon of its own. Dictators are called "word originators"; transcribers, "correspondence secretaries"; dictating equipment, "input equipment," and so on. Be certain, though, that if you use such terminology, you define it; for to many people these terms are meaningless.

8·A·11 Other labels

There are other terms used to describe words in our language. They are not dictionary labels but are further breakdowns, primarily of nonstandard usage, of previously discussed labels. These terms are vernacular, dialect, cant, argot, lingo, street language, and coined expressions. They are all informal language and are usually spoken rather than written.

8·B Language to avoid

There are several groups of words and expressions that, although they are not labeled in dictionaries, should for obvious reasons be avoided. These are some of those groups:

8·B·1 Overused and out-of-date expressions

There are many terms, such as trite, hackneyed, worn, cliché-ridden, and stereotyped, applied to words and expressions that are overused or out of date. At one time some of these expressions were quite acceptable, but either because of overuse or obsolescence, they should now be avoided. Unfortunately, many business writers seem to believe that including such expressions in writing makes it more "businesslike". Sometimes clichés are helpful; for instance, when used by skilled writers, they can be given a new approach.

EXAMPLE: Our garden cultivators get down to earth.

The following list contains only a few of the worn-out expressions still in use. Some come from old sayings, some are

SECTION 8 LANGUAGE USAGE PROBLEMS

comparisons, and many are, far too often, found in business letters.

allow me to . . .
any and all
as a matter of fact
as of this date
as per your order
as regards
as soon as possible
as the case may be
as the crow flies
assuring you of our prompt attention
at hand
at the present writing
at this point in time
at this time
at your earliest convenience
attached find (hereto)
avail yourself of this opportunity
awaiting your further instructions (order)
be in a position to
be kind (good) enough
beg to differ (acknowledge, advise, inform, state)
better late than never
bring to a head (end)
build a better mousetrap
by means of
by the same token
call a spade a spade
check to cover
contents noted
deem it advisable
desire to state
down to earth
due course
due to the fact that
enclosed herewith (please find)
every Tom, Dick, and Harry
fate worse than death
feel free to
few and far between
first and foremost
for the purpose of

for your convenience
for your information
goes on to say
gone but not forgotten
gone forward
happy as a lark
high and dry
hit the nail on the head
I have before me . . .
I wish to state
in a position to
in due course
in lieu of
in re
in receipt of
in response to same
in the amount of
in the last analysis
in the majority of instances
in the near future
in this connection
in this day and age
in view of the fact that
it goes without saying
last but not least
let me call your attention to . . .
looking forward to hearing from you
make a long story short
on behalf of
open-and-shut case
over a barrel
over and done with
permit me to say that
plain as day
please be advised that
pursuant to . . .
rack your brain
recent date
referring to . . .
regarding your communication
regret to advise
relative to
replying to your letter of . . .

ripe old age
rest assured
slip of the tongue
step in the right direction
take pleasure
take the liberty of
take this opportunity
thank you for your patronage
thank you in advance
this is to acknowledge your letter of . . .
this is to advise you
this letter is for the purpose of
to the bitter end
too cute for words
under separate cover
under the circumstances
undue delay
upon investigation
upon reviewing our records
valued favor (business)
we are in receipt of
we take pleasure in . . .
we wish to call your attention to the fact
we wish to inform (notify, advise) you that
we wish to say

Along with overused expressions, mention should be made of standard usage words that become very popular and for a short period of time are used excessively. These are fad words that seem to come into popularity for a limited time and disappear almost as quickly as they arrive. In addition to their overuse, they are often vague terms and sometimes not even used correctly. Presently there seems to be a tendency to use such words as *meaningful, viable, know-how, spelled out, phased out, breakthrough, target date,* and *chain reaction.*

8·B·2 Redundancies, repetitions, and gobbledegook

Wordiness, overwriting, redundancies, repetitions, gobbledegook—all of these are terms for writing more than is necessary. There are several ways in which wordiness can be expressed:

a. Using words when the meaning is already expressed in other words in the phrase.

EXAMPLES:
final outcome	surrounded on all sides
careful scrutiny	audible to the ear
completely destroyed	when first begun (started)
advance planning	raining outside
after the conclusion of	cooperated together
basic fundamentals	orange in color
dead corpses	reason is because

b. Using phrases or clauses that could be expressed in one word.

EXAMPLES:
at the present time	now
due to the fact that	because
in accordance with	according to
a small number of	few

SECTION 8 LANGUAGE USAGE PROBLEMS   65

    by means of.. by
    bring to a head .... end

c. Using *and* to make a compound of two phrases or words that have the same meaning.

EXAMPLES: help and assistance
each and every person

d. Using overwritten bureaucratic jargon, called gobbledegook by government officials. Although such writing is not confined just to government workers, it has come to be associated with much government writing.

EXAMPLE: Following is the first paragraph of a letter written by former Vice President Rockefeller to former President Ford (November 3, 1975): "The time is virtually at hand when you will be firming up your program for the Presidential primaries, the Republican National Convention and the Presidential Campaign of 1976. Involving, as this must, difficult calculations, considerations and decisions, it will clearly help you in this task if the range of options is simplified at the earliest time."

e. Included with wordiness is the problem of using long, multisyllable words instead of short, simple ones. Here are some examples of long words and substitutions for these words:

Avoid:	Use:	Avoid:	Use:
above mentioned		endeavor	try
above name	this	institute	begin
above referenced		lenient	easy
acquire	get or gain	maintenance	upkeep
advantageous	helpful	possess	have
aforementioned	this, these	previous	before, former
anticipate	expect, look for	preserve	keep
approximate	about		money,
ascertain	find out	remittance	check,
available	ready		payment
concerning	about	remunerate	pay
conclusion	end	render	give
determine	tell, find out	request	ask
efficient	able	retain	keep
eliminate	leave out, omit		

LANGUAGE CHOICE

8·B·3 Ambiguous and equivocal statements

A statement is ambiguous when the meaning is confused and could be interpreted in two or more ways. Ambiguity is usually caused by carelessness—by indefinite reference of pronouns, dangling or misplaced modifiers, or incomplete ellipses (see p. 35). Ambiguity can also be caused by asking a negative question to which either *yes* or *no* could be the answer.

EXAMPLES: Jean saw Cindy when she was at the library. *who was at the library?*

No dog shall be in a public place without its master on a leash. *who is on the leash?*

I do not know Leslie as well as Barbara. *as well as I know Barbara or as well as Barbara knows Leslie?*

You are not going to the meeting, are you? *yes, I am going or no, I am not going—which is the answer?*

If ambiguity is intended, the statement is also equivocal. No carelessness is involved; the statement is deliberately unclear.

EXAMPLE: The letter of recommendation that reads: "He tries very hard to get along with co-workers . . ." suggests all sorts of things: he has trouble getting along with co-workers; he tries to overcome his problems but is not successful; he is successful in overcoming his problems. Of course, the reader also wonders why the point of getting along with others needed to be raised.

8·B·4 Euphemisms

Euphemisms are accepted expressions that are used in place of terms considered impolite, unpleasant or offensive. They are synonyms for the unpleasant, vulgar, or distasteful. Language usage has made almost a complete circle from the Victorian days when *legs* were called *limbs* to the present time when the so-called street language has been brought into many homes. The four-letter words formerly found chalked on fences now seem to be incorporated into everyday language. When the purpose of a euphemism is to avoid vulgarity or offense, then it should certainly be used. One of the purposes of business writing is to create goodwill; this is not achieved by using words or expressions that offend. At the other extreme, euphemisms may offend too—not by their vulgarity but by their "cuteness." Such expressions as *powder room, little boys'* room, and *little girls' room* for *toilet* might be considered by some more offensive than the term that they are replacing.

When the euphemism glosses over something that some may prefer not to talk about—*laid to rest* for *burial* and *stretching the truth* for *lying*, for example—then the euphemism again becomes a communication problem. Mortuaries seem to have created a language of their own in an effort to avoid terms connected with dying—*slumber room, reposing room, loved one, grief therapy, memory gardens, funeral director, remains, service,* and *casket.* The hardware store that advertises *experienced chainsaws* for sale or the automobile dealer who sells *previously owned cars* may attract attention, but the choice of words may also make customers wary of the products.

8·B·5 Dysphemisms

The opposite of euphemism is dysphemism. Often such expressions are used more in disparagement than in attempting to substitute an offensive term for an inoffensive one. The man who refers to his Cadillac as a *heap* or the woman who calls her new designer's dress an *old rag* may merely be embarrassed by their possessions.

8·B·6 Insincere language

Insincerity is created in business writing when the tone of the language is artificial and presents a false impression. This may be difficult to avoid since the line is likely to be fine between the language that pleases or flatters or persuades and the language that is unbelievable and that makes the reader wary. Such language is often the language of the sales letter or the advertisement. The printed form letter that is being sent to "only a few of our favorite customers" is viewed with suspicion. Yet a letter that is individually typed and signed, even though it is the product of the automatic typewriter and the automatic pen, may contain the same language and not be viewed the same way. Not only, then, is the language likely to sound insincere but the method of communicating can also be suspect. Remember, too, that in written communication, there are no facial expressions or gestures that can make an unbelievable statement seem sincere. The words are there, to be reread if the reader desires, with no gestures, tone of voice, or smile that might convince someone that an outrageous exaggeration is in some way remotely connected with the truth.

Here are some of the ways insincerity in language is created:

a. Gross flattery This is language that makes use of terms such as *your impeccable taste* or *only you can appreciate* *the value of* or *your superior knowledge places you in a special category.*

b. Superlatives   This is writing in which everything is the most, the biggest, or the largest ever.

EXAMPLE: Our company has just had its biggest year ever—we sold four times as many television sets as any of our competitors. We are not taking all of the credit, however, for we know that without you, our very favorite customer, this tremendous leap in our sales could not have been possible. Therefore, we shall continue to give you our very best possible service. If at any time we make any mistake, even a teeny one, won't you please let us know? Only if we are truly aware of all of our customers at all times, is it possible to offer you the kind of service to which you are very rightly entitled.

Is this example more believable:

> Our company has in this past year topped its previous sales records by 40 percent. The television set that you purchased last November helped boost our sales, so we would like to return the favor. Should you have any problems with your set in the coming year, please call us. Remember, your set is covered by warranty for a full year. Again, thank you for selecting our shop for your television purchase.

c. Overhumility   This is language in which the writer not only apologizes but does not seem to know when to stop. Often, too, the writer makes promises that cannot be kept; for example, no firm can be certain that *this error will never occur again.*

EXAMPLE: All of us at Ace Corporation are so very, very sorry for the inexcusable error made in your last shipment. We shall do everything possible to correct the error and try never, never again to let such a thing occur.

d. Sweeping generalities   This is the language that bases

SECTION 8 LANGUAGE USAGE PROBLEMS

an all-encompassing statement on limited knowledge or experience; it is judging a whole by a part.

EXAMPLES: You can't trust anyone over thirty.
All attorneys write so that no one can understand their letters.

Avoid such words as *all, no one, everyone, always,* and *never;* these words do not allow for exceptions.

8·B·7 Inaccuracies and incorrectly used expressions

There are a number of words and expressions that are used either incorrectly or imprecisely—or actually do not exist so far as correct usage is concerned.

These are examples:

a. Malaprops (or Malapropisms) These are instances in which use is made of a word that sounds similar to the one that should have been used, usually with humorous or ludicrous results. The term originated from a character in Sheridan's play, *The Rivals,* who mistakenly substituted allegory for alligator and said: "An allegory on the banks of the Nile." It is a favorite device of writers of television comedies.

EXAMPLES: snipping the biblical cord
religious frenetic (*All in the Family* television program)

b. Wrong prefixes Errors can also be made by placing the wrong prefixes before roots of words. Some of these errors could be eliminated if the meanings of frequently used prefixes were known. For example, some of the common negative prefixes are *un-, im-, non-, dis-,* and *mis-*. However, though these prefixes have similar meanings, it does not necessarily mean that they can be used interchangeably. *Disinterested*—freedom from selfish bias or self-interest—and *uninterested*—without an interest—do not have the same meaning. Knowing prefixes can also be helpful in spelling. You will not confuse *anti-* and *ante-* if you know that *anti-* means against and *ante-,* before.

c. Illiterate usage These are words or phrases that have never been acceptable or that are incorrectly used as other parts of speech. Here are some examples:

Not acceptable: *alright* (this is a spelling problem only); *anywheres; anyways; irregardless; leastwise; leastways; muchly; thusly; somewheres; and/or.*

Incorrectly used for other words: *of* for *have*, *could* for *should*; *said* for *this* or *these*; *can't seem* for *seems unable*.

EXAMPLES: Avoid: The said person could not be found.
Use: This person could not be found.
Avoid: I could of done the work if I had had more time.
Use: I could have done the work if I had had more time.
Avoid: Robert was not to be found anywheres.
Use: Robert was not to be found anywhere.
Avoid: Joe can't seem to finish the job.
Use: Joe seems unable to finish the job.
Avoid: The secretary and/or the attorney can sign the contract.
Use: Either the secretary or the attorney can sign the contract.

d. Made-up words Words can be fabricated by adding syllables to otherwise ordinary words. Here are some examples: adding the suffix *-ize*: *finalize, focalize, maximize, cosmetize, inferiorize, normalize*; adding the suffix *-wise*: *weather-wise, cost-wise, expense-wise, value-wise, savings-wise, percentage-wise, time-wise*; adding the suffixes *-y* or *-ee*: *oniony, treesy, cutesy, returnee, standee, drawee*; adding the prefix *non-*: *nonsmoker, nonwhite, nondairy creamer, nonuser*; adding the prefix *de-*: *debrief, deplane, deprogram*. All of these examples are of questionable usage and doubtful preciseness.

Be careful about adding syllables such as *self-* and *re-* to words in which these syllables add nothing to the meaning—*self-addressed* and *self-confessed* are examples. Too, although you could easily *retype* a letter, you could not *recopy* it, and you could not *recheck an answer* unless you had previously checked it.

Generally, feminine endings are being dropped. Words such as *usherette, authoress, executrix*, and *benefactress* are no longer used. The masculine names, particularly those including *-man*, once used for titles of positions held by both sexes, are being replaced by one-name titles. The list is not only endless, but includes some most unusual combinations. A few examples are *businessperson, gentleperson, chairperson, serviceperson*, and *freshperson*.

Avoid shortened words such as *enthuse, emote*, and *biz*. There are, however, acceptable shortened forms such as *ad* and *phone*. Consult a dictionary if you are in doubt about using a shortened form.

e. Words with similar meanings Another group consists of words that have similar meanings but are not synonyms; therefore, they should not be used as such. Some of them are described below.

admission, admittance—somewhat interchangeable: *admission* means allowing entry or conceding the truth; *admittance*, making available certain rights and privileges.

EXAMPLES: Admission to the auditorium is by invitation only.
Admission of guilt by the defendant seems unlikely.
There is no admittance to the atomic research site.

advise, inform—*advise* means to give counsel; *inform* (or *say* or *tell*), to give information.

EXAMPLES: The attorney advised us to drop the case.

Avoid: Please advise when you can make shipment.
Use: Please tell us when you can make shipment.

allude, refer—*allude* implies indirect reference; *refer*, direct reference.

EXAMPLE: Melinda alluded to the newspaper story, but she did not refer to it.

anxious, eager—although usage of these two words tends to overlap, *anxious* is used when there is apprehension or concern involved; *eager* means desirous.

EXAMPLES: I am anxious over the outcome of the meeting.
He said that he was eager to see the new product.

apt, liable, likely—*apt* means an inherent tendency or quick to learn; *liable*, open to something disadvantageous or responsible for consequences; *likely*, probable or expected.

EXAMPLES: Leslie proved to be an apt pupil when learning to type.
It is likely that Mr. Peale will be liable for damages in the accident.

as, like—*as* is a subordinate conjunction; *like* is a preposition; therefore, *as* introduces dependent clauses and *like* is followed by an object—either a noun or pronoun.

EXAMPLES: Do as I say, not as I do.
I do not think his brother looks like him.

balance, remainder, rest—*balance* refers to accounts or bookkeeping; *remainder* and *rest* refer to something left over after other parts have been taken away.

EXAMPLES: The balance in the petty cash account is $25.
Michael spent the rest of the day trying to find the error.
For the remainder of his life, Ivan was an invalid.

bring, take—*bring* indicates movement in the direction of the speaker or writer; *take* indicates action away from the speaker or writer. When there is no movement, *bring* may be used in the sense of producing.

EXAMPLES: Bring all of the papers to the meeting.
Do not take any of the material when you leave.
The allocation of federal funds for the project will bring many jobs to the area.

can, may—*can* shows ability; *may*, permission.

EXAMPLE: If I may have your permission to work late, I can finish the project tonight.

conscience, conscious—*conscience* is the sense of right or wrong; *conscious* is an adjective meaning aware.

EXAMPLES: McNally's conscience would not allow him to hide the errors.
Val was not conscious of the errors in the work.

continual, continuous—*continual* means repeated at intervals (in terms of events); *continuous*, uninterrupted (in terms of time and space).

EXAMPLES: The continual ringing of the telephone was most distracting.
There was a continuous snowfall for more than twelve hours.

SECTION 8 LANGUAGE USAGE PROBLEMS

direct, directly—*direct* is both an adjective and an adverb; *directly* is always an adverb. For the sense of immediately or exactly, use *directly*. For the sense of without interruption, *direct* is more effective. *Direct* and *directly* are interchangeable in the sense of in a direct line or manner, or straight and without anyone intervening.

EXAMPLES: Ship the product direct to the consumer.
Ingersoll was directly reponsible for the entire report.
The pilot radioed that the jet was directly (or direct) on target.

first, former—use *first* to indicate the first of more than two; use *former* for the first of two.

EXAMPLES: We hired the first applicant who applied.
Of the two applicants, I prefer the former.

formally, former, formerly—*formally* means in a prescribed or customary form; *former*, coming before in place or order; *formerly*, beforehand, previously.

EXAMPLES: The new president was formally presented to the board of directors by the former president.
Formerly it was not our policy to accept returned merchandise.

hopefully, it is hoped/I hope/we hope—*hopefully* is generally misused. It is not a synonym for "it is hoped" or "I hope/we hope." It is an adverb and should be used as such. A real monster was created by one of the editors of a small newspaper when he wrote, "The planning department wishfully hoped...." Unfortunately, the misuse of *hopefully* seems to be gaining in popularity, for it is being used in this inaccurate sense by more and more people. It is also less awkward to use "I hope" than to say "I am hopeful."

EXAMPLES: Avoid: Hopefully Mr. Quinn can be persuaded to take the job.
Use: We hope that Mr. Quinn can be persuaded to take the job.

imply, infer—*imply* means to intimate, to insinuate, or to hint; *infer*, to deduce or draw a conclusion from facts or indications.

EXAMPLES: The newspaper article implies that prices will increase greatly.
Reading the paper caused Nell to infer that prices will increase greatly.

last, latest, latter—*last* means at the end; *latest*, most recent; *latter*, second in a series of two.

EXAMPLES: Carl made the last payment on his car.
Your latest payment leaves a balance of $250 on your account.
The latter plan seems better than the first.

leave, let—*leave* means to allow to remain; *let*, to allow. The distinction between *leave alone* and *let alone* seems to be disappearing.

EXAMPLES: Let me go.
Let her be.
Leave the papers on the desk.

party, person—in law, *party* is a person or group involved in legal proceedings; in ordinary usage, it is not a synonym for *person*.

EXAMPLES: Avoid: The party who called would not give her name.
Use: The person who called would not give her name.

quotation, quote—*quotation* is a noun; *quote*, a verb.

EXAMPLES: Avoid: The article consisted of quotes from a number of authors.
Use: The article consisted of quotations from a number of authors.

respectfully, respectively—*respectfully* means in a courteous manner; *respectively*, singly, in the order named.

EXAMPLES: The closing on the letter should be "Respectfully yours," not "Respectively yours."
The first and second highest scores went to Bob and Ann respectively.

8·C Choosing words for preciseness

The whole area of written communication depends upon a common understanding of language between reader and writer. The connotation of a word—that is, the implication in addition to the literal meaning of the word—can cause confusion. For example, the dictionary meaning of *cheap* is given as inexpensive; yet to most persons there is a vast difference.

Humor, too, is another area of writing that can cause a great deal of misunderstanding. Oral humor is assisted by facial expressions, gestures, timing, and many factors other than the actual words themselves; written humor must rely entirely upon the words and the images that they bring forth. Obviously, humor that is dependent upon the embarrassment or humiliation of others should be avoided. Humorous writing relies primarily upon a play on words, such as puns, spoonerisms, and malaprops. It possibly could attract attention in sales letters or perhaps, if all else fails, in complaint letters. Generally, though, use humor sparingly, and be sure that your humor is not only understood but understood in the manner you intended.

8·C·1 Homophones

Homophones are those words that are pronounced alike but spelled differently and have different meanings. Sometimes they are called *homonyms* although technically there is a distinction—homonyms can be spelled the same but have different meanings. Ordinarily these words are spelling problems rather than usage problems.

EXAMPLES: I could not hire any more employees.
The price is higher than we thought it would be.
Bear in mind that this is a net price.
Ralph cut everything from the budget but the bare essentials.

8·C·2 Sound-alike words

Many words are confused because their pronunciation is very similar. Here are some of them:

accede—to give consent
exceed—to surpass

accept—(verb) to take or receive
except—(prep.) with the exclusion of

access—entrance
excess—surplus

adapt—(verb) to make suitable
adept—(adj.) highly skilled
adopt—(verb) to take as one's own

addition—an increase
edition—form in which a written work is published

advice—(noun) an opinion or judgment
advise—(verb) to give counsel or opinion

affect—(verb) to produce an influence upon
effect—(noun) a result or outcome; (verb) to produce as a
   result, to accomplish

biannual—twice a year
biennial—every two years

choose—to select
chose—past tense of choose

coma—unconsciousness
comma—mark of punctuation

compose—to put together or arrange
comprise—to include or consist of

consul—(noun) an official appointed to a foreign country
council—(noun) an administrative body
counsel—(verb) to recommend a course or policy; (noun) a
   lawyer engaged to give legal advice

eminent—outstanding
imminent—near at hand

eraser—object used for removing ink or pencil marks
erasure—a place where an ink or pencil mark has been
   removed

loose—(adj.) not fastened
lose—(verb) to fail to keep
loss—(noun) the act of losing or failing to keep, the state
   of being lost

reality—the actual state of a thing
realty—real estate

than—(conj.) introduces statements of comparison or preference
then—(adv.) at that time, in the future or past

weather—(noun) state of the atmosphere; (verb) to expose to the open air
whether—(conj.) introduces an indirect question involving alternatives

8·C·3 Idioms

Idioms are expressions or phrases that, either because of grammatical structure or arrangement of words, cannot be translated literally. If each word in the phrase were defined, the meaning of the idiom still would not be known. Try defining "by the skin of my teeth," and the problem becomes obvious. Every one of us uses such expressions every day; they are the substance of our language. However, do at all times remember that they are generally used informally. Idioms present all kinds of problems for the person learning English as a second language, as they cannot be translated into another language. Ordinarily they are easily learned. The greatest problem is the idiomatic use of prepositions with certain verbs (see p. 45). Dictionaries are the best sources for help to tell you whether an expression is idiomatic and whether its usage is standard. Many idiomatic expressions are listed in dictionaries under the most important word in the phrase.

EXAMPLES: to hang in the air   to want in the worst way
to bend over backwards   to catch one's breath
to get under one's skin   how are you?

Because idioms are usually informal and often labeled slang, obsolete, or regional, you will have to make decisions about using them in business writing. You can, of course, avoid them entirely. If you do, your writing style is likely to become heavy or pretentious. If you use too many, the tone will sound informal and perhaps careless or even insincere. Be sure, too, that the idiom has not become a cliché—such as "tickled pink." The ideal is to write so that you sound sincere and natural and, at the same time, are easily understood.

EXAMPLE: We have bent over backwards to get in touch with you.
    Or: We have telephoned, written, and sent special messengers in our efforts to reach you.

8·C·4 Negative/positive terms

What terms are negative? In this instance, negative does not refer to the whole area of words that offend—the vulgar, obscene, insulting, biased, and distorted; these are known to be negative and should be avoided. What is meant is a group of words and expressions that are the opposite of positive. These words needle the reader, are subject to different interpretations, and put the reader on the defensive. They are, in general, the kind of expressions that are defended with "What's wrong with that?" or "He misunderstood me; I didn't intend it that way."

These are examples of words that are negative and could antagonize:

bad	dissatisfied	mistrust	uncalled for
blame	failure	misunderstood	unfair
careless	false	must	unjust
complaint	ignorant	negligence	unreasonable
disagreeable	incorrect	offensive	untrue
dishonest	misled	poor	worthless
displeased	mistake	unacceptable	

Phrases that antagonize include:

as you no doubt know (or are aware)	you overlooked
	your error
you are wrong	we cannot accept your statement that
you claim that	
you do not understand	we have been reliably informed that
you failed to	
surely you must have known	the mistake that you made
you neglected to	it is unreasonable of you

Here are some positive words that influence the reader to react favorably:

you	results	love
money	health	discover
save	easy	proven
new	safety	guarantee

Also consider the tone of the letter or writing. A positive tone puts emphasis on the favorable; a negative, on the unfavorable. Perhaps the writing is not so much unfavorable as it does not tell what the reader wants to hear or does not say what can be done.

Contrast these examples:

Avoid: We cannot ship your order before the end of next week.
Use: Your order will be shipped no later than Friday of next week.
Avoid: We cannot pay the invoice of $300 at this time.
Use: We will send our check in payment of your invoice for $300 within two weeks' time.

8·C·5
Concrete/
abstract
language

Concrete words are nouns that name persons and things that can be seen or touched—*house, letter, book*—as contrasted with nouns that name qualities, conditions, or actions—*education, consumerism, honesty, wealth*. Most business writing uses concrete terms; preferably, these should be terms that the reader knows. If there is the slightest doubt that meanings could be misunderstood, define precisely what you mean by a term and give examples. Consider this statement: *Mr. Conrad lost a great deal of money in the venture.* "A great deal of money" is abstract with its different meanings for different people. Change the statement to: *Mr. Conrad lost $50,000 in the venture.* Now it becomes concrete; you know exactly how much "a great deal of money" is.

4

beginning and organizing the business letter

Before writing any letter, there are things that you must do. Beginning any task is often more difficult than actually doing it, particularly if you have a feeling that you do not really know how to start. This is true for all persons who write business letters—from the executives of the company to the newly employed clerks—whether the business messages are written for a firm or for personal use. Follow the suggestions that are given here to eliminate false starts, paper shuffling maneuvers, and other subterfuges often employed to keep from getting on with the job.

SECTION 9 Beginning the business letter

In any writing situation, there are various considerations before beginning to write. You should not ask your secretary to take dictation, then begin reading the letters that you are going to answer. You can do this, of course, but this is wasted time. Remember, half of the letter-writing cost is made up of the time of the dictator and the secretary. Even if you are writing the letter without the assistance of a secretary, you should not roll a piece of paper into the typewriter or pick up a yellow pad and start writing. Whatever you do, don't laboriously write the message in longhand and then have it typed.

When you are just beginning to write letters, it may take a little longer to compose as you write or dictate than it does to write all of your letters first in longhand; but taking the time to train yourself in this all-important skill will eventually be well worth both the time and effort. In order to acquire this skill, it is most important that you plan a time, preferably a regularly

SECTION 9 BEGINNING THE BUSINESS LETTER

scheduled one—such as after the mail is distributed for the day—so that letter writing becomes part of your working routine and not something that is delayed as a burdensome chore.

9·A Answering letters

Letters that are being answered are, of course, written in reply to incoming mail. They are easier to write if they are in reply to letters that are clearly written and easily understood.

9·A·1 Reading and marking letters

The first thing you must do before you can prepare to answer any letter is to reat it very carefully. Underline key points—all dates and places—and make pencil notes (they can be erased later if you want) in the margin of the letter. If necessary, make notes and an outline on a separate note pad. As you read the letter, ask yourself—why was the letter written? If it needs a reply, what does the writer of the letter want to know? Does the letter need a written answer or would a telephone call be sufficient? Decide whether you can answer the letter or whether it should be sent to someone else. If you do not know what the writer of the letter wants, what questions will you need to ask to clarify the purpose of the letter?

9·A·2 Collecting background information

You will also need background information before you can answer the letter. Have you or your secretary pulled files or obtained computer print-outs so that you have all of the necessary information? Perhaps your secretary (or you, if you are the secretary) should routinely read the incoming letters and find the pertinent files for them. The incoming letter could then be attached to the file. If you need information that is not in the file, make a list of such information. Where can you get it? From other departments or persons in the firm? A telephone call to someone? Perhaps it will be necessary to consult references or library materials for additional data. Will you need enclosures for the letter that you are going to write? Such items as price lists, catalogs, and brochures of company products are often included. Make notes of any enclosures that you will need.

When you have collected all the needed information, make a simple check. Does the information answer who, what, why, when, and where? These questions must always be answered completely. Is the *when* complete with date and time? Is it necessary to indicate *a.m.* or *p.m.*? Is the *where* complete with room number, building, street address, city, state, and ZIP? Complete information means just that—everything that the reader needs to know is there.

This is an example of a letter that has been read and marked for reply:

September 15, 19—

Ms. Harriet H. Schwartz, Sales Manager
Empire Products, Inc.
385 Washington Street
San Francisco, CA 94904

Dear Ms. Schwartz:

<u>Some time ago</u> I wrote you asking for information concerning a <u>franchise for handling your products</u>. As I have not heard from you, I wondered if perhaps my letter had gone astray.

I told you in my previous letter that I am considering expanding my business and would like <u>to add a line of office equipment</u> to the products that I now carry.

Would you be interested in considering my firm as an outlet for your office-equipment products? You can get <u>financial information</u> about my firm from <u>Dun & Bradstreet</u>. I should also be willing to furnish additional information that you might require.

Please send me information concerning your contracts with dealers who handle your products. I should like to have such information as soon as possible.

Sincerely,

Carl L. Mason

Carl L. Mason

Probably the secretary checked the files before giving the letter to the sales manager. This would determine how to answer the writer's question about not receiving a reply to his letter. Such a question should always be answered, even if you must apologize for an oversight in your office. The lines under *franchise for handling your products* and *to add a line of office equipment* show the purpose of the letter. The lines under *financial information* and *Dun & Bradstreet* would note that a request for financial information should be made. The answering letter would: (1) acknowledge that the letter had been received and explain the reason for the delay in answering, (2) tell the person who wrote the letter what will be done—that a sales representative will call on him shortly and will bring complete information, and (3) thank him for his interest in the products. If additional letters are required—to Dun & Bradstreet and the sales representative—notes should be made to write these letters.

9·B Initiating letters

If you are initiating correspondence, the step of reading and marking is, of course, omitted. Instead, you will first determine the purpose of the letter—why you are writing—and then collect all of the necessary background information. For example, you might be writing a letter telling customers of a special sale —this is the purpose. What information would you need to know? Certainly you would need to know the details of the sale—when will it be held? Where will it be held—in our store or at a special place such as a warehouse? What is on sale—all merchandise or only certain items? What are the price reductions? What are the conditions of the sale—cash only, no returns, free delivery of items costing over $50? How long will the sale be in progress? You would also need to know who gets the letter—all charge customers, a special mailing list? Once you have all of the necessary information, you can outline what would be included in the letter.

9·C Purposes of letters

You have planned your letter, you have made a list of all of the facts that you want to include, and you have gathered all of the information that you will need. As you planned the letter, you told yourself the purpose of it. Is the purpose part of the outline?

Business letters are written for three main purposes—to get the receiver to respond, to give information, or to build goodwill.

9·C·1 To get the receiver to respond

The reader of any letter may respond in a variety of ways: by attending the sale that you are describing in your letter; by paying an overdue bill; by sending the information that you want; by answering your complaint or claim; even by saying *no* to your request. Or the reader may not respond in writing but by some action.

If response is the purpose of your letter, what can you do to make sure that the reader will do this? How can you create in the reader a desire to do what you want? How do you keep the reader from tossing the letter aside without even reading it?

One good way to make sure that the reader will respond is to make very clear what sort of response you would like. Tell the reader that you want payment of the overdue account by a certain date or that you want the reader to buy a product before the price rises.

There are devices, too, that make it easy for the reader to reply. They are such things as stamped, addressed return envelopes, reply cards that need only be checked, rewards such as an extra month's subscription to a magazine if the order is returned promptly, or free gifts for making inquiries.

9·C·2
To give
information

You respond in a variety of ways to requests for information: You quote prices for a product or service; you give information about an account; or you tell the person to whom you are writing how to qualify for benefits. Whenever you are giving information, make sure it is complete and accurate—and that you tell the reader precisely the information that was requested.

9·C·3
To build
goodwill

Actually all business letters have the purpose of building goodwill. Even when writing to a slow-paying customer, you write so that you do not antagonize the customer and lose future business. Often goodwill letters do not require responses. They are written to acknowledge a service, to thank a good customer for using your products, to invite someone to attend a special event, to extend season's greetings, to welcome a new customer, to congratulate someone on a promotion or winning an award, or to apologize for an error that has been made.

Undoubtedly there are letters that are written for more than one of these purposes. In fact, sometimes a letter serves all of these purposes. You might, for example, answer a request for price information on a product and at the same time try to get the reader to respond by purchasing the product. You build goodwill, for without it you probably would not get a response.

SECTION 10 Organizing the business letter

After you have completed the letter planning and have gathered the necessary information, how do you begin to organize the letter? How do you arrange the facts that must be presented?

A business letter is organized differently from other kinds of writing. It almost always follows the same format, which consists of three parts: introduction (or opening), body, and closing. Keep this format in mind as you plan or outline the letter, for it determines what you will include and the order in which the facts are presented.

These are the three parts of the business letter:

10·A Introduction

The introduction, or opening, is the headline of the letter. It starts with a clear-cut statement of what the letter is about, and if appropriate, how the subject of the letter is handled or what decisions have been made. It gives the conclusion of the subject at the beginning.

The opening paragraph sets the tone. It determines how the reader will react to the letter. There are three usual reactions: (1) positive—the reader is on your side, is favorably impressed, is interested, and wants to help or come to the sale or buy your product; (2) negative—the reader is annoyed, angry, dissatisfied, discouraged, or distrustful; the reader is not going to buy your product, is not going to help you in any way, will go to the appropriate authorities for action against you, and hopes you will not succeed in whatever you are attempting; and (3) "blah"—the reader does not react one way or another, is not interested, probably will not read all of the letter, and ignores you. Unfortunately, many letters are blah letters. Naturally you want a positive reaction. You get such a reaction by getting to the point immediately and by establishing a friendly, courteous tone.

Getting to the point immediately—presenting the message of your letter first, then developing details—is writing deductively. In negative letters, the process is reversed—the details are presented first, then the point of the letter is developed from the details. This is called writing inductively.

The opening, "Can you help us? Some needed information was left out of an accident report you recently sent us," involves the reader. The reader is not blamed for leaving out some information but is asked to help and probably will. The tone is courteous and friendly. If the opening begins, "You neglected to send us some needed information in your recent accident report," the reader might become defensive and annoyed and feel accused of doing something incorrectly, something that perhaps is not the reader's fault.

The introduction starts with a complete opening sentence, which does not contain useless information. Do not use a sentence fragment such as, "In regard to your letter of the 15th."

When a letter begins, "I am answering your letter of January 15 in which you ask about our new electric typewriter," it sounds as if the writer is not ready to begin. The reader knows what was written and when it was written; the reader wants an answer to the question, not to be told what is already known—that a letter was written. If you do not immediately get the attention of the reader, you will probably lose that reader before the end of the first sentence or paragraph. Even if the reader continues on with the letter, there is likely to be annoyance or prejudice against the writer.

Keep the first sentences short and easy to understand and keep the opening paragraph short, probably not more than two or three lines. A short opening paragraph is easier to read, and it does not intimidate the reader.

EXAMPLES:

(Read the opening sentences that are given in the first column. Then ask yourself: Are there things in these sentences that are unnecessary? Does each sentence get to the point immediately? Is this what the reader wants to know?)

(Read the sentences in the second column and ask yourself the same questions.)

I have before me your letter of March 5 in which you ask the price of our new Ease E Typewriter.	The price of our new Ease E Typewriter is $700; this includes all transportation and delivery charges as well as a year's guarantee.
Thank you for the deposit of $500 that was enclosed in your letter of June 1; we are pleased to add it to your account.	Your deposit of $500 has been added to your account.
We have received your check for $200 in payment of the order you placed on May 20 for office supplies . . .	Your order for office supplies was shipped today.

There are instances in opening paragraphs when you do not get to the point immediately; these occur wherever the letter contains negative or bad news—refusing credit or telling a job applicant that he or she was not hired, for example. The details that explain the bad news are given first (inductive writing) and, if possible, a substitute is offered. If a substitute cannot be offered, keep the opening statement neutral—sometimes even *thank you* will serve the purpose. By offering a substitute or a neutral statement, you can keep the tone of the letter positive. A rejection can be antagonistic; a substitution offers a positive, courteous solution to a situation that might otherwise be embarrassing to someone whom you do not wish to offend.

EXAMPLES: Avoid: We cannot extend credit privileges for a 30-day account to you at this time.
Use: Thank you for asking us to open an account for you. Would you consider permitting us to send C.O.D. shipments until you have established a credit rating?

10·B
Body

In the opening you have told the reader what the letter is about. The body of the letter develops the opening and adds any needed details. For example, the opening of a letter tells the reader that the order that was placed has been shipped. The body adds the details of how it is being shipped—parcel post or delivery service; when it can be expected; and any additional information—if the order is complete or if substitutions were made. It could tell how the billing will be done if payment did not accompany the order. The body contains all of the information that the reader needs to know to make decisions.

Like the opening, the body does not contain anything that the reader does not need or want to know. In fact, if unnecessary detail is added, it may confuse the reader about why such a fact is being included. For example, should you write, "We are shipping your order by Mountain Freight Company; we have never had any trouble with their service," the reader might wonder why such a statement about the shipping company is included. Suspicions might be aroused that the company is not dependable when ordinarily such a thought would not occur. Do not include any statement that might cause the reader to wonder why a fact is being included. It is merely rambling writing.

10·C
Closing

The closing is a short and courteous goodbye. It does not include anything that has not already been introduced. It makes action on the part of the reader easy. The closing is specific; it gives times and dates.

Avoid participial or fragment conclusions. There should be no "Hoping to hear from you," or "With best wishes, I remain . . . ."

The closing is the summary of the letter; it emphasizes the action that you want the reader to take; it states exactly what you want the reader to do, and it leaves the impression of courtesy. Like any goodbye, jog the reader's memory if there is something that you want the reader to do, but keep the closing short and friendly.

EXAMPLES: Making the action easy: Merely sign the enclosed card and drop it in the mail.

Giving a specific date: Be sure the card is postmarked by October 1 so that you may be certain that your order will arrive on time.

Jogging the reader's memory by using a positive statement: Avoid: If you do not order before August 31, the introductory offer will not apply.

Use: Don't forget that this introductory offer is in effect only until August 31.

On the next page is a letter sent to people who may want to sell their homes. It is a form letter, and the mailing list for the letter is unknown, compiled possibly from the city directory or from a list of homeowners for a certain area. Read the letter and answer these questions:

1. What is the purpose of the letter?
2. Does the letter follow the form of opening, body, and closing?
3. What does the writer want the reader to do?
4. Is the letter reader-oriented?
5. Do you think this letter accomplished its purpose?

The purpose of the letter, although it is not mentioned until the last paragraph, is to get the reader to list property with the agent who signed the letter. The letter appears to follow no form. The opening is a dull bragging paragraph that gives no clue to the purpose of the letter. The action part of the letter is in the last paragraph, which in most instances probably would not be read. The closing makes no attempt to make it easy for the reader to act: the telephone number appears in small print at the top of the letterhead and the salesperson's signature is

**HALL-DAVIS
AND COMPANY
REALTORS**

500 MARKET BLVD • KENTFIELD CALIFORNIA 94904 • (415) 120-3456
REAL ESTATE • PROPERTY MANAGEMENT • MORTGAGE LOANS • INSURANCE

Dear Homeowner:

Hall-Davis & Company sells more single family residential property than any other kind. Through our 48 residential sales offices located from Seattle..to..San Diego, we have sold over $300 million of residential property in 19--.

Traditionally, spring and summer are the most active periods of the year for residential sales.

The vast exposure of Hall-Davis & Company...one of the Nation's largest realtors...puts us in contact with highly qualified, well-motivated buyers; and now, with the prevailing favorable interest rates, we anticipate another record year for our expanded residential office.

If you are considering the sale of your home, now would be a most opportune time. I would appreciate meeting with you at your convenience.

                                        Sincerely,

                                        HALL-DAVIS & COMPANY

Actual Sales Letter Sent to Prospective Clients

unreadable. It puts the burden of action on the reader—to call the salesperson.

There is no appeal to the reader until the last paragraph—then "you" and "your" are used four times. Before that, the firm name is used twice and there are five personal pronouns referring to the firm. It is difficult to find any way in which the letter is oriented to the reader. Did it accomplish its purpose—to get the homeowner's property listed with this company? It is hard to imagine that it did.

The rewritten letter appears on the following page. In this letter the purpose is stated in the opening. The first paragraph of the body tells about the company, and the second paragraph explains why now is the time to put the house on the market. Count the number of you's and your's—the number has increased to ten. The closing makes it easy for the reader to act and is more positive. The reader is no longer "considering" selling his house; the reader is invited to talk about it with the realtor.

10·D Postscript

Usually the postscript would not be considered a part of a business letter, and it is certainly not included in every business letter. It does have a purpose, though, and that purpose is to attract attention. The postscript stands out in a business letter and often attracts the attention of the reader before the body of the letter does. It, like the closing, should not contain any new information; rather, it should serve as a reminder of an earlier point in the letter. It is most often used in letters that want the reader to do something—buy a product or respond to an appeal.

EXAMPLES: P.S. This offer is for two weeks only. After May 1 the price will be $19.95 instead of this special offer of $15.95.

P.S. If you return the enclosed card promptly, our sales representative will bring a gift package when he calls.

SECTION 10　ORGANIZING THE BUSINESS LETTER　　　　91

HALL-DAVIS
AND COMPANY
REALTORS

500 MARKET BLVD • KENTFIELD CALIFORNIA 94904 • (415) 120-3456
REAL ESTATE • PROPERTY MANAGEMENT • MORTGAGE LOANS • INSURANCE

February 25, 19--

Dear Homeowner:

OPENING { Are you planning to sell your home? Has your house become too large or too small? Are you being transferred to another city?

BODY { Every year thousands of families in Smith County decide to sell their houses; and they select our company, Hall-Davis, as the agent to handle these important transactions. Our company has 48 sales offices located from Seattle to San Diego, so, whether you want to stay in Smith County or move to another area, we can help you. As one of the nation's largest realtors, we meet many highly qualified, seriously interested buyers. In 1978 these clients bought over $900 million worth of residential property through our sales offices.
　　Now, too, is the time to take advantage of the real estate selling market. Not only is the spring and summer the time when most people decide to make changes, but the interest rates for home mortgages are at a three-year low.

CLOSING { Would you like to talk with me about selling your home? You can call me at the office--444-3322--during the business day or at my home--333-4433--any evening. An appointment can be made for any time that you would like.

　　　　　　　　　　　　　　　Sincerely,

　　　　　　　　　　　　　　　Nancy E. Edmunds

　　　　　　　　　　　　　　　Nancy E. Edmunds

Revision of Sales Letter (See p. 89)

5

business letters for specific purposes

Basically all business letters are written in the same pattern—the opening gets to the point immediately, the body develops what has been said in the opening, and the closing is a courteous goodbye that may emphasize some point in the letter. The only exception to this pattern is the negative or bad news letter. Too, all business letters are written for at least one general purpose: to get the reader of the letter to respond, to give information, or to build goodwill. Sometimes a letter will serve all three purposes. However, letters also have more specific purposes, such as ordering a product, selling a product or service, or collecting money.

Letters written for specific purposes include:

SECTION **11** Order letters

11·A
Placing orders

If it is at all possible, when you write to order a product, use an order blank. The reason is obvious; the blank asks for all the information necessary to fill the order properly and promptly. However, if you do not have a blank available, the order should contain the following information:

1. The exact name of the item that you are ordering; use a trade name if one is available
2. A catalog or model number or any other identifying number
3. Size, should more than one size be available, or any other specifications

SECTION 11   ORDER LETTERS   93

    4. Color, if there is a choice

    5. Quantity that you are ordering

    6. Unit price

    7. Sales tax and shipping charges, if these apply

    8. Method of payment, such as check enclosed or charge to a previously established account

    9. Method of shipment

   10. When and where the order should be delivered

Show the calculations by which you arrived at the amount you are enclosing. It is sometimes helpful if you tell where you found out about the item—an advertisement in a magazine, for example. Do not tell more than is needed, as anything written in the letter has to be read. If a fact is not pertinent, it merely gets in the way and slows the processing of the order. It is not necessary, for example, to add a paragraph about the problems of postal delivery or a paragraph explaining how you think the item that you are ordering will be used in your office. If the order you are placing is a follow-up of a telephone conversation, try to direct the order to the person with whom you talked.

EXAMPLE:

```
                              217 Western Road
                              Denver, CO 80200
                              January 15, 19--


Valley Dress Shop
230 Main Street
Salt Lake City, UT 84111

Ladies and Gentlemen
```

    Please send me three of the No. 444 Taylor-Maid Sports Shirts, which were advertised in the December issue of _Women_. I should like one each in red, white, and green, all in size 12.

    I am enclosing my personal check for $32.50 for the three shirts at $10 each, plus $2.50 for shipping charges.

If, for any reason, you cannot ship the shirts immediately, would you please let me know.

Thank you.

                              Sincerely,

                              Margaret Cole

                              Mrs. Margaret Cole

Enclosure: Check

Notice that the items orders are identified, the size and colors are given, and calculation for the amount enclosed is itemized. It is a courteous letter, containing both "please" and "thank you." The company should have no difficulty filling the order.

11·B Acknowledging orders

When order letters are received, they should be acknowledged. Even if the order is sent within a short time of its receipt, acknowledge the order. First-class mail, such as letters and postal cards, usually travels more quickly than parcel post or other shipping methods. By notifying the person placing the order, you are confirming that the order has been received, that it will be or has been filled, and that the order will arrive shortly. Such acknowledgments should be done routinely. Often a postal card is sufficient to acknowledge the order. Certainly, if there is any delay in shipment, this fact should be told to the person placing the order; otherwise, the person is left wondering if the order was received and if it has been shipped.

11·C Placing orders for services

Order letters include not only orders for products but also orders for services—hotel reservations, for example. Hotel reservations can, of course, be made by telephone. In fact, it is often better to telephone, as it is not necessary to wait for confirmation from the hotel. However, if you are writing for hotel reservations, either for yourself or for a member of your firm, the letter should contain certain facts. State specifically the kind of accommodations that are desired—double, single, twin beds, suite; how many will occupy the room; the price range that you wish to pay; and dates that you wish the room. If you are attending a meeting or convention, say so, for often special rates are in effect for such meetings. Include the time of arrival

SECTION 11   ORDER LETTERS

or departure only if the time is earlier or later than usual check-in or check-out times. Usually in American hotels it is not necessary to specify a room with bath, but room with bath should probably be requested in foreign hotels. Ask for a confirmation and to be told whether or not a deposit is required. Do not contribute unnecessary information such as the name of the airline on which you are traveling or the flight number. Address the letter to "Reservations" or "Reservations Clerk"; this speeds the letter to the proper desk.

As with other kinds of orders, hotels normally have order forms (often post cards) that can be completed and returned to the hotel for reservations. If such forms are available, take advantage of them.

EXAMPLE:

```
                              217 Wood Road
                              San Diego, CA 91000
                              January 3, 19--


Reservations
Boston Hotel
2100 Front Street
Boston, MA 02000

Ladies and Gentlemen

   Please reserve a single room with bath for the
nights of February 1, 2, and 3. I shall be attending
the National Secretaries Convention that is being
held at the Boston Hotel on those dates. It is my
understanding that the daily room rate for this
convention is $30.

   Would you please confirm this reservation and let
me know if a deposit is required.

   Thank you.

                              Sincerely,

                              Mary Ann Johnson

                              Miss Mary Ann Johnson
```

Hotels reply by letters or form post cards to notify guests concerning their confirmations. Confirmations should always be carried when checking into any hotel.

SECTION 12 Request for information letters

Letters are written to obtain all kinds of information—requests for catalogs, brochures, price lists, and other printed matter. They are also used to obtain facts about products and services (such as where a product is available); prices of products and other sales information (method of payment, acceptable credit cards, and so on); details of an account (such as amount owed and when payments were made); and checking-up letters (when was the order sent and why was a reply not received to a letter).

So that requests for information can be answered as quickly and easily as possible, follow these points:

1. Make the request in the opening sentence. Sometimes a subject line is helpful, as it tells the reader what the letter is about.
2. Give as much information as you have. Usually this is placed in the body of the letter.
3. Close with a summary of the request and thank you or other amenities.

EXAMPLE:

```
                    223 West End Drive
                    Omaha, NE 68130
                    December 15, 19--
```

```
Home Magazine
230 Fifth Avenue
New York, NY 00231
```

Ladies and Gentlemen

Would you please tell me the name of the manufacturer of the candlesticks that were pictured on the December cover of Home Magazine.

SECTION 13   FAVORS OR ASSISTANCE LETTERS

The candlesticks appear to be brass and were shown on the mantel of the fireplace in the Christmas scene cover. I am interested in purchasing similar candlesticks if it is possible to do so.

I shall be grateful for your sending me the name and address of the manufacturer.

Thank you.

                Sincerely,

                Sara Cartwright

                Mrs. Donald T. Cartwright

Notice that the opening sentence identifies the information that is wanted. The body gives further information, and the closing is a courteous summary of the request.

Letters requesting information are often opportunities for the recipient of the letters to create business; therefore, these letters should be answered promptly and positively. Perhaps the letter can be answered by writing across the bottom of it. If the desired information is not readily available and may take several days to locate, it would be well to write a brief note explaining this to the writer of the letter. In any event, this is an opportunity to create goodwill; if you take advantage of it, your firm may have a new customer.

SECTION 13 Favors or assistance letters

13·A Requesting favors or assistance

Letters are also written to ask for favors or assistance. Large organizations generally comply if the requests are reasonable, chiefly as a means of building goodwill. Often the requests for favors are made by nonprofit organizations (schools, charities, and the like). Typical requests are for speakers, permission to visit offices and factories, copies of printed matter, free samples of products, and so forth.

Here are some hints for writing letters requesting favors:

1. Be sure, first of all, that your request is reasonable.

2. Identify what you would like and give as much information as possible.

3. Identify and tell something about the group that you represent.

4. If someone has suggested your contacting the firm to whom you are writing, use that person's name (with permission, of course).

5. Make your request as far in advance as possible. This gives the company time to make arrangements.

6. Make it easy for the recipient to reply—give a telephone number and times that you can be reached or be sure that your address is easily found on the letter.

7. Ask for alternative help. If the person to whom you are writing cannot comply with your request, perhaps an alternative suggestion can be made.

8. If possible, write to a person in the firm rather than to the firm itself. If the letter is addressed to a firm, it will have to be routed to the person taking care of such matters. This becomes both time-consuming and less personal.

9. The tone of the letter should be friendly and courteous, but avoid flattery and other insincere language.

EXAMPLE:

```
                              3745 Willow Street
                              Phoenix, AZ 85010
                              January 5, 19—
```

Miss Linda Harris, Office Manager
River National Bank
345 Tenth Avenue
Phoenix, AZ 85011

Dear Miss Harris

Would it be possible for you to speak to the Business and Economics Club of State College on Tuesday, February 17, at two o'clock? Mr. Paul Mann, who works with you, suggested that we write you.

The Business and Economics Club consists of forty members who are business majors at State College. Our club holds monthly meetings to which business people, selected from various organizations in the

SECTION 13 FAVORS OR ASSISTANCE LETTERS   99

community, are invited to speak. Our February meeting will be concerned with women in the field of banking. Mr. Mann, who assists our faculty adviser, thought that you would be particularly qualified to speak on this topic. The time allocated to the speaker is 45 minutes; usually part of the time is spent in a question-and-answer session. The meeting is held in Room 400 of Madison Hall.

    I can be telephoned at 333-1111, Ext. 40, any afternoon between two and five; or if you prefer, you may write me.

    We do hope that you can be our guest speaker.

                Sincerely,

                Roberta Scott

                Roberta Scott, Secretary

13·B Answering requests for favors

The reply to a letter requesting a favor, whether the answer is yes or no, should be gracious and friendly.

If the answer is positive, begin with this fact:

    I shall be delighted to speak to the Business and Economics Club on Tuesday, February 17, at two o'clock.

Not only is this to the point, but it confirms the time, the place, and the organization. The tone is positive and friendly.

The next paragraph, the body, should explain any details:

    Because students are usually interested in a topic that applies to their particular interests—in this instance, how women can succeed in the field of banking—I should like to talk about River National Bank's program for women in banking. I should also like to show some slides made in our bank. Do you have a projector and screen available? If not, I can bring them with me.

The confirmation is in the closing:

    My telephone number is 777-1111, Ext. 333. I shall plan to be at Room 400 of Madison Hall a few minutes before two o'clock.

SECTION **14** **Sales letters**

Letters that try to persuade a customer or client to buy a product or service are, of course, sales letters. They may be solicited (written in answer to a request for information), or they may be unsolicited (written on the initiation of the writer and sent to selected names). Sales letters may be individually written letters and go only to one person, or they may be reproduced in quantity and go to many persons. Whether they are carefully read or discarded after a quick glance determines their effectiveness.

Direct mail, which is a package of promotional material (generally including a sales letter, an illustrated leaflet, and a reply form) sent to a large mailing list, is a field quite apart from the ordinary sales letter. Entire college courses are devoted to this aspect of sales writing. Direct mail is more likely to be a part of advertising than of business writing; therefore, it is not included in this discussion.

The sales letter considered here is the letter sent from a business office as an answer to an inquiry or as a follow-up to a customer's visit or is initiated as the result of some special event such as a sale, a new product, or the opening of a new office or store. It can simply be an appeal to get new business or clients. These sales letters are not written in order to make an appeal to thousands of people across the country; they are instead tailored to individuals or small groups with similar interests or desires. Such letters have the same ultimate goal—to persuade someone to buy a product or service. They should, however, be easier to write as the attraction does not have to be so broad and often the letters are written in reply to requests for information—they are solicited.

In any sales letter, the first goal is to arouse interest. If you do not immediately get the interest of the reader, chances are that the letter will not be read or, at best, will be hastily scanned. Assume that the letter is well presented—the letter is appealing; the paragraphs are short, as is the letter itself; and the reader is attracted. Where, then, do you start to arouse interest? Perhaps an unusual salutation will attract attention, but ordinarily it is the opening where reader interest is aroused. The opening sets the tone for the letter—it must make the reader receptive to the rest of the letter. To be effective, the opening should get right to the point, arouse curiosity, be positive, and not tell something that the reader already knows. These are some of the kinds of rational appeals that arouse interest: monetary—saving money or getting a bargain; personal—improvement of health, appearance, and surroundings; emotional—sympathy, pride, concern for family, patriotism, or concern for other persons.

You know what you must do—arouse the reader's interest —but how do you start? Before you begin writing or planning, know as much about your product or service as possible; you can't sell a product unless you know all about it. Next, know as much as you can about your reader. If you are answering a request for information, it is easier than writing to an unknown customer; but even if the customer is unknown, you can tailor your letter to a certain group—the graduating seniors of the local high school, for instance. Use empathy—how would you react to the opening you have written?

Perhaps there should be a warning about having a too-unusual approach in writing sales letters. Be careful about using things that emphasize or are superlatives. That means be sparing with exclamation points, ellipses (three periods), underlining, all capitals, and other devices that attract attention but do not necessarily hold it. Remember that superlative language can sound insincere unless you use it judiciously. Other attention grabbers are using more than one color, putting pictures on the letter, printing words in large letters of boldface type, and gimmicks—a penny or swatch of material glued to the letter, for example.

A short sentence or question can often be used effectively. Here are some examples:

```
Would you spend five minutes to save $100?
Do you look as young as you feel?
We invite comparison--compare our all-new Ace
    Television with any other set on the market.
Our staff of experts wants to work for you.
```

You arouse the reader's interest in the opening; the body should supply the details to convince the reader that purchasing the product or buying your service is desirable. You will lose the reader, though, unless the body is geared not to a description of the product or service, but to the self-interest of the reader—what the product or service can do for that person.

This is the opening of a sales letter. The rest of the letter will be added later.

```
Here is good news--our sales representative will
demonstrate the Apex Vacuum Cleaner in your home
free of charge!
```

BUSINESS LETTERS FOR SPECIFIC PURPOSES 102

The appeal is made to money-saving and convenience. The reader does not have to go to a store; the cleaner will be brought to the home. It is easy and there is no charge for this service.

Supply the details in the body of the letter. Develop the appeal of seeing this vacuum cleaner in the convenient setting of the home. Don't make the mistake of going into an elaborate description of the product—the horsepower of the motor or the superiority of the materials used in making the cleaner. Rather, tell the reader how it will help personally. Emphasize any money-saving features, how it will help improve the appearance of the reader's home, and how it will save time and effort—all very important points so far as the reader is concerned.

Avoid the trite and obvious. Use specifics in sales letters; for example, use the brand name, not such a vague term as "our product." Use positive words and phrases that will help sell.

In the body of the letter make the reader want to see the cleaner. Add this body to the opening:

```
Our all-new Apex Vacuum Cleaner can go to work in
your home any time that you wish. You can see for
yourself--right in your own living room--just how
well this powerful cleaner will chase the dust and
dirt. The Apex can slip under furniture and capture
dust from all of the hard-to-get-into corners. You
will find how lightweight the Apex is--over bare
floors or shag rugs, the Apex glides easily.
    The Apex would be a bargain at its usual price of
$89; but for two weeks only--it's an even bigger
bargain--we've cut the price by more than 10 per-
cent! See our vacuum cleaner and, if you buy within
the next two weeks, we'll take $10 off the price for
your promptness. The price of the vacuum, delivered
to your door, will be only $79.
```

Assume that you have aroused interest and convinced the reader that this product is desirable. Go to the closing to get the reader to act. Make replying as easy as possible—enclose a stamped reply card or emphasize a local telephone number. Sometimes a special premium or bonus can be offered to the reader who replies promptly.

This is the closing for the vacuum-cleaner letter:

```
Either call us at 123-4567--an operator will take
your message and arrange for an appointment any time
between nine and five--or sign the enclosed postage-
```

paid card and drop it in the mail today. We will
respond promptly. If you reply within the week, our
sales representative will bring a gift of a new spot
remover when she calls to demonstrate the vacuum
cleaner. The gift is yours without obligation.
You've heard from us—we want to hear from you!

Perhaps you have one more point that you want to make. Add a postscript. It is an effective place to attract attention, for often the reader's eye goes there first.

Here is the postscript for the letter:

P.S. Perhaps you don't have cash right now for a
vacuum cleaner. We can arrange for payment over
three months without carrying charges of any kind.
This is the plan: A down payment of $19 and $20 the
first of the month for three months are all that is
required.

Put the letter together, and this is the result:

Dear Mrs. New Customer:

Here is good news—our sales representative will
demonstrate the Apex Vacuum Cleaner in your home
free of charge!
Our all-new Apex Vacuum Cleaner can go to work in
your home any time that you wish. You can see for
yourself—right in your own living room—just how
well this powerful cleaner will chase the dust and
dirt. The Apex can slip under furniture and capture
dust from all of the hard-to-get-into corners. You
will find how lightweight the Apex is—over bare
floors or shag rugs, the Apex glides easily.
The Apex would be a bargain at its usual price of
$89; but for two weeks only—it's an even bigger
bargain—we've cut the price by more than 10 percent. See our vacuum cleaner and, if you buy within
the next two weeks, we'll take $10 off the price
for your promptness. The price of the vacuum, delivered to your door, will be only $79.
Either call us at 123-4567—an operator will take
your message and arrange for an appointment any time
between nine and five—or sign the enclosed postage-
paid card and drop it in the mail today. We will

respond promptly. If you reply within the week, our sales representative will bring a gift of a new spot remover when she calls to demonstrate the vacuum cleaner. The gift is yours without obligation. You've heard from us; we want to hear from you!

      Sincerely,

      Roger Agent

      Roger Agent, Sales Manager

P.S. Perhaps you don't have cash right now for a vacuum cleaner. We can arrange for payment over three months without carrying charges of any kind. This is the plan: A down payment of $19 and $20 the first of the month for three months are all that is required.

 Check the letter by answering these questions:

 What are the appeals the letter makes?
 Is the letter "you" oriented?
 What are the benefits of the reader's replying promptly?
 Is the language specific?
 Is the letter oriented to what the product will do for the reader?
 Do you think the reader will reply?

SECTION 15 Claim or adjustment letters

Claim or complaint letters are written to tell an individual or a firm that something is wrong with a product or service. It may be that a product has not been received, that it was received but in damaged condition, that the wrong product was sent, that the product or service does not do what it is advertised to do, or for a variety of other reasons.

15·A Initiating the claim or complaint

Before you complain, do these things: First, and most important, be sure the complaint is accurate and reasonable. Check the original order; by any chance, did you or someone in your firm make the mistake? Gather all of the information that you can. If the package arrived in damaged condition, check the packing. Look at the documents—shipping order, bill of lading, packing slip, and anything else that might be available—to see what facts you can find. Check dates, numbers, and names.

SECTION 15 CLAIM OR ADJUSTMENT LETTERS

When was the order or shipment sent? Were the necessary numbers (order, requisition, model) given? Do the numbers correspond or match? Are the forms signed? Who was responsible for packing, shipping, or delivery? The more information that you can supply, the easier it becomes to settle a claim. If possible, address the letter to a person within the firm rather than to the firm alone. Perhaps you telephoned about the order; if so, ask for the name of the person with whom you spoke so that the follow-up letter can be directed to that person.

Once you have all of the information that you need, plan your letter. Begin with a factual description of the problem. Enclose photocopies (not originals; those should be kept as proof) of any documents. Whatever you do, try to keep the goodwill of the reader of your complaint letter; there should be no threats, accusations, or antagonizing expressions.

Assume that you placed a routine order for stationery and office supplies. You asked that the order be delivered by the end of the year to assure that you would not run out of stationery. You received the invoice for the stationery on December 28, but you still have not received the order by January 5. A telephone call to Mr. Robinson at the stationery company did not give you much information. He merely said that you should have received the order. You are almost out of memorandum forms and other stationery supplies are getting quite low. Because you are angry, you dash off the following letter:

```
    We have been ordering stationery and office sup-
plies from your organization for over ten years.
Usually the service has been satisfactory, but this
time you have really goofed on a simple order. Last
October we placed our regular order and asked that
it be delivered before the end of the year. Your
salesman assured us that there would be no problem.
Well, I am now assuring you that there is. It is
January 5 and still no order. Not only that, but you
sent us a bill for $475.13 for this stationery. We
are not, repeat not, paying this.
    If we do not have our stationery by January 10, we
are canceling our order and taking our business
elsewhere. Our orders may not be as large as other
companies', but we do pay our bills on time; that
should count for something.
    Please get something right and send our order
immediately.
```

How is the recipient going to respond to this? Of course, they want your business, but they do not want your abuse. Perhaps losing one customer is not that important to a successful firm.

Compare the angry letter to this:

```
On October 20 we ordered from Mr. Robinson, the
salesman for our territory, stationery and office
supplies for use in our office. We asked that the
order be sent before the end of the year. The dupli-
cate sales order that we have is No. 3455. We have
not yet received the order, even though it is past
the promised delivery date. We did, however, receive
an invoice for $475.13.
     Would you please check to see the reason for this
delay. We are getting quite low on certain items in
the order; and unless we receive this order soon, it
will be difficult for our office to operate prop-
erly.
     Is it possible to send this order so that it
reaches us by January 10? We are, of course, holding
your invoice for payment until we receive the order.
     Please let us know immediately, either by tele-
phone or special-delivery letter, what has become of
our order and how soon we shall receive it. We are
sure that you will take care of the difficulty
promptly.
```

This letter begins by stating the problem; facts and names are given. There is no threatening or antagonistic language. The writer states what is desired. The ending expresses confidence that the firm will handle the matter.

A claim or complaint letter follows this outline:

1. The opening states the problem and gives as much information as possible.

2. The body gives any additional information—why it is necessary to write, why you are inconvenienced, etc.

3. The body also states what you want done—what you consider a reasonable demand to satisfy your claim.

4. The closing expresses confidence that the company will handle the matter satisfactorily and fairly.

SECTION 15 CLAIM OR ADJUSTMENT LETTERS

15·B Answering claim or complaint letters

First of all, any claim or complaint letter should be answered promptly. If there is a delay in making a decision about the claim or adjustment, let the writer know that the letter has been received and that the problem will be taken care of. A slow response only antagonizes someone who is already dissatisfied about a product or service.

15·B·1 Agreeing to writer's request

The answer to a claim letter is easy if you are agreeing to the writer's request—you are refunding money, sending a replacement shipment, or doing whatever it is that the writer wants. This is a positive letter that begins with the good news.

Here are some openings:

```
We shall be glad to accept for credit the coat
that you recently purchased from us and that you
wish to return.
    Of course you can return for full credit the lamp
that has a broken base.
    Our check for $10 is enclosed. This is the amount
that you were overcharged on our recent invoice.
```

The body of such a letter supplies details—how the merchandise should be returned or whether the overcharge is being credited to the customer's account or returned in a cash refund. The body may even include a paragraph about a new product or an explanation of how the firm is attempting to keep this problem from happening again. It probably includes an apology and a promise that the company will try to prevent such things from recurring.

A warning should be added against writing adjustment letters that are too casual. If a mistake has been made, the letter correcting the error and apologizing for it should be a dignified explanation. An opening such as, "Oh, boy, we goofed this time!" does nothing to create confidence that the firm is capable of conducting business in a responsible manner.

The closing should be courteous and might contain a request for future business.

15·B·2 Making adjustment of writer's request

The in-between answer to a claim letter is one in which the writer is making some adjustment or concession, but the demand is not entirely met. For example, instead of replacing a damaged garment, the firm is offering to repair it. You cannot begin the letter with what you are willing to do because this is

Markby's
Department Store

New York   Pittsburgh   Cincinnati   Baltimore

June 8, 19--

Mrs. Francis L. Norton
2435 East 107 Street
Olympia, WA 89501

Dear Mrs. Norton

Of course you may return for full credit the microwave oven that was damaged in shipment.

American Delivery Service will pick up the oven on Friday, June 17. If you would like us to replace the oven with another like it, the delivery service will exchange a new oven for the damaged one on June 17. However, if you would prefer, we will credit your account for $308, the purchase price of the oven plus sales tax. Just write a note on the bottom of this letter telling us what you would like us to do. There is a postage-paid envelope enclosed so that you can send us the letter easily and quickly.

Thank you for telling us that the microwave oven was damaged when it was delivered. By letting us know when these things occur, we can correct problems and, we hope, keep you as one of our satisfied customers. We should like to serve you again soon.

                            Sincerely

                            MARKBY'S DEPARTMENT STORE

                            Ross Carson

                            Ross Carson, Sales Manager

RC/abc
Enc.

Letter Granting Customer's Request

SECTION 15 CLAIM OR ADJUSTMENT LETTERS

not what the customer wants. Instead, you must convince the customer that this is a reasonable settlement of the request. The opening will begin with a thank you or an apology and a specific statement of the claim or complaint.

Here are some examples:

Thank you for telling us the problems you have encountered in using our Halo Electric Hair Dryer.

We are sorry that the coat you purchased had a button missing.

Would you please return the coat you recently purchased and that has tear in the sleeve? Then our tailors can determine what must be done.

The body of the letter explains why the demand is being handled in this way, why it is fair, what company policies are, and how this is a reasonable settlement for both the firm and the customer. Use specifics, such as sale merchandise is not returnable, merchandise on sale is sold as-is, all returned merchandise must be accompanied by a sales ticket. Again, you are trying to build goodwill; you are not accusing the customer of being negligent or dishonest. Try in some way to assume part of the blame—perhaps the firm should have tags that are more readable or perhaps the tag was lost from the garment.

The closing is courteous. It can include an invitation to visit the store sometime soon; or it could be a hope that the customer is satisfied with the adjustment. Remember, a closing does not contain anything that has not been previously discussed in the letter.

Look at this letter that was written in response to the claim letter on p. 106. Before the answering letter could be written, certain facts had to be determined. A check was made to see if the order had been received, why it was not shipped as promised, and how the invoice happened to be mailed before the shipment. If getting the information is going to take more than a day, the customer should be written saying that a check is being made and that the information will be sent as soon as it is available. Whatever else is done, an acknowledgment of the claim letter, at least, should go out quickly; the customer should not be left uninformed and, therefore, probably angry. Only after all of the facts are determined, is the letter written.

First, the customer is told what happened:

We are very sorry that your Order No. 3455 for stationery and office supplies has not yet arrived.

We checked with our shipping department; the order
was sent by Mountain Auto Freight on December 1.
We then checked with the shipping company. Unfortunately, there was a strike called at Mountain Auto
Freight on December 2, and all shipments were left
in their warehouse. We were not notified that your
order was left in Mountain Auto Freight's warehouse.
The strike has not been settled, and there seem to
be no prospects of a settlement very soon.

An alternative suggestion is offered:

Because we want you to have the order immediately, we have duplicated it. The order will leave
our shipping room today by a special delivery van.
It should arrive and be delivered in at most three
days.

Please do not pay the invoice until you have
received the shipment.

The closing is a repeat of the apology and a reassurance that the customer's business is wanted.

We regret this unfortunate mix-up, and we hope
that your work has not been seriously disrupted by
the delay in receiving your order. We value you as
a customer and would like to continue supplying your
office needs. Please let us know if the shipment
does not arrive within three days or if there is
anything further that we can do.

15·B·3 Rejecting writer's request

There are times when a customer's request must be rejected. "No" letters are difficult to write because you must both refuse the customer's request and retain the customer's goodwill. First, put yourself in the customer's place—perhaps the customer realizes that the request is not a reasonable one. In that case, your refusal will not be annoying. Second, usually along with the refusal you can suggest an alternative that the customer will find reasonable. Here is an example: "Please return the coat with the missing button to our tailoring department. If they cannot match the button, they will replace all of the buttons for a charge of $2." Third, sometimes it is a matter of language—instead of writing in a negative tone, try to make it positive. For example, avoid writing, "We cannot accept your

SECTION 15 CLAIM OR ADJUSTMENT LETTERS

request for a refund for the coat that you wish to return." Instead, try, "We wish that we could accept your request for a refund for the coat that you recently purchased."

If the letter contains negative or bad news, do not begin with the bad news in the opening. You can thank the customer for writing or perhaps say that you are sorry for the dissatisfaction.

Here are two openings:

```
We are sorry that the lady's coat that you pur-
chased at our Saturday Surprise Sale had a cut in
the fabric.
    Thank you for telling us about the problem that
you encountered when you used Zip Fabric Bleach.
```

Explain why the request is being refused in the body of the letter. If at all possible, offer an alternative. Also, if possible, tell the customer what you are doing to prevent the problem from being repeated.

This is the body that would accompany the first opening given in the preceding examples:

```
Most of our customers who shop Saturday Surprise
Sales know that the sales merchandise is not return-
able. We post signs telling our customers of this,
and we mark all of the sales tickets, too. Perhaps
our signs need to be more prominently displayed.
Although we cannot accept the return of the coat,
we can offer you the services of one of our expert
tailors. Simply take this letter and the coat to our
Alterations Department and ask for their help.
Usually repairs such as the one we think your coat
will require cost no more than $7. Ordinarily the
coat that you purchased would cost $100, but at our
special sale the price was only $59.95. Even with a
small alteration charge, the coat is still below its
usual price.
```

The closing is a summary and a request for the customer's future business:

```
We hope that you will consider this to be a rea-
sonable solution to the problem. We value your
```

patronage and want you to return and shop at our store. Thank you for letting us serve you.

15·C Writing to prevent claims or complaints

Often it is possible to prevent claims or complaints by anticipating that a planned action may be unfavorably received and by writing to customers or clients that such an event will occur. You are, in effect, adjusting the claim before it occurs. Such negative actions might be price rises, added charges for services that had previously been free, interrupted service, items that are not the same as advertised (substitution of a plastic part for a metal one, for example), slower delivery of an order than originally promised, or cutbacks in service. If a letter is written in advance telling why such negative action is necessary, a great deal of customer anger can often be prevented. Such an advance-notice letter should be clearly stated in precise language so that the action appears justifiable and not arbitrary. It is also possible that you can include in such a letter information about your products or services so that the letter, in addition to letting the customer know the negative news, becomes a kind of sales letter. You might, for example, suggest that the customer place an order before the date when price increases go into effect so that the increase can be delayed.

Following is an example of a letter written to explain the price rise in the home delivery of a newspaper:

Dear Customer:

On March 1 we must raise the price of the home-delivered Gazette by 75 cents per month—from $6.75 to $7.50.

We are reluctant to raise prices; however, the price of the newspaper to the distributor has risen almost 10 percent, and labor costs for delivery services have also increased approximately 10 percent. We find, therefore, that we must for the first time in over a year raise prices.

In spite of rising prices, home delivery of the Gazette is still less expensive than newsstand prices; and there is the added convenience of having the Gazette at your doorstep each morning.

We shall, of course, continue our same dependable service. If, for any reason, you have a problem, please call 765-4321. An operator will take calls any time between 6 a.m. and 11 a.m.

We sincerely regret the necessity for raising prices. We hope that you can understand why this increase is necessary and that you will permit us to continue serving you.

Sincerely,

Robert D. Agent

Robert D. Agent

SECTION 16 Collecting overdue account letters

Because very few persons or firms pay for their purchases as they make them, they accumulate debts. If these debts are not paid when they are due, letters are written to ask these people for payment. Often a series of letters is necessary to get customers or clients to pay. Many firms have a time schedule for sending such letters. The first letter is sent when the account is delinquent for a certain period of time; the second, so many days later; and so forth.

Collection letters have two purposes: first, to collect the past-due account and, second, to keep the customer's goodwill. Even if a firm successfully collects its past-due accounts, it needs to keep the customer buying from that firm. It cannot operate without repeat business; therefore, a firm cannot afford to antagonize its customers.

Descriptions of the various steps in collecting overdue accounts are given here. However, different firms follow different collection policies and procedures; for example, some are more lenient, while others speed the process by writing fewer letters.

16·A First reminder

The first notification in collecting overdue accounts is generally a reminder. It can be as simple as a rubber stamp or a printed notice or a gummed sticker over the statement; it is not usually a letter. If it is a computer billing, the machine has been programmed to add a line telling the customer that the account is overdue. You are assuming that the obligation has been overlooked; therefore, you are sending a reminder. Writing a collection letter at this point would risk losing the customer's goodwill and also incur the expense of writing the letter.

16·B Second communication

The second step in the collection series is a letter written to ask why the company has not been paid. You assume that there is

BUSINESS LETTERS FOR SPECIFIC PURPOSES 114

a reason for not paying and that something is wrong. The letter should have a helpful tone. Every attempt should be made to make it easy for the customer to pay—enclose a return envelope or ask the customer to call or to communicate in some way.

EXAMPLE:

The opening reviews the situation:

We have not received the December payment of $44 that was due on your television set, and it will soon be time for the January payment.

The body begins with an offer of help and then explains what is wanted. The closing is a courteous goodbye:

Because you have met previous payments promptly, we think something must have happened that has prevented you from making the December payment. If so, can we help in some way?

Would you please send us your check for $44? You may also include the January payment by sending your your check for $88. If you cannot pay the entire amount at this time, would you please explain your difficulty to us and let us know your plans for making these payments.

Should your check already be in the mail, please accept our thanks.

In this collection letter, do not suggest reasons for the nonpayment, such as that the statement did not arrive or that it was overlooked in the rush of Christmas holidays. Too, do not suggest that the product or services were unsatisfactory; if they were, the customer would have complained before the account became past-due. Let the customer explain the nonpayment to you.

**16·C
Third communication**

The next letter in the series will be stronger. It will attempt to get the customer to pay by appealing to such things as sense of fair play, desire for a good reputation or credit standing, or security. You are not offering in this letter to help; you want the bill paid.

This is an example of an appeal to maintaining a good credit standing:

We wrote you three weeks ago asking that you send us your check for $88 to cover the December and

SECTION 16   COLLECTING OVERDUE ACCOUNT LETTERS   115

January payments on your television set. We have not heard from you.

Because you have always made your payments promptly, you have a fine credit standing with our company. We are sure that you wish to maintain this rating. Therefore, won't you please send us your check within the next five days?

Use the enclosed envelope for your check. When we receive your payment, your credit rating will again be rated highly.

16·D Fourth communication

If appealing to the customer brings no response, usually one more letter is written before the threatening, last-chance letter. This letter is more demanding; every effort is used, however, to avoid the final threat.

EXAMPLE:

We are sure that you have received our previous letters asking for payment of your delinquent account. We know that your credit rating is excellent, as we made a routine check before extending credit to you.

Now that credit rating is threatened by your not paying our account, which amounts to $132. If this amount is not paid, the resulting loss of your good credit rating will restrict further credit purchases and force you into the inconvenience of paying cash for all of your purchases.

Because your account is so long overdue, we must ask our Legal Department to take over. Should this happen, there will be additional legal costs.

We will not turn this account over to our Legal Department for seven days, for we are sure that your check will be here before that time. The enclosed envelope is directed to my desk for immediate attention. Please use it to send us your check.

16·E Final communication

When none of the previous appeals has produced payment, the last letter is "pay now or face legal action." Building goodwill is no longer an important consideration; you would like to keep the customer's business, but you want to collect what is owed. There should be no abusive or angry language, but the tone of the letter should be strong, firm, and clear.

The final letter should review what you have done in an attempt to collect the account. It should tell what effect nonpayment will have on the customer's credit standing, and it

BUSINESS LETTERS FOR SPECIFIC PURPOSES 116

should state precisely the steps that you will take if the account is not paid.

EXAMPLE:

We have written you four times over the past three months in our efforts to collect $132 that is now six months past-due.

As you have not replied to any of our reminders or letters asking for payment, we are forced to take legal steps to collect this overdue account. Are you aware what this will do to your credit standing? We must, when we take legal action to collect any account, notify the credit bureau of our action. They, in turn, will change your credit rating accordingly.

Therefore, unless we receive your check for $132 by May 1, we will notify our Legal Department to proceed with a suit to collect this amount. If this involves court action, costs will be added.

We hope that you will not force us to take this unpleasant action.

16·F Using special postal services

Using some of the special postal services is sometimes effective in collecting slow-paying accounts. The importance of the letter can be emphasized by sending it by certified mail with or without a requested return receipt. A return receipt furnishes proof that the letter was actually received. You can, too, for payment of an additional fee, restrict delivery to the addressee. The cost of sending telegrams to collect overdue accounts makes it impractical in most instances.

16·G Form collection letters

Often firms compose a series of form collection letters. Sometimes these are programmed into the computer. At certain predetermined intervals, the computer writes letters to customers with overdue accounts. This can antagonize because, not only is the appearance of the letter usually mechanical and impersonal, but the computer does not take into consideration any replies that the customer may have written. In addition, the computer can send collection letters to persons who either do not actually owe the debt or who, because of a question concerning the account, are withholding payment of the bill.

16·H Duplicated collection letters

Collection letters with names and amounts added to duplicated forms are impersonal; therefore, they are more likely to be disregarded. They might be effective, though, as first reminders because they are so impersonal and would, as they are intended to do, gently remind customers of overdue accounts.

SECTION 17 Credit letters

Letters are written to ask for credit, to check credit references, to reply to credit checks, and to grant or refuse credit. To establish personal credit, most persons complete a form that is supplied by the firm granting credit. This will be discussed in the section on personal business writing (see p. 179).

Because credit is such an important part of business, most firms have routine procedures. In addition, credit information is available to companies through agencies and firms that operate both within the United States and internationally. In most instances, such information is available in a very short period of time once credit has been established. Firms reciprocate—XYZ Company will tell you about Robert McNamara if you will tell the XYZ Company about Julia Kidd. Credit ratings of firms are also available from companies such as Dun & Bradstreet that specialize in such information.

17·A Requesting credit

A short letter is generally sufficient when a firm makes a request for credit and its credit rating is already established.

The opening of the letter contains the request; often an order accompanies the credit request.

This is a sample opening:

```
Will you please extend credit to our firm by
filling the enclosed order on a credit basis?
```

The details of the request are given in the body. Financial statements are enclosed, and sources from which credit information can be obtained are given.

EXAMPLE:

```
The enclosed financial statements will give you
information about our firm. You can also check with
these three firms from whom we purchase on a credit
basis:
    1. James and Quan, 411 Front Street, Chicago, IL
       25550
    2. Parker Company, 400 East River Drive, Boston,
       MA 02100
    3. Morris Manufacturing Company, 100 World
       Center, Chicago, IL 25550
```

Should additional information be required, please write to us.

The closing is a summary:

We hope that you can extend credit to us and fill our order promptly.

17·B Requesting credit information

When the company receives a letter requesting credit, it routinely checks the credit references. The letter requesting credit information begins by identifying what the letter is about and the name and address of the credit applicant. Also included is the fact that the credit applicant has given the recipient as a reference. A subject line can be helpful. Most credit request letters assure the recipient that the information will be kept confidential. If the specific information that you wish to know is set forth in tabulated form, it is easier to read and to answer. Close the letter with *thank you* and an offer to give the recipient similar information.

EXAMPLE:

May we have credit information about Keith Jordan? As president of Jordan Manufacturing Company, 192 West 52 Street, St. Louis, MO 63108, he has applied for credit and has given your name as reference.

You can, if you wish, complete the blanks after the questions and return the letter to us. Your reply will, of course, be kept strictly confidential. Please use the reverse side of the letter for additional information.

1. Length of time this company has done business with your firm_____
2. Highest credit extended this firm_____
3. What is the balance currently due _____
4. Is any of the balance past-due _____
5. How does the company pay? Within discount period? _____ Within net period? _____ How many months?_____
6. Remarks _____

Thank you for your help. We shall be glad to give you similar information whenever we can.

17·C Replying to credit check

When you are replying to a credit check, complete the form if one is available. You may wish to keep a carbon or photocopy of your reply. If no form is available, write a simple reply. The information contained in such a letter should be factual; the recipient is not interested in your opinions. Do not merely write: "It is my opinion that Mr. Jordan is a good credit risk." Include specific information about the customer's paying habits.

EXAMPLE:

We are happy to tell you that we consider Mr. Keith Jordan, about whom you requested confidential information, to be an excellent credit risk.

Mr. Jordan has been one of our credit customers for six years. The balance in his account has been as high as $25,000, and we have not placed a limit on his credit. His payments have always been made within our usual credit terms of thirty days. We understand that he is planning to expand his business.

We hope that this information will be of value to you in establishing an account for Mr. Jordan.

17·D Granting credit

Letters that grant credit are easy to write. They begin with the positive news that an account is open and usually something about how the decision was made. The body explains the credit terms of the account. The body can also include promotional material—something about a new product, for example. The closing is a courteous request to use the account soon.

EXAMPLE:

We are very pleased to tell you that an account for your firm has been opened with us. The order that you recently sent is on its way and charged to your new account. We checked the credit references that you gave us and found that you are highly rated.

Our credit terms allow for payment of the invoice thirty days after delivery. Please do not pay until you receive a statement.

When you discover how well our stationery and office supplies sell, we think you will want to consider other products that we manufacture. Our new spring catalog is enclosed.

We are also enclosing a supply of order forms. Thank you for buying from Empire Products.

**17·E
Refusing
credit**

Letters refusing credit are much more difficult to write. Because they are bad news, do not get to the point in the opening. Begin, instead, with a *thank you* to the customer for wanting to buy from the firm or a remark about the popularity of the product that the customer ordered. If the bad news opens the letter, the recipient may see only that fact, become angry, and read no further. Even though you are refusing a request for credit, you still would like to maintain the customer's goodwill and possible future business. Offer an alternative if possible—the customer could place a C.O.D. order or pay in advance, for example. Remember, too, that slow-paying customers are often aware of their credit ratings; therefore, if the letter is tactful, goodwill can be maintained. The language should be polite but impersonal.

EXAMPLE:

```
    Thank you for your order and for applying for
credit with Empire Products.
    Although we should like very much to open an
account for you, our routine check of the credit
references that you sent us indicates that you are
having difficulties in paying some of your creditors
and that some of your accounts are as much as three
months overdue. Two of the firms with whom we
checked told us that this was a recent occurrence.
Perhaps there is an explanation that you would care
to supply.
    In the meantime, may we fill your order? We can
send it either as a C.O.D. shipment or, upon receipt
of your check for $285.15, as a prepaid order.
    Please let us know whether you would like the
order shipped. As soon as we receive your instruc-
tions, the order will be on its way.
```

SECTION **18**   **Routine letters**

There are many short routine letters that have to be written. There are situations that require a letter of acknowledgment. For example, the person handling certain matters is out of the office, and the writer of the letter must be notified that the matter will be taken care of when that person returns. Or there might be a request for information not readily available, and the writer of the letter must be notified when the information will be sent. Orders and payments are acknowledged so that the senders know that they have been received. Routine letters of

SECTION 18   ROUTINE LETTERS

Pylon Corporation

824 Faunsworth St., Atlanta, GA 30305
404/677-4774

January 12, 19--

Mr. J. R. Brown, Agent
Sun Insurance Company
211 West Main Street
Los Angeles, CA 90100

Dear Mr. Brown

I am enclosing the Loss Claim form that you sent us. This form describes the loss that we had when fire burned furniture in our office on January 9.

As you requested, we had three estimates for the repair of the damage. They are listed on the reverse side of the form in the blanks that are provided.

We should like to have the work done quickly so that work in our office will not be disrupted any more than necessary.

Thank you so much for your help.

Sincerely

J. T. Martin

J. T. Martin
Office Manager

JTM:abd

Routine Letter of Transmittal

transmittal or covering letters are written to tell a recipient what is being sent, why it is being sent, and who sent it; for example, a covering letter accompanies a check made in payment of an insurance claim. Reminders are other routine letters. A customer is reminded of an appointment, a payment that will be due, or a shipment that has arrived and can be picked up. These messages are handled by form postal cards or letters.

SECTION 19 Goodwill letters

Although all business letters have the goal of building goodwill, certain kinds are written specifically for this purpose. These letters do such things as show appreciation to an old customer, welcome a new customer, thank a customer, extend an invitation to a customer, congratulate a customer, extend season's greetings, and express condolences, apologies, or regrets.

Goodwill letters usually do not require replies. They are sincere, carefully written, friendly letters that convey the intended meaning; otherwise, they convey the idea that the firm is using such a situation to sell itself or its products. For most of these messages, it is better to write a letter or note than to use a printed card. They should be brief. If possible, have the letters signed by a high-ranking official of the company.

These are some of the specific situations in which such messages might be written: to show appreciation or thanks when a time contract, note, or mortgage is paid, a new account is opened, a gift or favor is given to an organization, or bills are paid on time; to extend an invitation to visit a new office or shop; to congratulate those who have been promoted, won a prize, been elected to an office—in a professional, civic, or social organization or to a public office, purchased a new home, were graduated from school, or for any of a variety of happenings that are worthy of commendation; to extend greetings—not only at the time of Christmas holidays, but also on birthdays, anniversaries, and other holidays; and to extend condolences and sympathy at times of illness or death.

EXAMPLE:

Congratulations, Mr. Conklin!

   Mrs. Greaves, who is the head of our Mortgage Department, has just told me that you have made the final payment on your home mortgage. She has also told me that, in the fifteen years that the mortgage covered, not once have any of your payments been late.

We should like to commend you on your splendid record and to tell you that your credit standing with our bank is excellent. If, in the future, you need money for any purpose, we should like to be of help.

Thank you for dealing with Valley National Bank; we hope that it has been a mutually satisfactory experience.

Sincerely
Jack R. Curtis
Jack R. Curtis, President

SECTION 20 Interoffice memoranda

For communications within the company or within the branch offices of the company, use interoffice memoranda. A special memorandum form is ordinarily available. It contains, in addition to the letterhead, a heading that usually has four items: *To*, *From*, *Date*, and *Subject*. Because there is no salutation, complimentary close, signature, or personal titles such as *Mr.* or *Mrs.* in the heading, it is quicker to write. The writing line is usually long—six inches—so no time is consumed in margin setting. If the message is short, the body can be double spaced. It is usually typed in block style. It is often addressed to a group within the company, such as *All Salespersons* or *All Mail Room Personnel*.

SECTION 21 Letter-writing shortcuts

Letter writing is the usual way of communicating in business. We write letters to complain, to order, to tell a customer about a sale, and for many other purposes. Letter writing is expensive; presently the cost is about $6.70 for the average business letter. Often letter writing is time-consuming; by the time the letter is dictated, transcribed, signed, and mailed, several hours have gone by. Consider some of the ways that the time and expense of letter writing can be cut down.

21·A Telephoning

One of the ways of cutting letter writing is to telephone and to avoid letter writing entirely. The telephone has become so

College Production **Harcourt Brace Jovanovich, Inc.** 757 Third Ave., New York 10017

TO All Personnel

FROM Joanne Barnes, Office Manager

DATE April 16, 19--

SUBJECT Salutations of Letters

Within our company all letters addressed to individuals should have salutations that include the name of the person addressed; for example, in a letter addressed to "Mrs. Linda Wade," the salutation should be "Dear Mrs. Wade." Do not use a salutation such as "Dear Madam" or "Dear Sir." Try also to avoid addressing letters to job titles--<u>sales manager</u> or <u>director of personnel</u>, for example. Salutations for letters addressed to companies should be either "Gentlemen" or "Ladies and Gentlemen"; never use "Dear Sirs."

Will you also avoid using attention lines; instead address a letter to a person rather than to that person's attention.

We hope that by following these practices all of the letters from Empire Products will be uniform. Please call me if you have any questions.

Thank you.

J. B.

JB/abc

Interoffice Memorandum

much a part of business that there are some who now think that it has replaced writing. Based on today's letter-writing costs, it can be argued that telephoning, if not actually cheaper, at least costs no more than writing. Telephoning is, of course, faster; you can get the message or answer right away, and it certainly saves time for both persons involved in the conversation. In addition, a telephone conversation cannot be ignored or forgotten as easily as a letter.

What, then, are the advantages of writing? First of all, there is the possibility that the person you want to talk to is not in the office so you will either have to call again or depend upon the other person to call you. Second, you may need verification or proof in writing (an oral agreement does not prove a thing). Third, a correctly written letter eliminates the chance of error or misunderstanding or just plain forgetfulness. Fourth, both the writer and the reader of the letter have time to consider all of the information—the writer can choose words carefully and rewrite if necessary; the reader can reread. A telephone call must be answered and dealt with immediately. A letter may even prevent a negative answer. The reader has time to think about the message of the letter rather than give an immediate answer after an oral request has been made.

Both the telephone and letter writing are means of business communication; each has its place. Certainly, if all you want to know is whether a product is available or the cost of an item sold by a company, telephone. However, if, for example, you are placing a complicated order for a product with precise specifications—or if you are asking for information or for a favor that might be negatively received—write a letter.

21·B Postal cards

The postal card is an excellent way of communicating quickly. Business uses both types of cards: the government postal card and the picture post card. The government postal card is 5½ by 3¼ inches and can be purchased at any post office for several cents less than letter postage. As an alternative, cards this size can be printed or typed and stamped or metered. One side of the card is for the message; the other side, for the address. It is sent as first-class mail. The post card usually has a picture on one side; the other side is divided in half, one half for the message and one half for the address.

Postal cards contain short messages that fit easily on the card. They are used for those times when the message is general enough so that it does not need to be sealed in an envelope. It is an informal means of communicating.

Postal cards can be used in such instances as an announcement of a sale, a notice that a special order has arrived or work has been completed, a request for brochures or other information, a reminder of an appointment, a notice of a meeting of an organization, an acknowledgment of an order, or an announcement of a new business that is opening. Picture post cards can be used to send both a picture and a message; for example, an automobile dealer might use a post card with a picture of a new model and a message on the other side telling the recipient about the car. Sometimes the card becomes a ticket of admission to an exhibit or display.

The advantages of postal cards are that they are quicker to write and mail than a letter, they are easier to read, they can be pinned to a bulletin board, they might be slipped into a pocket or purse as a reminder, and they are less expensive.

The disadvantages are that they are not private—the message is open and can be read by anyone seeing the card; there is no file copy to give proof that a communication was sent; they are easier to overlook or to lose in the mail; and they are difficult to file.

Here are some reminders for using postal cards:

1. Always date postal cards.
2. You need not use an inside address and usually not even a salutation or complimentary close.
3. Check the message to be sure that it contains all of the information.
4. You may not need to sign the card but be sure that it contains your name and address.
5. You need not put your return on the address side of the card if the message side contains it.
6. Do be courteous—even though the message is brief, it should contain *please* and *thank you*.

Notice that the example of the postal card is dated, that it contains complete information—what is wanted and where it was advertised, the complete name and address of the writer—and that both *please* and *thank you* are used.

21·C
Answering on bottom of letter

Another short-cut means of communicating is to write an answer on the bottom of a letter. Perhaps you have received a letter that needs only a one-line answer; the exact name of a book, for example. It is not correspondence that needs to be filed. Therefore, you can write in a couple of minutes in long-

SECTION 21   LETTER-WRITING SHORTCUTS   127

```
                            January 15, 19—

    Please send me the brochure, Investment Planning,
    that you offered in the January 12 issue of the Wall
    Street Journal.

    Thank you.
                              Miss Marjorie K. Benton
                              415 East 17 Street
                              Denver, CO 80100
```

Postal Card Requesting Brochure

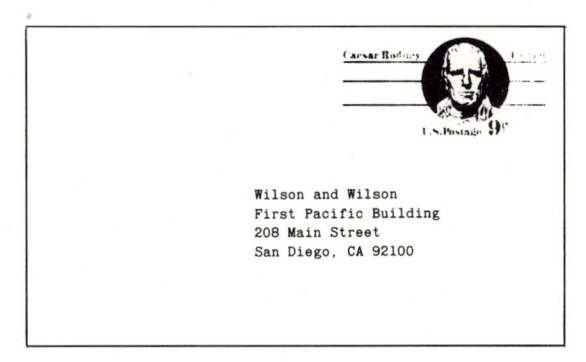

```
                                        Caesar Rodney
                                        U.S.Postage 9¢

    Wilson and Wilson
    First Pacific Building
    208 Main Street
    San Diego, CA 92100
```

Address Side of Postal Card

hand the needed information across the bottom of the letter, address an envelope (or ask your secretary to do so), and the answer is on its way. Nothing has to be dictated; nor are there any file copies.

21·D Multicopy memorandum forms

Still another method of saving time and money is the multicopy memorandum form. It is a preassembled snap-out memo form, usually consisting of an original and two carbon copies. After the memo is typed, the second carbon is kept for the writer's files, and the original and one carbon are mailed. The recipient writes a reply in the designated space on the original and retains the carbon for the files. The original is returned to the writer of the memo. When the memo with the original message plus the recipient's reply is received, there is no file searching or checking for previous correspondence. This method saves time and stationery, and all of the information is on one piece of paper.

21·E Other short forms

There are other forms used within the company, such as routing slips, message slips, and small memo forms that read "From the desk of . . ." When using these, the main considerations are that they be accurate and contain all of the necessary information. Often they are written in longhand; if this is the case, be sure that the handwriting is legible.

21·F
Form letters

Form letters are another way of saving time in offices. There are several ways of handling form letters:

1. A printed letter (for example, the kind that magazine publishers send to subscribers when their subscriptions are about to expire) that is usually not dated, has no inside address, contains a salutation that could go to many persons, such as "Dear Subscriber," has a general message in the body of the letter, and has a duplicated signature. There are variations; the current date and inside address and salutation can be filled in and the letter signed, but this takes time.

2. A typed form letter that is made up of form paragraphs. Usually these form paragraphs have been written to cover all possible situations. Not all of the paragraphs would be used, but selections would be made so that the letter is tailored for each situation. It saves time since the paragraphs do not have to be composed.

3. A letter that is typed from a previously written form letter. It has the advantage of appearing to be an individually dictated letter rather than a form letter. A typed letter is more likely to be read than an obviously printed form letter. The disadvantage is that, if it is copied from a form, it will be written too generally to cover a specific situation.

With the increased use of word-processing centers, printed form letters are likely to be replaced by letters that appear to have been individually typed; actually they have been typed by automatic typewriters. The letter or form is typed by an operator and recorded on magnetic tape or card for future use. The typewriter will then play back the letter that has been typed, typing at speeds from 150 words per minute upward. The material can be corrected or edited merely by finding the spot where the error or revision occurs and retyping. The tape will activate the typewriter to type the corrected material as many times as wished.

The tapes can be filed and used over and over again. Form letters are assembled from the stored paragraphs—even inside addresses can be put on tapes—and the machine does the typing. One of the problems is, of course, that the machine types what is stored on the tape so the original typing must be error-free.

There are also machines that write signatures. It is possible, therefore, to receive a typed and signed letter that is produced entirely by machines. Even the form paragraphs may have been selected by computers. Such choices are based on computer-stored facts about the recipient of the letter.

Occasionally a form letter is a printed page consisting of a number of paragraphs with boxes in front of each paragraph. The pertinent boxes are checked so the recipient "reads" the letter by reading only the checked boxes. Try to devise another form letter; these checked paragraphs are awkward and confusing to read as the unmarked paragraphs are distracting.

21·G Printed forms

Printed forms are used for a great many purposes—job applications, credit applications, insurance claims, orders, requisitions, questionnaires, employee ratings, to name a few. Using such forms is another shortcut. Sometimes the forms are computer cards that, after they have been marked, can be put into the computer and have data compiled from them.

The advantages of using forms are that they are timesaving. All of the needed information is asked for; all of the questions are placed in the same position (so that the forms can be checked easily for specifics); they are easier to read than letters; they are easier to file since the size is uniform; and they ask for no unnecessary information.

If you are completing a form, be sure that your answers are legible, particularly if handwritten; spelling is correct; facts and figures are accurate; and all of the blanks are completed. If one of the questions does not apply, mark it to that effect but do not leave it blank. In addition, directions such as *use pen* and *put last name first* should be followed carefully.

When completing a form, it is often advantageous to include a letter of transmittal. Such a letter permits you to direct the form and letter to a specific person (perhaps the person who sent you the form), which will probably speed the processing of the form. It also permits you to say *thank you* if that person has been helpful.

6

employment writing

All writing dealing with hiring employees is employment or personnel writing, whether the writing is done by the applicant or by those doing the hiring. As such writing determines who is hired and who accepts positions, it forms the foundation for employer-employee relationships. Therefore, it is obviously important writing for everyone concerned.

SECTION **22** ## Employment writing for employers

From the employer's point of view, employment writing refers to preparing application forms for job applicants, writing letters to applicants and checking their references, evaluating employees on the job, and writing letters of recommendation for employees. Among the various letters to applicants are those answering letters of application, setting up appointments for interviews, offering jobs, and telling applicants why they were not hired for positions.

22·A Application forms

Almost every company has an application form for prospective employees. It may consist of only one or two pages, but generally it is from four to six pages long. It may have been designed very carefully to give the company the pertinent information and to be helpful in the job interview; or it may have just happened over a period of time and not have been revised for many years. The Civil Rights Act of 1964 provides that an application may not ask for information having to do with race or religion and may not require a photograph. The form must also be designed so that it does not discriminate against applicants because of sex, age, handicaps, color, national origin, or ancestry. In addition, many states have legislation governing discriminatory hiring practices.

What information is useful in helping companies reach decisions about hiring applicants? Most of the information requested is factual: name, address, age, citizenship, physical condition, education, special qualifications, job history, and personal references. Special qualifications include such skills as proficiency in a foreign language, photography, sports, or music. Subjective questions include such things as why the applicant would like to work for the company or a discussion of the capabilities of the applicant. Any questions on an application blank should be included for only one reason—to find information that will help the personnel people make decisions about the abilities of applicants. Whoever prepares the application form has a responsibility to eliminate irrelevant material. Forms should be evaluated periodically to see if they can be improved and perhaps shortened.

22·B Letters to applicants

If it is at all possible, telephone the job applicants. It is faster, gets the answer right away, does not require additional correspondence, and is probably cheaper. If someone has requested a job application, the form should give enough information so that a covering letter is not necessary. If letters to job applicants are necessary, consider using form letters that can be copied and do not have to be dictated. Even form postal cards can be used for such things as notifying job candidates when and where qualifying tests will be given. Never, of course, put confidential information on a postal card.

Letters to applicants should be short and contain only the essential information. Check the letter when it has been written to see that it contains who, what, why, when, and where. With the exception of the bad news letter—an applicant is rejected, for example—the subject of the letter is given in the opening.

Examples of openings:

```
Could you come for an interview for the position
of secretary with our company? An interview has been
scheduled for nine o'clock on Friday, March 15, with
Miss Lee in the personnel office, Room 202.

We are pleased to offer you the position of
secretary with our firm.
```

The negative letter should begin with a thank you to the job applicant or perhaps something about the job.

EXAMPLE:

    Thank you for submitting your application for the position of secretary with our firm. So many well-qualified people have applied that it has made selecting a very difficult task.

    The body of the letter adds additional information to the opening. If it is a letter setting up an interview, tell the applicant any necessary details, such as listing items that need to be brought to the interview (the completed application blank, for instance) or that the applicant will be expected to take performance tests at the time of the interview. Supply any information that will be helpful to the candidate. It puts the candidate at ease and makes interviews progress more smoothly and quickly.

    The letter telling the applicant that he or she did not get the job could be helpful to that person if the letter makes suggestions for future applications. Including useful information could also build goodwill for the company.

EXAMPLE:

    Although we selected another applicant for this position, we should like you to know that we were extremely impressed by your qualifications. In fact, we thought that your qualifications were much better than the job demanded. Have you considered applying for a position of administrative assistant rather than that of secretary?

    The closing of the letter is a summary; it is courteous and contains no new material.

**22·C
Letters checking references**

Checking personal references of job applicants requires a letter similar to that of checking credit references. The letter begins by telling what the letter is about and giving the name and address of the job applicant. The letter should include the fact that the applicant gave the person's name as a reference. If the person to whom you are writing is a former employer, it is helpful if you give the dates that the applicant worked for that employer. Also tell the recipient of the letter the job for which the person is applying. The body of the letter should ask any specific questions that you would like answered and assure the recipient of the confidentiality of the reply. The closing is courteous and includes an offer to reciprocate.

EXAMPLE:

Mrs. Ellen Lee of 211 Pine Street, San Francisco, has applied for a position as secretary with our firm. She has given your name as reference. Mrs. Lee has told us that she worked as your secretary from May, 1971, until July, 1973.

We are considering Mrs. Lee for the position of secretary to the personnel director of our firm. The position involves a great deal of confidential information, a heavy load of shorthand and typing, and meeting the public. We should like to know your opinion of Mrs. Lee's qualifications for this kind of position. We shall, of course, hold your reply in strict confidence.

Thank you for your help. Please ask us for assistance in similar situations.

22·D Letters of recommendation

If you are writing a positive letter of recommendation, begin with the good news in the opening. A negative letter follows the usual form for bad news letters—the details are given before the bad news.

Usually solicited letters of recommendation (those which you are asked to write) are positive, for ordinarily job applicants give as references the names of persons who would respond favorably toward them. Most personnel people are, however, aware that letters of recommendation are likely to be slanted toward the job applicant. Even those letters written by persons who were not given specifically as references are, if not highly complimentary, at least neutral or say nothing that is actually detrimental about the job candidate. In most instances, personnel people are not interested in general letters of recommendation carried by the job applicant, for no one is going to present a letter that is known to be negative.

22·D·1 Recommendation considerations

There are certain points to consider when writing letters of recommendation:

a. The letter should be as fair and accurate and honest as possible. To err in either direction—to overpraise the applicant's capabilities or to downgrade that person's capabilities—is an injustice to both the applicant and the prospective employer.

b. Deal in specifics rather than generalities. State precisely what the applicant can or cannot do. Answer any questions that are contained in the letter requesting the information. A letter written in general terms has an evasive tone and tells very little about the applicant.

c. Write in positive language. A sentence such as, "Mrs. Dalton was rarely absent from her job," creates a negative tone. Write instead, "Mrs. Dalton had a very good attendance record." The first statement suggests that, although she was usually at work, perhaps she took days off when she had no reason to do so. Usually the reader is not sure whether the writer of the letter is deliberately vague or is not a precise writer.

22·D·2 Positive letters

The opening of the positive letter of recommendation begins by identifying the applicant and by giving a positive recommendation. The body develops the details, such as how long the applicant was employed, what the job involved, and answers any specific questions that are asked. If there are positive details that can be added, do so. The closing summarizes the strong points of the applicant.

Here is an example, recommending Mrs. Nancy Dalton. The opening identifies the subject and states the writer's recommendation. It repeats that this is a confidential reply:

```
Mrs. Nancy Dalton, about whom you requested con-
fidential personnel information, is an excellent
secretary.
```

The body answers any questions:

```
As she told you, Mrs. Dalton worked as my secre-
tary from June, 1973, until July, 1975. She is an
extremely competent secretary. Her shorthand and
typing skills are excellent. She took all of my
telephone calls and made my appointments so that I
was relieved of much of the burden of meeting the
public. She handled all of my files discreetly and
confidentially.
```

The body also adds details:

```
Mrs. Dalton was also punctual, and I cannot
recall any days that she was absent from the office.
She was courteous in dealing with our customers and
was well-liked by other employees. She left our firm
because of an illness in her family.
```

The closing is a summary:

> Mrs. Dalton's excellent secretarial skills and her personal qualifications make her a fine choice for handling a secretarial position. It is a pleasure to recommend her so highly.

22·D·3 Negative letters

Often the negative recommendation is handled verbally, for many businesspeople are reluctant to commit themselves in writing. Any negative letters should be factual and contain supporting evidence. The language should not be emotional or exaggerated. A statement such as, "Mrs. Dalton was never on time," is obviously an exaggeration. However, the statement, "Mrs. Dalton was at least a half hour late two or three mornings each week," is factual and specific.

Negative letters about an applicant are difficult to write. If you do not want to reply about an applicant, do not ignore the letter asking for information. Instead write a short note acknowledging the request but stating that you would prefer not to comment on the applicant. Undoubtedly, this will be damaging to the applicant.

22·E Evaluations of employees

One of the difficult tasks confronting those who supervise other employees in large organizations is employee evaluation. In small firms this is not a problem; most large organizations, however, and government agencies in particular, require that all employees be evaluated by a supervisor. Time limits such as annually or every two years are ordinarily set. Usually these evaluations are in writing. A typical evaluation can involve a rating scale covering a variety of subjects—appearance, punctuality, performance, as well as subjective areas such as ability to get along with others, responsibility, initiative, and dependability.

Employee evaluations must, like letters of recommendation, be done as objectively as possible. The language must be both specific and positive. If there are areas in which the employee rates average or below, the evaluation should then include suggestions for helping the employee. The good and superior evaluations are easy to write; it is the average and below average that cause difficulties. Usually the report is discussed with the employee, who has the right to agree or disagree with the report.

Begin an evaluation with the positive points about an employee; then, if necessary, go to the points where the employee is weak. If possible, make specific suggestions for improvement—attend classes given within the company or at nearby schools or eliminate the reasons for chronic absenteeism. There is the possibility, too, of changing jobs within the company if the employee is unhappy or not performing satisfactorily at a particular level or job.

EXAMPLE:

Nancy Dalton has worked as my secretary in the Personnel Department for the past two years. Her duties have involved handling the mail, dictation, filing, answering the phone, meeting callers, typing from rough draft, keeping my appointment calendar, as well as many other duties. Mrs. Dalton is a very competent secretary. She is punctual and rarely absent. She is well-groomed and a very pleasant person with whom to work.

My only suggestion for improvement would be that she learn to delegate routine jobs to one of the clerks within the department. As with most highly competent people, she tends to assume the responsibility for more work than she can do with the result that work is sometimes not done as promptly as it should be. I have talked with Mrs. Dalton about this. She is aware of the problem and is devising a system so that work is completed on a priority system and routine work is given to others and checked by Mrs. Dalton as a final step. We both think this will eliminate any problems.

I recommend that she be given the higher rating that she has earned after two years of very satisfactory employment with our company.

SECTION 23 Employment writing for applicants and employees

The writing that you do to get a job is, as far as you are personally concerned, the most important writing that you will do. The first contact that you have with a firm is usually the application letter; or if there is no application letter, the completing of the job application form. The letter or completed form may very well determine how your application is considered. It undoubtedly will form the basis for the interview.

23·A Data sheet

Before you begin making applications for jobs, get together as much information about yourself as you can. Make a list of your education and training together with dates. Do the same for your work experience. List all of the jobs, either full or part-time, that you have held. Include the dates of these jobs. Have precise information about what you can do. Do you *think* that you can type 60 words per minute or do you *know* that you can? If you were given a typing test, would you be embarrassed because you had overestimated your typing skill? If you plan to give names as references, do you have permission to do so? Do you know how to spell the names correctly, and do you have the correct addresses?

When you have collected all of the information that you need, then begin to plan the data sheet.

The data sheet is a summary of your qualifications for employment. (It may also be called a résumé, personal profile, summary, or qualification sheet.) The heading of a data sheet tells what the form is, the name of the applicant, the date, and perhaps the name of the company for which the sheet was prepared. Usually the data sheet is divided into four sections listed in this order: Education or Special Training, Work Experience, Personal, and References. There may be further breakdowns within these sections. From the data and facts that you have assembled, prepare a data sheet that is no longer than two pages and preferably one. Certainly those applicants for entry-level jobs should be able to get all of the material on one page. The data sheet should be factual; do not list such things as job goals or other subjective data.

23·A·1 Education section

In the Education section, begin with your most recent education. Give the names and addresses of the institutions that you attended, degrees granted, and dates. Give any honors or awards that you have won. Give your grade point average only if it is B or above. If you can use a grade point average, such as 3.5, explain it. If you list specific courses that you have taken, use the catalog titles if those titles tell what the courses are about. For instance, Advanced Typing is explanatory, but Modern Office Procedures probably should include a description of what was in the course. If you attended college, do not include information about your high-school education other than the name and address of the school. If you have measurable skills, list them; for example, typing, 70 words per minute. Include any special training, such as having taken a six-week computer programming course.

23·A·2 Work experience section

Work experience should be listed with the most recent experience first. Give the names and addresses of firms for which you worked as well as the names of immediate supervisors. Give the dates when you worked for these companies. If you are a recent graduate and do not have a great deal of work experience, list part-time and nonrelated jobs. It is a good idea to describe just what duties you did perform in a part-time job. Nonrelated jobs show that you have been employed and therefore know what is expected of employees.

23·A·3 Personal section

The personal data section has to do with you. It includes your name, address, telephone number, age, date and place of birth, and health and physical defects, if any. Do not include information about race or religion. Including a picture on the data sheet is of doubtful value. Employers are prevented by law from requiring a photograph on an application—your appearance is usually left for the interview.

23·A·4 Reference section

In the reference section, give the names, addresses, and telephone numbers of three persons who know you well enough to vouch for your personal characteristics and abilities. Never use a name as reference unless you have that person's permission. Personnel representatives sometimes prefer character and educational references to work references. Business and professional people are best choices, and the longer they have known you, the better. Obviously, any names, numbers, and spellings should be correct. Some applicants do not include names of references but put a statement that references will be furnished upon request.

23·A·5 Other information

Type the data sheet and, by all means, arrange it attractively to present the best possible appearance. If you are not a good typist, have someone else type it for you. Carbon copy and some of the less attractive means of duplication should be avoided as it gives the impression that you are sending applications to many firms. However, some of the photocopy machines do excellent reproduction work and their copies would be acceptable.

There are professional services that will prepare resumes for you and then usually photocopy them in fairly large quantities. Most personnel people can spot the professionally prepared resume and might wonder why someone applying for a job in business should seek such help. Certainly at entry-level jobs it should not be necessary. When you prepare your own resume, you are well aware of what it contains. Keep the data sheet up-to-date and revise it as facts change.

23·B Application letters

After preparing the data sheet, write the application letter. Consider it to be a sales letter and use the same principles as for a sales letter. You are trying to sell yourself and your serv-

SECTION 23   EMPLOYMENT WRITING FOR EMPLOYEES

DATA SHEET FOR KAREN LEE CASTLE

June, 1978

EDUCATION	Community College:	Crane College, 2435 Mountain Road San Mateo, CA 92090 A.A. degree, June, 1978, in Business with major in secretarial studies, A- average (3.7)
	High School:	San Mateo High School San Mateo, CA 92090

Courses taken at Crane College:

Secretarial	Business	General
Shorthand	Business Mathematics	English
Typing	Business Law	U.S. History
Business Writing	Data Processing	Political Science

	Secretarial Skills:	Shorthand, 120 words per minute
		Typing from straight copy, 60 words per minute
		Office Machines: IBM Executive
		                   rotary calculator
		                   10-key adding machine
		                   CPT word-processing equipment

	Honors:	Member of Alpha Gamma Sigma, scholastic honorary at Crane College
	Special Interests:	Hobby: Photography Activities: Secretary and President, Photo Club Secretary, Senior Class, San Mateo High School
WORK EXPERIENCE		Stenographer at Registrar's Office, Crane College, part-time and summer, 1976 to present Duties: took dictation, answered telephone, did filing and other clerical work
		Cashier at Playhouse Theatre, San Mateo, part-time, 1974-76
PERSONAL INFORMATION	Address: Telephone: Date of Birth: Place of Birth:	340 Addison Road, San Mateo, CA 92090 (410) 345-5959 May 30, 1958 Age: 20 years Chicago, IL
REFERENCES (by permission)		Mr. D. M. Lee, Registrar, Crane College, 2435 Mountain Road, San Mateo, CA 92090 Mr. David Hyatt, Manager, Playhouse Theatre, San Mateo, CA 92090 Mrs. Jean Ryan, Instructor, Secretarial Studies Department, Crane College, 2435 Mountain Road, San Mateo, CA 92090

Example of Data Sheet

ices instead of a product. As in the sales letter, you would like a response.

The opening of the application letter should tell where you learned of the vacancy. If you were told of the vacancy, use the name of the person referring you. Include also in the opening the name of the specific job for which you are applying. Do not say that you will do "anything." Be as precise as you can—use "secretary" rather than "office worker," for example. If you are writing to inquire whether the firm has any vacancies, say so.

In the body of the letter stress some outstanding qualification that is listed on the data sheet. Because you will probably include with the letter a data sheet, do not repeat facts that are listed on the sheet; rather call attention to facts that are listed there. The body of the letter shows how your education and work experience fit you for a specific job. It should also show that you have some knowledge of the firm and its products or services.

End the letter with a request for an interview. Tell where you can be reached by giving your telephone number and the times when you are available. Be sure, too, that your address is given. You can also suggest times when you could come for an interview.

Since the application letter is an attempt to get a response, you can also end the letter with suggestions for how the reader might express interest. You might ask the reader to check your references for additional opinions about you, or you might offer to supply additional information if it is requested.

Here are some suggestions for the application letter:

1. Address the letter to a person rather than to a firm or department. Try to find the name of the personnel director; however, a letter addressed to "Personnel Director" is better than one addressed to "Galaxy Manufacturing Company."

2. Be meticulous about correct spelling and typographical accuracy.

3. Be sure that the letter is attractive. Place the letter correctly on the page and type it in a conventional letter style (modified block is probably best). The ribbon should be dark and the type clean. Use plain white bond paper of a good quality (no onion skin and not your present employer's letterhead) with a matching envelope. Letters should be individually typed and not duplicated or photocopied.

SECTION 23   EMPLOYMENT WRITING FOR EMPLOYEES   141

4. Be sure that your letter is original. Do not copy a letter from a text or other reference source.

5. Avoid writing *I*, *we*, *my*, and *mine*.

6. Base your application on qualifications, not on need, a bid for sympathy, or whom you know.

7. Don't forget to include your address and don't forget to sign the letter.

8. Be careful about sending a gimmick-type application. If you are tempted to put your application in the form of a wanted poster, for example, be sure that the people who will read your application look favorably upon this type of approach. Perhaps a novel attention-getting device will do just that—attract attention—but you want an application that will persuade the prospective employer to call you for an interview. Generally, businesses are fairly conservative and, particularly with entry-level jobs, prefer a conventional application. Too, avoid clever or cute expressions or phrases as well as those that you consider humorous. Remember, your reader will probably be unknown to you and may find this kind of expression offensive.

EXAMPLE:

>   340 Addison Road
>   San Mateo, CA 92090
>   June 10, 19—

Mrs. Linda Miller, Personnel Director
Empire Products, Inc.
345 Washington Street
San Francisco, CA 94100

Dear Mrs. Miller:

    Please consider my application for the position of correspondence secretary with Empire Products. Mrs. Jean Ryan, my secretarial studies instructor at Crane College, has told me that you have a vacancy.

    As you will see from the enclosed data sheet, I have completed courses at Crane College in both word processing and office practice. I have also been trained to use CPT word-processing equipment. My education has included extensive training in English skills, which I think will be most helpful in using word-processing equipment.

    May I come for an interview? You may call me at 345-5959 any afternoon after four o'clock. I hope that I may have an opportunity to talk with you about the position of correspondence secretary.

                    Sincerely,

                      Karen Castle

                    Karen Castle

23·C Application blanks

Undoubtedly, as a job applicant, you will be asked to complete an application blank. This is a most important form. It may be mailed to you before you go for an interview; you may be asked to complete the form at the time of the interview; or it may be given to you to take home, complete, and return. The blank may be several pages long. If you are asked to complete the form when you make application or go for an interview, use a pen. Be prepared for this by carrying a pen; a list of references with names and addresses; an outline of information such as dates of education or employment, Social Security number, and anything else that you think might be asked for; and a small pocket dictionary.

    Before you begin to complete the form, read it through carefully. If you are completing it other than at the time of application, type the answers. Answer all of the questions; some may require "no," "none," or "does not apply" answers, but do not leave any of the questions unanswered. If some questions are not clear, ask about them. If you write your answers, be sure that your handwriting is legible and that your pen writes clearly, preferably in a dark ink. If you type your answers, use the variable line spacer on the typewriter to align the typing. The ribbon should be dark and the type clean. Correct all errors; do not strike over or "x" out. Proofread carefully to eliminate typographical errors. Consult the dictionary for spellings—do not guess. Most employers check the application form carefully; therefore, take plenty of time and effort. Careless errors could cost you a chance to be considered for the job.

SECTION 23   EMPLOYMENT WRITING FOR EMPLOYEES   143

Here are several points to remember when completing an application blank:

1. Birth date means the year born, not the date of your last birthday.
2. An item such as "have you ever been refused a surety bond?" refers to the practice of firms insuring employees against losses caused by the employee's negligence or theft.
3. Be sure that you date and sign the application.
4. Be sure that you have permission to use names as references.
5. Answer all questions.
6. Write or type legibly.
7. Proofread the completed application carefully for spelling or typographical errors.

23·D Thank-you letters

If your data sheet and letter of application are successful in getting you an interview, write a thank-you letter after the interview. The thank-you letter is a follow-up that shows that you are still interested and want to pursue the application. It might possibly give you a slight advantage over other applicants who do not write such letters. Write promptly, either the day of the interview or no later than the day after. It should be a courteous short letter expressing your appreciation for the time that the interviewer gave you.

When you write the thank-you letter, be sure that you have the correct name, title, and address of the interviewer. Be sure, too, that you mention the title of the job for which you are applying. Try to make some comment about the interview to remind the interviewer which candidate you are. If you are returning an application blank after the interview, include the thank-you letter with the application.

EXAMPLE:
Dear Mr. Andrews

Thank you very much for the time that you spent with me yesterday discussing the programming job in the Advertising Department.
It is very interesting to learn about your com—

EMPLOYMENT WRITING

pany's plans for a new computer. I am glad that I am starting my career as a programmer at a time when there are so many new and exciting innovations in the field. It is both stimulating and challenging.

If I can supply you with further information about my training and work experience, I shall be happy to do so. Thank you again for talking with me.

               Sincerely,

               Martin Sullivan

               Martin Sullivan

23·E Acceptance letters

The letter of acceptance is an easy one to write. Begin by accepting the position, give any necessary or requested details in the body, and close with a friendly comment about your pleasure in going to work.

EXAMPLE:

    I am delighted to accept your offer of the job as programmer in the Advertising Department.

    I shall report to work Monday, April 15, at nine o'clock, and I shall bring with me a copy of my birth certificate and the completed health form from my doctor.

    After seeing the offices and talking with other employees at Empire, I am sure that I shall enjoy working there.

23·F Refusal letters

Because the refusal letter is a type of negative or bad news letter, do not begin with the point of the letter—that you are not accepting the job. Begin with a courteous, positive statement about the job that you are refusing. The body should tell why you are not accepting the position and what your future plans are. The closing is a courteous thank you. Write the letter promptly so that the company can offer the job to someone else.

EXAMPLE:

    I am very pleased that you selected me for the position of secretary with Empire Products. I was particularly impressed with the new word–processing center that your firm is developing.

As you told me at the time of the interview, opportunities for secretaries who wish to get into this new area will be very great. However, after considering all of the factors and possibilities, I think that I would prefer to work in a smaller office where I would have more contact with people. I am, therefore, accepting a position with Crown Equipment Company, where I shall be secretary to the vice president.

Thank you for offering me the secretarial position with your firm and for the time that you spent with me.

23·G Resignation letters

When you are resigning a position, do so as courteously and tactfully as possible. Because the letter becomes a part of your employment file, it may be important to you in future years should you need references or need to answer why you left the company.

EXAMPLE:

I have recently been asked to accept the position of executive secretary to the senior vice president of Fraser Corporation.

As you know, I have just successfully passed the CPS examination; and I am eager to demonstrate my knowledge and skills. I also know that Empire has few positions for executive secretaries and that there are not likely to be any openings for quite some time.

Would you please, therefore, accept my resignation from my present position as secretary in the Advertising Department. I should like to leave the 31st of this month. If this timing is not convenient, I can either stay a week or so longer or leave earlier.

I have enjoyed very much the three years that I have been employed at Empire. I have gained a great deal, and I hope that I have also contributed to the firm.

7

business report writing

All business reports have the same purpose; that is, to convey information. After that, all similarity seems to disappear, for the variety of reports seems to be as great as the people who request and compile them. The information may be requested; it may be routinely supplied; or it may appear almost spontaneously from no known source. A report can be made orally to the person concerned with the information; but other than for relatively simple requests for information, reports are generally in written form. The form may be simple—a one-page letter or memorandum—or it may consist of hundreds of pages and be printed in thousands of copies—*The United States President's Commission on the Assassination of President Kennedy,* for example. Some reports are confidential or top-secret; others are printed for nationwide distribution. Some are prepared and written by professionals and are highly technical; others are reports on fairly trivial matters and are prepared by one person.

Report writing is a different process from letter writing, but the principles of writing remain the same. Perhaps the chief difference in presentation is that most letters are written deductively with the point of the letter presented in the opening, the details of the point or decision are given in the body of the letter, and the closing is merely a summary. Reports, however, are often written inductively—the information or details are presented first, then the point or points (conclusions or recommendations) are drawn from the details and presented.

What is the role of the average business writer in report writing? It is unlikely that most office workers are going to write, for example, the sophisticated, expensive annual reports that most corporations send to their stockholders. Although the purpose of these reports is to give financial information about the company to the stockholders, usually these reports also promote the company and its products. Often the advertising department or advertising agency of the corporation does a great deal of the preparation of the annual report. The long formal reports are usually done by the professionals, even to the extent that sometimes outside consulting firms are hired to collect information and write reports. That leaves the writing of the short informal reports for the average office worker.

As you were told earlier, the purpose of any report is to give information. Some reports are analytical—they interpret the information—while others, in addition to giving information and interpreting information, make recommendations. Reports are usually made to help a person or a number of persons make decisions, such as whether a project is feasible, or whether a proposed action should be taken, or which is the best procedure to follow. They may also, as in the case of financial reports, provide permanent records that will assist those writing future reports and provide proof should it be required. In any event, every report does have a purpose, and that purpose should be defined and kept in mind as the report is prepared. Before any report is requested, though, be sure that it will be of value and that it will be both read and considered. Routine reports that are written for specific periods such as quarterly or annually should also be reviewed frequently to determine whether they should be continued. Writing useless, unneeded reports is both expensive and time-consuming.

Two names used to describe reports are informational and analytical. There are terms that describe length—short and long; frequency—annual, biannual, monthly, weekly, and daily; formality—informal and formal; and type—progress, justification, preliminary, periodic, and special. Reports are also classified as internal and external. The internal reports have to do with the operation and administration within a company and external, outside of the company. These names are also subject to interpretations by the people who initiate (ask that the report be made) the requests for reports and the people who do the work and submit the reports. Reports travel within a company—up to the president; down to the employees; and laterally from department to department.

Informal reports are often made on prepared forms. For example, an office worker who handles calls from the public may make a report on each call, listing the purpose of the call and the disposition of the request. If the employee is taking telephone calls about the company's products, such routine report forms can be very helpful in future sales campaigns. More formal reports can also be prepared from the information collected in these reports.

Meetings and committees produce reports. Meetings, as a matter of procedure, often have an *agenda,* which is a report of the things the organization wants to do or discuss at its meetings. The meeting itself is recorded in *minutes,* a written account of what happened at the meeting, what motions were introduced and whether or not they were passed, the topics discussed and any business that was transacted. Committees are formed to investigate or get information about a certain topic, with the desired information presented in a report.

SECTION 24 **Preparation for writing the report**

Regardless of name or classification, all reports do have common characteristics—the information must be presented accurately and objectively and the report must be organized to be easily understood.

There are steps involved in preparing for any report. In very simple reports some steps can be omitted or at least cut down. Generally, however, this is the procedure that is followed:

**24·A
Recognizing
and defining
the job**

The first step in making any report is to recognize and define what has to be done. You need to know exactly what is wanted and what use will be made of the report. You need to know for whom the report is intended and who will read the report. What are the limitations? How long do you have to complete the report? How much money is available? What is the size of the staff available for the job? Find out if similar reports have been made; look in the files to check for previous reports. Unfortunately, reports can be buried in files and remain unread and forgotten. Earlier reports can often provide a great deal of help. Even if they are not pertinent, they at least serve as models for the report that you are doing.

Assume, for example, that your employer—Mr. Benton of International Insurance—asks you about word processing. He has read about word-processing centers and asks that you get more information. He wonders if the equipment would work well for the company. He suggests that you do some investigating and give him a written report about it.

You would have to work with him to define the problem. What are the questions that you would ask? You would probably want to know how long you had to complete the report. You would want to know when he wanted you to do the work. If you were to carry on your regular duties, would it be possible to get some help on the report? How detailed should the report be—for example, should it include a plan for installing a center, complete with layout of equipment, where it would be placed, and personnel involved; or would a preliminary report of costs, recommended equipment, and training of present personnel be sufficient? You are asking what kind of report is wanted—a long formal report or a short preliminary one. By asking for all of the information, you are defining the situation. Perhaps you would need time to determine the questions to ask. You would most certainly need to think through what you have to know before beginning the task.

The example just given is an oral request or authorization; some authorizations are written in letter or memorandum form. If you receive such a written authorization, go over it carefully —underline the main points. Perhaps you will want to write a summary of the problem as it is defined in the letter. After you have read the letter or memo, make a list of the questions that arise. Then ask questions—preferably in person or over the telephone—of the person requesting the report. Be sure that you keep the original authorization. It might be a good idea, too, to reply in writing, listing all of the points, particularly those about which you have questions. This defines the problem for both you and the originator of the request and prevents future misunderstandings because you did not understand what was wanted.

**24·B
Obtaining the information**

After determining what is to be in the report, decide how you are going to collect the information necessary for completing the report. There are a number of sources of information. You may be able to find all the information you need in one source; or, more than likely, you will need a combination of sources.

Information is divided into two kinds: primary and secondary. Primary information is data obtained firsthand by asking questions, doing surveys, reading company reports or files, conducting experiments, and making personal observations. Primary information has not been interpreted nor analyzed by others. Secondary information is obtained through library research. Because primary sources can be limited and subjective, as well as both time-consuming and costly, consult library sources first—the information that you want may be there; or, if not, it will at least help you in starting the primary research.

Start library research within your company. Many large companies have libraries and research departments available, and almost all companies have some reference material—even telephone and city directories can in certain instances be extremely useful.

College Production **Harcourt Brace Jovanovich, Inc.** 757 Third Ave., New York 10017

TO James Paige, Purchasing Department
FROM Diane Lester, Transcription Department
DATE May 23, 19--
SUBJECT Word Processing Center

    We are finding it increasingly difficult to get mail out as quickly as dictators would like, to finish reports when they are needed, and generally to keep up with our work. We have tried employing temporary help when the work has accumulated in unusual amounts, such as the times when quarterly reports are due, but this has not always been satisfactory. We are now considering a word-processing center.

    Do you have or could you get information concerning cost, suitable equipment for our department, personnel needs for such a center, and whatever information would be useful to us in making a decision to request a center.

    I know that you will need a great deal of information from our department before you can make specific recommendations. If you will let me know what information and figures you need, I shall be glad to collect any needed data and cooperate in any way that I can.

    If we decide to make a budget request for a word-processing center, we must make the request by June 30. We should, therefore, like to have such information, if possible, by June 15.

                                                  D. L.

DL:feo

Request for Information in Memorandum Form

SECTION 24 PREPARATION FOR WRITING THE REPORT   151

Libraries that are readily available are the public libraries and those in schools, colleges, and universities. Many of these, in addition to general sources, have special collections. Almost all libraries can borrow for you from other libraries through interlibrary agreements. Libraries can also supply information about private collections and special libraries which you can visit with permission.

Library research is fairly easy, as it is no longer necessary to copy long passages and to make detailed notes; photocopying machines, which are available in most offices and libraries, make copies quickly and accurately. (Warning: Be sure, when making copies, that copyright laws are not violated.) In addition to photocopying, 3 x 5 cards are helpful for making both bibliographic and information notes.

Librarians are most helpful in locating materials and helping you use information sources.

Primary information can be gathered in a variety of ways: (1) surveys, such as personal pollings of employees within the company or questionnaires submitted to selected persons; (2) observations, such as watching the processing of mail to see whether improvements could be made; (3) experiments, such as those conducted within the firm in a laboratory—more simplified experiments would be trying a machine for a week or comparing two brands of carbon paper; (4) consulting other companies for such things as product information or information concerning their experiences in handling a similar situation.

In the example of finding information about a word-processing center, where would you start gathering information? Probably you would go to the manufacturers of such equipment. Before you approached them, you would have to know what questions to ask. Before you could do that, you would need some background information. Books and periodicals in the library could prove helpful. Take notes and indicate the sources of the notes. Prepare a list of questions before talking with the various manufacturers. The equipment brochures that the manufacturers supply might also give information. Perhaps you know people who work in offices that use word-processing centers and would tell you of their experiences with the various brands. One of the officers or members in an organization such as the American Management Society might be helpful. There are many sources of information, but you are going to have to know what questions to ask and how to ask them. You cannot make a vague statement such as, "Tell me what you know about word processing."

24·C
Establishing a schedule

A very important step in report writing is establishing a schedule. If you have a deadline, plan back from that date. If you do not establish a schedule, you are likely to come up to the deadline with much of the work yet to be done.

Setting up a schedule is part of the original planning. If a deadline is set or you are consulted about the time needed, outline what has to be done and determine the time each step will require. After making a schedule, keep to it. If there are unexpected delays, you may need extra time. Whatever you do, do not miss deadlines without talking it over with the person requesting the report.

24·D
Organizing material

As you collect information, you will have to organize it. Go over the material as you acquire it. Sometimes, by reading what you have, you will get ideas for further information. Put material into categories—start files if necessary. Sometimes a chronological record of how a report is developed is helpful. It is probably not a good idea to discard data until the report is completed, but certainly the seemingly unimportant material can be put aside.

Return to the report on word processing. You have gathered a lot of information. You have seen most of the products of the major manufacturers. You have prices. You have even tried much of the equipment. You have visited three offices that have different word-processing centers. By now you have more information than you probably can use. Your problem is eliminating the excess so that your report will contain only what your employer wants to know. You will waste everyone's time if you include too much.

You then decide to organize the material into a report on three different systems. You organize each category with its price, exactly what it does, advantages and disadvantages, and opinions of the persons who are using the equipment.

24·E
Analyzing data

The final step before writing the report is to analyze what has been collected and to arrive at a solution to the problems that you have been investigating. This step would be omitted if the purpose of the report is only to give information and not to draw conclusions. You are, of course, objective; you present the facts the way they are—not the way anyone has predicted or demanded. You will attempt to fit your findings into language that will be understood by the reader.

Again, back to the word-processing report. By the time all of the data have been collected, you would probably be ready to make a recommendation: the firm should have a word-processing center and the recommended equipment for the center is Technomatic. You back your recommendations with reasons that are objective—such as the merits of the system for your company. Perhaps you can present more than one solution—do so if you can. Have you written the report on the basis of what your employer asked you to find out? Did you include prices and costs? (Most businesspeople are very conscious of this factor.) Did you make suggestions about leasing rather than purchasing?

SECTION 25 Writing the report

After the preparation, the next part is the actual writing of the report—communicating the information that you acquired. The format of the report will be determined by the instructions you received when you were asked to write the report.

25·A Forms of reports

Usually reports are made in one of these four forms: memorandum, letter, short informal report, and long formal report. Most reports that you will be concerned with will fall into one of the first three categories. The report in either memorandum or letter form is both short and informal. Usually the letter form is a little more formal than the memo. The memo is used for intercompany reports. The letter might be used if you were writing a short report that would go to the higher levels of management—the president of the company, for example, or it could be used for reports going outside of the company. The short informal report is usually no longer than ten pages. The long formal report is structured to a definite pattern and is ordinarily prepared by specialists—sometimes brought into a company just to prepare the report—or by an outside agency. These reports may take long periods of time to prepare, cost hundreds of thousands of dollars, and run hundreds of pages in length.

25·A·1 Memorandum

The memorandum form of report is the simplest to write. Such reports are usually written deductively—the point or conclusion that has been reached is put into the opening. The body adds details and the closing is a summary with perhaps an offer of further information or assistance if the reader wishes it. It should be one, or no more than two, pages in length. It includes a summary of the original request to remind the reader of the purpose of the report. It does not ordinarily include conclusions or recommendations; it is simply an informational report.

BUSINESS REPORT WRITING

College Production **Harcourt Brace Jovanovich, Inc.** 757 Third Ave., New York 10017

TO All Dictators
FROM Lynn Adams, Administrative Secretary
DATE May 15, 19--
SUBJECT Machine Dictation

At the request of some of the division directors, we have made a survey of machine transcribers to see what could be done to improve both the quality of transcripts and the speed with which the work is completed. These are their suggestions:

1. Both dictators and transcribers should be familiar with the dictating and transcribing equipment. A manual is available for every machine; it explains how to use the equipment.

2. It would be helpful if all dictators would:

    a. Mark the indicator slips with special instructions and corrections. Mark the slips, too, to show the length of the letter or report.

    b. Spell any proper names as well as technical or unfamiliar words.

    c. Control their voices so that the dictation is neither too loud nor too soft. Be sure to enunciate clearly.

    d. Supply as much information as possible--number of copies, type of message, and identity of dictator. It would also help if salutations and subject lines, when used, were dictated.

    e. Indicate when you would like the dictation completed and which dictation is _rush_.

3. Machine transcribers will complete transcription by the day following the receiving of the tape unless the dictation is marked _rush_--then every effort will be made to complete the work when it is wanted.

Please let me know if you have further suggestions. I should also like to know if these suggestions result in better transcripts.

                                                              L. A.

LA:DEH

Report in Memorandum Form

Many companies urge their employees to use written memoranda because written statements reduce misunderstandings. There are also indirect reasons for writing: it places the responsibility on the writer, it may force the writer to write more carefully than if the message were spoken, and written messages are less likely to be ignored. However, because they are written, care should be taken to see that they convey exactly what the writer intended and that they are not treated casually because they are "only interoffice memos."

25·A·2 Letter

A report in letter form is much like the memorandum report. The tone, though, of a letter report is more formal than that of the usual business letter or memorandum. Like the memorandum, the letter report is both factual and informational. It may include tables, charts, or other graphic presentations that substantiate facts and conclusions included in the report. The inside address, salutation, and complimentary close may be omitted; letterhead stationery is ordinarily used for the first page. Headings, subheadings, and visual aids are used to make reading easier. A subject line can be valuable.

25·A·3 Short informal report

The short informal report is the usual form that most reports take. Certainly it is the form that the average business writer will use most often. The short report (usually no more than ten pages) differs from memorandum and letter reports in content, length, and form. Like the memorandum and letter report, though, short report topics are limited and frequently quite simple.

A short report may include some or all of these parts: (1) a title page; (2) a summary of findings with conclusions and recommendations; (3) authorization letter or a statement that the authorization was made informally; (4) the purpose or problem of the report; (5) a statement of findings, conclusions, and recommendations. Other items that might be added include graphic illustrations such as tables or charts and bibliographical information. Headings and other typographical display devices might be used to make the report easier to read. The report in its final form may be unbound or bound either at the top or side.

25·A·4 Long formal report

The formal report is structured in a definite pattern, and it differs significantly from the other reports discussed. It is presented in more detailed form; that is, it is longer, more complex, and has more parts. Because of its length, it contains more reading aids in the form of headings, subheadings, graphs,

COLLEGE OF MARIN

KENTFIELD
CALIFORNIA 94904
TEL (415) 454-3962

June 15, 19--

Dr. James Dawes, Dean
Continuing Education
Carson College
2300 Ninth Street
Any City, CA 94300

Dear Dr. Dawes

You wrote us asking for information concerning our experience with community college television. Our school has participated in the Community College Television Series for the past two years and has provided television instruction to almost 2,100 students. The following data summarizes our experiences in this program.

Description of Program

The programs, provided by the Community College Television Series, are shown over one of the local networks. Enrollment procedures are those suggested by the Series. Most of the television classes are shown twice--once in the early morning and once in the afternoon or evening. Our college also provides a service of videotaping each lesson at the Audiovisual Center so that students can review them in the Video Lab at their convenience. The programs vary in quality from class to class; generally, however, they seem to be informative, academic, and well-done. The quality seemed to improve in the second year.

Student Profile

From surveys we determined these factors about the participating students:

	1976-77	1977-78
1. Age		
Under 20 years	15%	8%
21-30 years	34%	22%
31-45 years	34%	47%
46-65 years	17%	23%
Over 65 years	0	0

Conclusion: Television students are older students who are probably full-time employed, married, have children, and are part-time students.

Report in Letter Form

Dr. James Dawes   -2-   June 15, 19--

	1976-77	1977-78
2. **Sex**		
Women	52%	59%
Men	48%	41%

<u>Conclusion</u>: The trend of more women returning to college appears to hold true in Classes by Television as well.

3. **Occupation**		
Full-time Homemaker	21%	23%
Full-time Employed	42%	43%
Part-time Employed	29%	26%
Retired	8%	8%

<u>Conclusion</u>: The goal of College for Television of reaching full-time employed and homemakers who would otherwise find it difficult to attend campus classes is being realized.

4. **Educational Level**		
No High School Diploma	1%	2%
High School Diploma only	7%	12%
1-30 Units of College	36%	35%
31-60 Units of College	41%	31%
Bachelor's Degree	12%	16%
Master's Degree	3%	4%

<u>Conclusion</u>: Both regular full-time and part-time students enroll in the television classes with an increasing number of other students participating.

<u>Summary</u>

College by Television is a valuable service to the community. The enrollments have varied from year to year depending upon the type of classes provided by the Series and the amount of publicity given the classes at both the local and national levels. As the quality of the television program continues to improve and new instructional techniques developed, the effectiveness of televised instruction will also increase. We plan to continue with the Series.

Should you require additional information, we shall be happy to supply it. We are glad to share our experiences.

            Sincerely

            Roberta Marshall

            Roberta Marshall, Assistant Dean
            Community Services Department

RM/tc

RECOMMENDATIONS FOR INCREASED USE OF DICTATION SYSTEM

EMPIRE PRODUCTS, INC.

    This report was prepared under the supervision of Mrs. Carla Martinez, administrative secretary of the word-processing center, to determine the reasons for the restricted use of the new dictating equipment that was recently installed at Empire Products and to suggest means of increasing the use of this equipment.

    <u>Problem</u>: Three months ago a new dictating system was installed at Empire Products. The system consisted of direct lines to the word-processing center enabling dictators to use existing telephones to dictate reports, correspondence, and other material. The system was thoroughly checked before installation; surveys were conducted to determine whether employees were infavor of the new system (90 percent were), and whether work loads justified the purchase and installation of such equipment. It was decided that such equipment would be valuable to the company.

    After two months of using the equipment, these are the figures on actual usage. Approximately seventy-five people should be dictating over the lines; so far about half--53 percent--of these people are actually doing so. Some who use the equipment admit to writing the dictation in longhand and then dictating over the lines. Those who are not using the dicatation equipment often bring longhand drafts with oral instructions to the word-processing center. A few come to the center to dictate to one of the transcribers. This causes confusion as well as delays in the transcription of all work. The transcribers are having problems with the

Informal Short Report

2

quality of the dictation--some of it is difficult to understand, which results in a lot of unnecessary correcting and retyping. This, in turn, takes extra time for both dictator and transcriber.

What has happened is that a system that we had anticipated would save time, cut costs, and improve the quality of our transcripts not only is not doing so but is actually creating additional problems.

<u>Survey</u>. Questionnaires were sent to both dictators and transcribers concerning the problems. These are the results:

	Number Responding	
	Dictators	Transcribers
75 Questionnaires to Dictators.	69	
10 Questionnaires to Transcribers		10
Reasons for Problems:		
Unfamiliarity with equipment.	17	2
Prefer dictating to secretary than to impersonal machine	21	--
Difficulty in dictating long or technical reports or letters	33	--
Speech peculiarities or distorted dictation causing difficulty in understanding dictation.	2	6
Inconvenience of use: dictator cannot ask secretary to read back; easier to give oral instructions; transcriber has difficulty asking questions when they arise in transcription.	37	2
Work brought into the center is often expected to be completed out of scheduled order.	8	6

```
                                                                    3

Recommendations:

1. Prepare in booklet form thorough written procedures for both
   dictators and transcribers on how to use the equipment.
   Distribute these booklets to all personnel involved.

2. Incoming mail should be processed--that is, files should be
   checked and information gathered--before the mail is given to
   the dictator.

3. Set up a training program that can be given at regular intervals
   for both new employees and those who have questions or need
   additional training.  Perhaps videotaped dictation sessions
   might prove helpful.

4. Ask dictators to be very aware of speaking properly, pacing
   their delivery, and avoiding personal distractions such as
   smoking or eating or moving about the room while dictating
   so that all dictation is easy to understand.

5. Dictators should not expect the transcribers to stop their
   work and take shorthand dictation.

6. Ask transcribers to follow adopted schedules--do not take work
   from dictators out of schedule merely because the dictator
   brings it into the center and waits for it.

7. All transcription should be supervised by the administrative
   secretary in charge of the word-processing center.  No work
   should be given direct to transcribers.

8. A follow-up study should be conducted within two months to
   determine if use of the equipment is increasing.
```

charts, and other visual aids. It should be typed or printed in uniform style. Often it is prepared by specialists, either inside or outside the company. It is rarely the responsibility of the average office worker.

This is a detailed listing of the parts found in a long formal report; not all are used or even necessary. Infrequently used parts are starred.

*a. Cover (binder)—a folder or covering used to protect the report. It usually bears the name of the report and other title-page information.

*b. Flyleaf—blank sheets of paper placed at the beginning and end of the report. Such pages provide space for written notes.

*c. Title fly—a page bearing only the title. It is usually typed in all capitals and placed in the upper third of the page.

d. Title page—a page bearing the complete title and subtitle (if there is one), the name and title of the reader (probably the person requesting the report), the name and title of the writer, the firm and its address, and the completion date of the report. If no cover is used, the title page is often written on heavy or colored paper. The title page is considered to be the first page of the report.

*e. Letter of authorization—the letter requesting that the report be made. If no written request was made, then the oral request should be included in either the letter of transmittal or the introduction.

*f. Letter of acceptance—a written answer to the authorization letter. It is rarely included in the report.

g. Letter of transmittal—a letter on letterhead stationery written after the report is completed. It accompanies the report as a kind of preface or foreword. It may give the purpose of the report, a summary of conclusions, a mention of problems or limitations, and an acknowledgment of the help of others.

*h. Acknowledgments—used only if there were a number of persons helping with the report; otherwise, acknowledgments are included in the letter of transmittal.

i. Table of contents—an outline of the headings of the report and page numbers on which the headings appear. It is a complete breakdown of headings and subheadings as they are listed in the report.

*j. Table of illustrations—a listing of graphic materials. It is included only if the illustrations are extensive. A short listing of illustrations could be combined with the table of contents.

k. Abstract (summary, synopsis, digest, or preface)—a condensing of the report; it is usually 5 to 10 percent of the full report. Its purpose is to save the reader's time. It is written after the report has been completed.

l. Body of the report—the text of the report, consisting of three parts—introduction, text, and conclusions or recommendations. The introduction usually contains the purpose or reason for the report and something of the methods used in obtaining the information and material (research). The text shows the organization, presents the facts that were found, and leads the reader to the findings (conclusions or recommendations). The conclusions and recommendations are the result of the research presented in the text. If the report is written deductively, the conclusions are placed right after the introduction; if written inductively, they are placed after the text of the report. The text makes up 75 to 80 percent of the report.

WORD-PROCESSING CENTER:

AN ANALYSIS OF NEEDS
AND A
PROPOSED PLAN

Presented to

David H. Walker, Vice President
Empire Products, Inc.
San Francisco, CA

By Janet L. Sherman

June 15, 19--

Title Page

SECTION 25 WRITING THE REPORT

TABLE OF CONTENTS

INTRODUCTION..	1
CONCLUSIONS...	3
RECOMMENDATIONS...	3
SURVEY OF PRESENT TRANSCRIPTION SERVICES................	5
SHORTCOMINGS OF PRESENT SERVICES........................	7
PROPOSAL OF TRANSCRIPTION SERVICES NEEDS................	8
Methods of Determining Needs:	
Market Survey of Available Systems.............	15
Survey of Three Existing Services..............	20
Factors in Determining Needs.......................	23
SUGGESTED WORD-PROCESSING CENTER........................	24
Justification for Selection of STR System..........	30
Plans for Integrating Word-Processing System into	
Existing Facilities...........................	34
CHART OF LAYOUT OF STR SYSTEM...........................	39
APPENDIX	
Cost Factors of Available Systems..................	41
Staff Needs for STR System.........................	43
Flowchart of System................................	46

Table of Contents

*m. Appendix—the supplementary material that the reader does not need to read but that might be of interest. Such things as correspondence or survey forms used in preparing the report might be included.

*n. Bibliography—a listing of reference sources consulted.

25·B Steps in writing reports

Before the actual writing of any report is undertaken, there are many things that must be done first. These things have been discussed: the purpose of the report must be known and the problem defined; all the necessary information must be accumulated; and the data have to be organized and conclusions determined. After completing these preliminary tasks, you are ready to begin the actual writing of the report.

25·B·1 Outline

The first step in writing either a short or long report is to make an outline. As you were collecting information for the report, you organized the data. From that organized data, you can make the outline.

Probably the most familiar outline is that arranged by numbers and letters. It begins with Roman numerals, goes to capital letters, then Arabic numbers, and then lower-case letters. Variations with certain headings in all capitals can be added. It is also possible to use a decimal system for an outline. The advantages of this system are that it permits an almost unlimited breakdown and it shows interrelation better.

In any outline, headings or subheadings must be broken into at least two items; there must be, for example, both A and B under I. The reason is that, if something is divided, it must be divided into at least two parts.

The rules of parallel construction should be observed when making an outline. Make sure that the outline covers all of the points that should be made. An outline can be a procedure for organizing material and ideas. It can also force you to limit your thinking, particularly if you tend to write too much.

Examples of the number-letter outline and the decimal outline:

Number-Letter

I. Major heading
   A. Subheading—1st degree
   B. Subheading—1st degree
      1. Subheading—2d degree
      2. Subheading—2d degree
         a. Subheading—3d degree
         b. Subheading—3d degree

SECTION 25 WRITING THE REPORT

<u>Decimal</u>
1. Major heading
    1.1 Subheading—1st degree
        1.11 Subheading—2d degree
        1.12 Subheading—2d degree
            1.111 Subheading—3d degree
            1.112 Subheading—3d degree
                1.1111 Subheading—4th degree
                1.1112 Subheading—4th degree
    1.2 Subheading—1st degree
2. Major heading
    2.1 Subheading—1st degree
    2.2 Subheading—1st degree

25·B·2
First writing

After preparing an outline from information that you gathered, you are ready to begin the first draft of the report. Decide whether you wish to present the material inductively or deductively. Use a simple, straightforward writing style. Keep the report impersonal—avoid the use of personal pronouns (even *you*), since it makes the report sound as if it were the opinion of the writer rather than the presentation of objective data. Informal reports can use *I* or *we*, but formal reports rarely include first-person pronouns unless the writer is a person of authority (possibly hired specifically to prepare the report). Passive voice can be used in place of personal pronouns.

    EXAMPLES: Avoid: We conclude that the company should take steps to correct the situation.
        Use: These conclusions <u>are presented</u> so that steps <u>can be taken</u> to correct the situation.

Write objectively—avoid words such as *outstanding*, *fascinating*, and *overrated*, that tend to persuade or to give unsupported evaluations. If you comment that a system is *expensive*, you are making a judgment. Present the cost factors and let the reader decide if the price is expensive.

25·B·3
Second writing

Write the entire report before you do any revising. You will most likely have to do a rewriting of the first draft before the report is ready for its final typing. It is in this second writing that you concern yourself with style, clarity, and conciseness. Check mechanics—spelling, punctuation, grammar—and detail. Are names and dates correct? Do not discard any of the notes that you made when you were collecting information. You may want to check them later to be sure that the facts in the report are accurate.

25·B·4 Format of report

The format of the report will vary. The letter and memorandum forms go on regular office stationery. The short or long report will be placed on plain bond paper. Whether the report is single or double spaced depends partly upon the wishes of the reader and the purpose of the report. Double spacing is easier to read; and, if someone wishes to make changes or notes, there is room for editing. It does, however, take more paper and is less attractive than single spacing. Pages should be numbered. Covers and bindings vary with the length of report, number of copies, how long the report will be used, who is getting the report, and cost. The number of copies will depend upon the purpose to which the report will be put; always keep at least one copy for the files. The final typing should have an attractive appearance because the reader is influenced by the appearance of the report. Use paragraph headings; they serve as guideposts and make a report easier to read.

Use paper of good quality, usually 8½ by 11 inches, and use a black ribbon. Pica type is preferred because it is more readable. Margins are a minimum of an inch; wider margins may be used but not narrower ones. The top margin on the first page should be at least two inches. If the manuscript is to be bound at either the top or the left side, allow an additional half inch for this.

25·B·5 Documentation of report

Documentation of a report means that references are given for quoted sources. This is accomplished by both footnotes in the text and bibliographical references at the ends of chapters or at the end of the report. It is important to give credit whenever reference sources are used. This prevents the writer from being accused of plagiarism and provides a chance for the reader to refer to original sources.

a. Footnotes Footnotes give credit for quotations, explain terms in the text, and call attention to other parts of the report. They are usually placed at the bottom of the page that includes the reference. They are numbered consecutively with superior figures (numbers typed slightly above the line of writing).

EXAMPLES:

[1]Sigband, Norman B., Communication for Management

and Business, 2d ed. Glenview, IL, Scott Foresman, 1976, p. 187.
[2]Sigband, p. 264.

Another method that is becoming popular is to place the reference to the source in the body of the report so that the reader is not distracted by having to look at the bottom of the page.

EXAMPLES:
Zinsser points out (William Zinsser, On Writing Well, Harper & Row, New York, 1976, p. 13) that . . .

A second reference to the book is made this way:

(Zinsser, p. 18)

A short title should be added if more than one work by the same author is referred to in the report.

There is still another method of citing sources of information. Number the listings in the bibliography that is at the end of the report. Refer in the body of the report where the citation occurs to the bibliography number plus the page number of the reference being quoted. It would appear this way: (17:245). Explain this method in a footnote the first time it is used: "17:245 means page 245 of Item 17 in the Bibliography."

The practice of using Latin terms and abbreviations in footnotes is disappearing. Instead of such Latin terms as *ibid.*, *loc. cit.*, and *et al.*, English words and abbreviations are now being used.

b. Bibliography The bibliography is a listing of the source materials used by the writer of the report. It is placed either at the end of the report or after each chapter or section. It should be arranged alphabetically and include this information:

1. Name of the author, surname first. If the source material has two or three authors, invert the name of the first author but give the names of additional authors in normal order. If more than three authors, give the first author's name followed by *and others* (not the Latin *et al.*).

2. Title of book and name of periodical in italic type (or underscored).

3. Title of magazine article in quotes.

4. Place of publication, name of publisher, and date of publication for books. You may give a shortened form of the publisher's name if the name is clear.

Style and forms for bibliographies, like those for footnotes, vary greatly. Consult the *MLA Style Sheet.* 2d ed. Washington: Modern Language Association of America, 1970, or Kate L. Turabian's book, *A Manual for Writers of Term Papers, Theses, and Dissertations.* 4th ed. Chicago: University of Chicago Press, 1973.

This is a sample bibliography that has been adapted for use in business reports. Check other style manuals if you are preparing a bibliography in another area.

BIBLIOGRAPHY

BOOKS

Hanna, J. Marshall, Estelle L. Popham, and Rita S. Tilton, Secretarial Procedures and Administration. 6th ed. Cincinnati: South-Western, 1973.

Zinsser, William. On Writing Well. New York: Harper & Row, 1976.

BULLETINS AND PAMPHLETS

Stock Guide. New York: Standard & Poor's Corporation, March, 1977.

What Mailers Should Do to Get the Best Service. U. S. Postal Service Publication 153. Washington: Government Printing Office, 1970.

ENCYCLOPEDIAS

"Mencken, Henry Louis." The New Columbia Encyclopedia, 1975, 1745.

"Typewriter." Encyclopedia Britannica, 1958, XXII, 644-646.

SECTION 25   WRITING THE REPORT   169

MAGAZINES AND NEWSPAPERS

Meyer, Peter. "A Short History of Form 1040."
<u>Harper's</u>, 254, No. 1523, April, 1977, 22-24.

"A Businessman for Her Deputy." <u>New York Times</u>, 8 May
1977, Section 3, p. 1, col. 1.

FILM

<u>Mail It Right!</u> (Washington: U.S. Government: Postal
Service, 1974) film No. 30.

LECTURE

Daniel Schorr, "The Public's Right to Know," lecture
presented at the University of California, Davis,
18 May 1977.

PERSONAL INTERVIEW

Interview with S. I. Hayakawa, United States
Senator, Washington, 1 June 1977.

RECORDING OR TAPE

Doyle, A. Conan, "Stories of Sherlock Holmes," with
Basil Rathbone (New York: Caedmon), recording
TC 1208.

TELEVISION PROGRAM

"The Prophets and Promise of Classical Capitalism,"
in <u>Age of Uncertainty</u> series, with John Kenneth
Galbraith (San Francisco: KQED-TV 19 May 1977).

**25·B·6
Graphic and
visual aids
for reports**

Charts, graphs, tables, drawings, pictograms, and pictures are some of the more frequently used visual or graphic aids for presenting material in reports. Consider a situation in which you are trying to read written directions for driving to a certain destination. Compare the difference in following the directions with the help of a map. By being able to visualize where you are going, it becomes a much simpler process. The same applies when you are trying to assimilate a mass of figures or statistics.

If they are presented in graphs or charts, it is much easier to understand the figures and to see relationships.

EXAMPLE:

Read this paragraph; then look at the same figures presented in bar graph form. It is quite obvious which is easier and quicker to read and understand.

Gross sales for the past ten-year period are: 1966—$976,000,000; 1967—$1,000,000,000; 1968—$1,156,000,000; 1969—$1,271,000,000; 1970—$1,382,000,000; 1971—$1,527,000,000; 1972—$1,689,000,000; 1973—$1,898,000,000; 1974—$2,183,000,000; and 1975—$2,409,000,000.

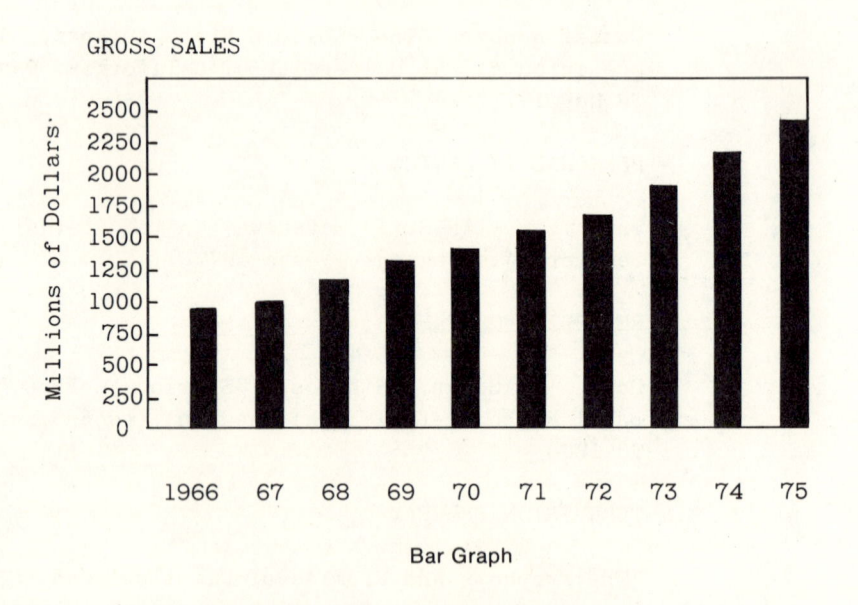

GROSS SALES

Bar Graph

Do not include graphic aids merely to make the report look impressive and do not expect graphic aids to replace the written text. Label the graphs or charts and place the written description close to the graph or chart. Be sure, too, that the information given is complete. Do not leave out information to make the aid show what you want. Do not present a false appearance by distorting the width of the graph; that is, do not make the graph very narrow so that it presents a sharp rise or fall—or make it very wide so that changes seem gradual.

SECTION 25   WRITING THE REPORT

Prepare a rough draft of any chart or graph first. It may be necessary to use graph paper along with such aids as protractors, lettering guides, and lettering pens.

Decide what kind of graphic aid will best present the data and how detailed or complex the aid should be. If a complex graph giving data in various colors cannot be easily understood, it might be better to use separate graphs to present each item of information. Graphic aids should, of course, be designed for those who will read the report and look at the aids. Obviously the complex graph that requires technical engineering knowledge would not be appropriate for the average office worker.

Graphs and charts have limitations. One limitation is the number of facts that can be presented—four or five are maximum; more than that should be presented in a table. Another limitation is that the figures are usually approximate; that is, they are rounded off. If you are dealing in millions of dollars, for example, thousands of dollars may be rounded.

Some of the frequently used graphs are shown in the examples.

The bar graph shown on page 170 presents quantities and time periods by using horizontal and vertical bars. The quantity usually begins with zero, and the time element begins with the earliest date shown. Such graphs are sometimes typed by using upper case characters such as M, N, O, W, and X; or by repeatedly striking the same letter or character to make a solid line.

The circle or pie graph (p. 172) shows quantity divided into sections. To make this graph, the circle represents 100 percent, and the parts are converted to percentages. Chart the largest part first. Identify each section within the graph if space permits. Type the labels horizontally.

The line graph (p. 172) compares changes over a period of time. Usually it compares such things as sales, expenses, profits, or production over a period of time. Such a graph should be prepared on graph paper and transferred to plain paper. The time period is placed horizontally at the bottom of the graph, beginning with the earliest date. Show no more than five lines on the graph and include a legend or key so that the various lines (solid, broken, dots) can be read easily.

The pictograph uses symbols instead of lines or bars to represent units of quantity. In the example (p. 173), the figures represent farm workers.

BUSINESS REPORT WRITING

EMPLOYED PERSONS--PERCENT DISTRIBUTION, 1975

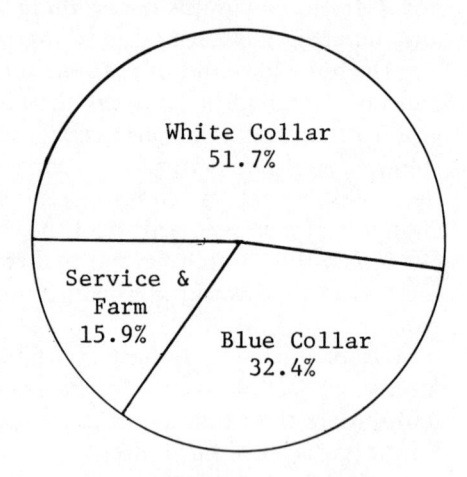

- White Collar 51.7%
- Blue Collar 32.4%
- Service & Farm 15.9%

Source: Statistical Abstract of the United States, 1976

Circle Graph

AVERAGE ANNUAL INCOME OF SELECTED OCCUPATIONS

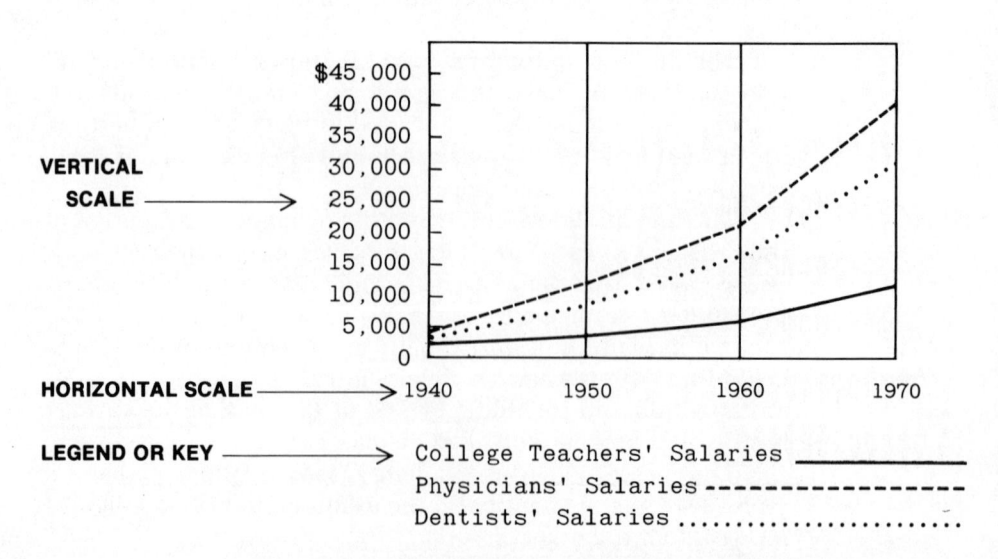

VERTICAL SCALE ⟶ $45,000 / 40,000 / 35,000 / 30,000 / 25,000 / 20,000 / 15,000 / 10,000 / 5,000 / 0

HORIZONTAL SCALE ⟶ 1940   1950   1960   1970

LEGEND OR KEY ⟶ College Teachers' Salaries _____
Physicians' Salaries -----------------
Dentists' Salaries ....

Source: Statistical Abstract of the United States, 1976

Line Graph

SECTION 25   WRITING THE REPORT

DEATH RATE BY RACE AND SEX: 1900-1970
(Number of Deaths per 1,000 Population)

		Death Rate					
		White			Black and Other		
Year	Total	Both Sexes	Male	Female	Both Sexes	Male	Female
1970	9.5	9.5	10.9	8.1	9.4	11.2	7.8
1960	9.5	9.5	11.0	8.0	10.1	11.5	8.7
1950	9.6	9.5	10.9	8.0	11.2	12.5	9.9
1940	10.8	10.4	11.6	9.2	13.8	15.1	12.6
1930	11.3	10.8	11.7	9.8	16.3	17.4	15.3
1920	13.0	12.6	13.0	12.1	17.7	17.8	17.5
1910	14.7	14.5	15.4	13.6	21.7	22.3	21.0
1900	17.2	17.0	17.7	16.3	25.0	25.7	24.4

Source: Historical Statistics of the United States, 1976

Table

CHANGES IN FARM POPULATION, 1940 TO 1975

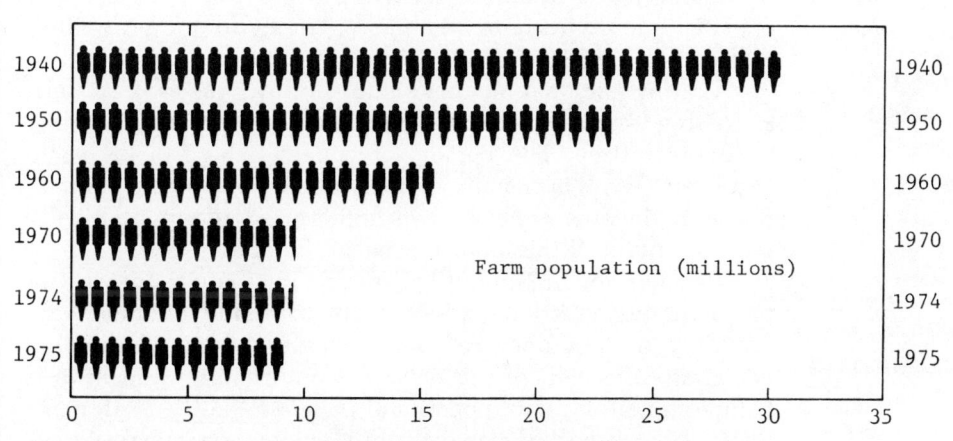

Source: Statistical Abstract of the United States, 1976

Pictograph

8

personal business writing

A personal business letter is any letter that you write having to do with your own personal business affairs—to a department store concerning your account or purchase, to a mail-order firm asking about an order, to a hotel asking for reservations, as well as an endless number of other letters having to do with personal affairs. You write business letters asking for information about a new product or service or how to use that product or service; you write to your elected representatives to express your opinion on how they should vote or sponsor legislation; and you write to editors of newspapers and magazines expressing your opinions on matters of public interest. Often writing business letters begins at an early age—premium offers with box tops and order letters, for example—and continues throughout a lifetime. You write for the same reasons that businesses do—to get information, to get a response, to give information, and to build goodwill. All too often, because you consider such writing to be a chore, letters do not get written and you lose because of it.

Writing personal business letters follows the same pattern as writing letters on the job. You collect information, you plan, and you outline. The personal business letter has the same three parts and is usually written deductively—the point is placed in the opening. Bad news letters are written inductively, with the point of the letter placed in the body.

Because you are quite likely to procrastinate about writing personal business letters, see if you can find another way. Should you telephone? Yes, but be sure that when you phone, you first collect all of the necessary information and have it before you, along with pencil and paper so that you can make notes. Get names of persons with whom you speak. Long-distance calls may be easier and quicker, take less time, and actually save money over letter writing. If you have the time and are nearby, it may be easier to call in person or make an appointment to talk with someone at the store or business. Nevertheless, there are many times when you must write.

SECTION 26 **Pointers for personal business writing**

Here are some pointers for writing personal business letters:

1. The personal business letter follows the same plan and is written the same way that firms write their business letters. You are writing for the same reasons.

2. Your letter is more likely to be read if it is typed. Make sure, of course, that your typing is readable—the ribbon dark, errors corrected, type clean, and no strikeovers. Keep a copy of the letter that you write—either make a carbon copy or use one of the commercial copiers. Also copy any documents that support the facts in your letter —canceled checks (both sides), receipts, order forms, and the like—and send the copies with the letter; never give up originals. Always keep such documents when you receive them. They are invaluable evidence if you have future questions.

3. If possible, address letters to persons rather than to organizations or titles within the company. Libraries have reference sources, such as Standard & Poor's, that give names of executives of companies as well as complete addresses of firms. Check addresses and ZIP Codes as these help get your letters to their destinations.

4. Sometimes pictures, drawings, or diagrams are helpful. A picture of damage may support an insurance claim, for example. Sometimes it is necessary to get information from experts, such as an estimate of the cost of repairs or the extent of damage. Gather such information before you write.

5. As in other business letters, do not use threatening or abusive language.

6. Use an acceptable business-letter style for a personal letter. Do not use your employer's letterhead; it only causes confusion concerning who is the writer of the letter. If you use plain paper, put your address above the date. Always date letters (use month, day, and year in full) and sign them with your legal name. Type your name beneath your signature so that the recipient has

no trouble knowing who wrote the letter. Include your address even if you do not wish a reply; there are so many similar names that often your address is necessary to identify you. Use account numbers if they are available.

7. Check the letter when you have written it to be sure that it contains who, what, why, when, and where. Once again, be careful that your name and address are included. It is amazing how easy it is to overlook one of those important facts.

SECTION 27 **Specific personal writing situations**

Here are some of the personal writing situations that differ somewhat from business writing situations:

27·A
Direct mail

Direct or so-called junk mail consists of promotional letters or brochures that fill most people's mailboxes with offers of an unlimited selection of products and services, opportunities to enter contests and perhaps win unbelievable prizes, persuasive reasons for voting for political candidates, and chances to make tax-free contributions to a whole range of charities and worthwhile causes.

Any person who registers to vote, owns a car, buys or donates anything through the mail, belongs to a profession or trade union, or subscribes to a magazine is likely to be on a mailing list. In fact, that person is probably on at least fifty of the 21,000 mailing lists available to companies or organizations wanting to reach you through the mails.

Direct mail for some persons creates a problem—how to stop receiving it. If you want to stop it (or start or get more; after all, some people like such mail), you can write to the Direct Mail Marketing Association. Two thirds of all mail-order business in the United States is done by firms that are members of the Direct Mail Marketing Association. The address to write to stop or start the third-class mail is: Mail Preference Service, 6 East 43 Street, New York, NY 10017.

27·B
Consumer complaints

When something goes wrong in dealing with a company—whether in regard to an order or a service—if at all possible, do your communicating by telephone or in person. Many of the large corporations have toll-free telephone numbers (prefixed by 800) that you can call. In most instances these companies have the matter taken care of promptly. When you must write, gather all the pertinent information and document your facts carefully. If you have an account number, use it. If it involves a magazine or other subscription, send the label from the publication. Supply all of the dates, names, and facts that you can—when did you purchase the item, from whom did you purchase it, what was the purchase price, what is the model number? If your letter is a follow-up to a telephone call, address the letter to the person with whom you spoke. Specifics in complaint letters are much better than generalities.

More and more state, federal, and local laws and ordinances are being enacted to protect consumers. There are also a number of agencies that can help you once you have exhausted your own resources. Telephone calls to city or county or state or federal consumer protection agencies can help. Most of them can supply information telling you what to do next. The local Better Business Bureau is often of service. If the complaint involves possible fraud, ask the district attorney or state attorney general's office for help. Radio and television stations as well as magazines and newspapers also offer help to the consumer. Libraries have publications such as *Consumers Complaint Guide* available for your use.

One of the problems in writing to companies is that often you do not get a reply. The widespread use of computers is partly to blame for this. If your complaint is attached to a computer card, chances are that it will not be read. Sometimes, if you fold, staple, or make holes in the computer card, the machine will not automatically accept it and human attention can be attracted.

When complaint letters are unanswered, go to the library and find the name of one of the officials of the company—the higher ranking the better—and write to that person. Attach copies of previous letters and explain your problem. Avoid abusive or threatening language. State your problem clearly and say what you would like done.

27·C Thank-you notes

Business thank-you notes and letters of appreciation are often neglected. These are the notes that are written to persons who have written letters of recommendation, to firms expressing appreciation when an employee has been particularly helpful or an extra service has been performed, or to anyone who has given service or has assisted in any way. Perhaps, for example, a librarian has spent a great deal of time helping you find a reference source. A letter of appreciation to this person is a courteous, thoughtful gesture for doing more than was expected. A copy of the letter to the librarian's supervisor as well is a good idea.

274 Martin Court
Any Town, NJ 08200 } ADDRESS AND DATE INCLUDED
July 1, 19--

ADDRESSED TO PERSON { Mr. Thomas J. Worth
Executive Vice President
Popular Book Club
250 North Avenue
New York, NY 00123

Dear Mr. Worth

ACCOUNT NO. { Subject: Account No. 4732122

Because the letters that I have written to the Popular Book Club have not been answered, I am writing to you for help.

In May I received a book, Great Stories from the Past, that I did not order. I returned the book the next day with a letter explaining why I was returning it. A few days later, I received a statement for $12.85; since I had returned the book, I ignored the statement. On June 10 I received another statement marked "past-due." I returned this statement with a note telling what had happened. Today I received a threatening letter about my past-due account. } PROBLEM STATED

Perhaps the problem is caused by a computer error or by my letters going to the wrong person. In any event, I hope that you can straighten things out. Would you please let me know what has happened. } WRITER'S REQUEST

Thank you.

Sincerely

Wilma L. Brooks

Mrs. Wilma L. Brooks } TYPED NAME

Personal Business Letter

Such letters should be brief. Give the person's name, state specifically the service that was performed, and express your gratitude. Open the letter with the point—that you wish to thank the person addressed for being so helpful. Address the letter to the person you are thanking and send a carbon copy to that person's supervisor.

**27·D
Completing
credit appli-
cation forms**
In almost all instances the person applying for credit will be asked to complete a credit application form. The information supplied should be accurate and truthful; be sure all names are spelled correctly. Do not leave any of the blanks on the form unanswered. Since the application does become a part of your general credit file and the information is shared by the firms where you have credit, the information contained in all application forms should agree. The application is also a signed contract in which you agree to abide by the credit terms of the firm from which you are seeking credit.

9

punctuation

The purpose of most punctuation is to make the reading of sentences easier. Some punctuation seems unnecessary; some is debatable; and some is left to the discretion of the writer. However, most punctuation is placed according to rules that can be applied mechanically.

SECTION 28 **End-of-the-sentence punctuation**

The period, question mark, and exclamation point are used to end sentences. Occasionally, these marks are used within sentences for other purposes or are placed after words or phrases that are not considered to be sentences.

28·A
Period (.) A period is used most frequently to indicate the end of a sentence. If the sentence is a direct question or is a statement with strong feeling or emotion, a question mark or exclamation point is used.

28·A·1
At the end Use a period at the end of any declarative or imperative sen-
of sentences tence and after simple requests and indirect questions.

        EXAMPLES: This letter should be retyped.   *declarative*
                      Keep your eyes on the copy.   *imperative*
                      Will you take care of this   *simple request*
                          matter.
                      I wonder whether Cynthia   *indirect question*
                          heard me.

28·A·2
Special uses Use a period after initials, abbreviations, numbers or letters in outlines or enumerations, and a few contractions. Usage varies in placing periods after letters in abbreviations.

SECTION 28   END-OF-THE-SENTENCE PUNCTUATION   181

        EXAMPLES: Inc.   A. Punctuation
                       R.S.V.P. *or* RSVP   1. Period
                       Dept.   2. Question Mark

28·A·3
Ellipsis   Three spaced periods are used to indicate an ellipsis (an omission of words within a sentence) in quotations or to show hesitation in dialogue or narrative. They are sometimes used in advertising copy or sales letters to separate statements or to indicate emphasis.

        EXAMPLES: The so-called debtor class . . . are not dishonest because they are in debt.
                                —Grover Cleveland   *omission in quotation*

                 Our travel agency offers rare trips for the sports enthusiast—hiking in the Swiss Alps . . . swimming in South Pacific waters . . . skiing on Austrian slopes . . . fishing in Scottish streams —at incredible bargains.   *setting off points of sales letter*

28·B
Question
mark (?)   Use question marks after direct questions and tag questions. A special use of the question mark is to enclose it in parentheses to show doubt or approximation.

        EXAMPLES: Will Connie receive the promotion?   *direct question*
                       He did finish the work, didn't he?   *tag question*
                       The first school in this area was built in 1825(?).   *approximation*

28·C
Exclamation
point (!)   Use exclamation points after sentences or expressions that show strong feeling or emotion. Use exclamation points sparingly and never use double or triple exclamation points.

        EXAMPLES: Help!
                       My trip to Rome was the best vacation that I have ever had!

28·D
Warnings   Notice these points about end-of-the-sentence punctuation.
28·D·1
Double-ending
punctuation   Double-ending punctuation, such as two periods or a question mark and a period, is never placed at the end of a sentence.

        EXAMPLES: I work for Lawson & Hall, Inc.
                       My boss asked, "When will you finish the report?"

PUNCTUATION

28·D·2
Courteous requests — Periods are placed after courteous requests or after questions to which answers are not expected.

> **EXAMPLES:** Will you let me know whether my account has been credited with the correct amount.
> May we hear from you soon.

SECTION 29 Internal punctuation

Internal punctuation marks are those found within the sentence.

29·A
Comma (,) — The comma is the most frequently used of all of the internal punctuation marks. It serves two purposes in sentences—to separate and to set off.

These are the rules for commas that separate:

29·A·1
Clauses of compound sentence — Separate clauses of a compound sentence by a comma when:

  a. the clauses are joined by coordinate conjunctions—<u>and</u>, <u>but</u>, <u>for</u>, <u>or</u>, <u>nor</u>, <u>yet</u> (The comma is always placed before the conjunction.)

  b. neither clause contains internal punctuation

  c. each clause has its own subject (A sentence that does not have a second subject is not a compound sentence; it is a simple sentence with a compound predicate.)

> **EXAMPLES:** We ordered typewriter ribbons a month ago, <u>yet</u> we still have not received them.
> I worked last Saturday, <u>and</u> I probably will work next Saturday. *each clause has its own subject*
> I worked last Saturday and probably will work next Saturday. *not a compound sentence because the second part does not have its own subject*

29·A·2
Items in series — Separate words, phrases, or clauses in a series when:

  a. the series consists of three or more items

  b. there is no internal punctuation in the series

The comma before the conjunction in the series is optional.

SECTION 29   INTERNAL PUNCTUATION   183

EXAMPLES: Mr. Bernstein called New York, Boston, and Los Angeles before he could find a distributor for the product. *the comma after* Boston *is optional*

What she will do, what she will say, or what she will expect are completely unknown. *series of clauses; comma after* say *is optional*

29·A·3
Coordinate adjectives

Use a comma to separate coordinate adjectives of equal importance that come before a noun and are not joined by a conjunction. Test whether adjectives are coordinate by placing <u>and</u> between the adjectives; if the phrase sounds natural, a comma is needed.

EXAMPLES: the good and old days; **use:** the good old days *not coordinate*

a stupid and little mistake; **use:** a stupid little mistake *not coordinate*

But: an old-fashioned and honest approach; **use:** an old-fashioned, honest approach *coordinate*

These are the rules for commas that set off:

29·A·4
Introductory words, phrases, and clauses

Set off an introductory word, phrase, or clause that, because it precedes the subject of the sentence, is out of its natural sentence order. The phrases are usually infinitive or participial; the clauses, adverb.

EXAMPLES: Yes, you may return the stereo for credit.

Outside, the building gave the appearance of great size.

Remember, our guarantee is in effect for one entire year.

By working overtime, David finished the report.

Standing on a shelf by itself, the clock could not be seen by the customer.

To hear the announcement, Ellen had to stop typing.

If it is possible, Miss Schultz would prefer the order sent by United Parcel.

After the campaign was over, the senator went to Europe.

Short introductory prepositional phrases are not followed by commas; long phrases may be.

PUNCTUATION   184

>   EXAMPLES: On January 31 our company will celebrate its
>   fiftieth anniversary.
>   During the last five years of his life, Sheldon lived
>   in Boston.

29·A·5
Restrictive/   Set off any nonrestrictive elements by commas. Nonrestrictive
nonrestrictive elements are those words, phrases, and clauses that can be
modifiers   taken out of a sentence without affecting the identity of the
                item described. Restrictive elements are necessary to identify
                the item described.

These are elements that are either restrictive or nonrestrictive:

>   **a.** Most restrictive and nonrestrictive elements are adjective clauses or phrases.

>   EXAMPLES: My father, <u>who retired recently</u>, has moved to
>   Florida. nonrestrictive—*the adjective clause is
>   not necessary to describe* <u>my father</u>
>   All secretaries <u>who work overtime</u> will receive
>   additional pay. restrictive—*the adjective
>   clause is necessary to limit* <u>all secretaries</u>
>   Julie, <u>hearing her name called over the intercom
>   system</u>, went into Mrs. Kane's office. *nonrestrictive participial phrase*

>   **b.** Appositive elements that come after nouns (or pronouns) and rename or supplement the noun (or pronoun) are also considered to be either restrictive or nonrestrictive.

>   EXAMPLES: My sister <u>Meg</u> left for New York this morning. <u>Meg</u>,
>   *not another sister*
>   Do you mean Richard Burton <u>the explorer</u> or Richard Burton <u>the actor</u>? *restrictive elements*
>   My employer, <u>Mr. Johnson</u>, is the new president of
>   the Chamber of Commerce. *nonrestrictive
>   element*

Nonrestrictive elements are words, phrases, or clauses that interrupt the sentences in which they occur. These elements may explain, contrast (usually containing *not*), or amend some part of the sentence; but they are not necessary to the sentence.

>   EXAMPLES: His brother, <u>not his cousin</u>, has been appointed to
>   the new post. *contrast—nonrestrictive*
>   This information is not, <u>so far as I know</u>, classified.
>   *qualifying—nonrestrictive*

SECTION 29   INTERNAL PUNCTUATION   **185**

>We can, I think, hire two new secretaries. *qualifying—nonrestrictive*

29·A·6
Explanatory
elements

Explanatory elements include geographic names, dates, degrees or titles, Inc. and Ltd., and explanatory expressions accompanying direct quotations.

>**EXAMPLES:** Eric sent the letter to Salem, Oregon, rather than to Salem, Massachusetts.
>Friday, March 15, is the last day to submit quotations.
>Martin Luther King, Jr., was killed on April 4, 1968.
>"I am concerned," Gretchen wrote, "that you did not receive my order."

If the date consists of the month and the year, it is not necessary to set off the year; usage varies.

>**EXAMPLE:** Mr. Todd will retire in January 1979.

Do not set off numbers such as II or 3d after personal names.

>**EXAMPLE:** Queen Elizabeth II is the queen of England.

29·A·7
Miscellaneous
uses

a. Use commas to separate repeated words, two numbers coming together, numbers of four or more digits, tag questions, and inverted names.

>**EXAMPLES:** In 1990, 5,000 acres of land will be sold from the ranch.
>I can still file an application, can't I?
>No, no, that is not right!
>Anderson, Kathryn

Do not use commas in numbers of four digits or more if the numbers are years, page numbers, house numbers, telephone numbers, serial numbers, decimal fractions, or ZIP Codes.

>**EXAMPLES:** page 1675   Requisition No. 43567
>4227 Laurel Avenue

b. Use commas to set off direct address and to show omission of words.

EXAMPLES: Thank you, Mrs. Harriman, for paying your bill so promptly.

In 1976 our company paid a yearly dividend of $3.40; in 1977, $4.15; in 1978, $4.35.

29·A·8
Warnings Notice these points about commas:

a. Do not use commas between subjects and verbs.

EXAMPLES: Avoid: The story that Tracey heard, is entirely different.
Use: The story that Tracey heard is entirely different.

b. Do not use commas between verbs and direct objects or complements.

EXAMPLES: Avoid: The reason for his departure from the haunted house was, the appearance of a ghost.
Use: The reason for his departure from the haunted house was the appearance of a ghost.

c. Do not place a comma between the last adjective in a series and the noun that is modified.

EXAMPLES: Avoid: The bright, handsome, child is extremely popular.
Use: The bright, handsome child is extremely popular.

d. Do not place a comma between two items in a series that are joined by a coordinate conjunction.

EXAMPLES: Avoid: I wanted to finish the work, and to leave early.
Use: I wanted to finish the work and to leave early.
Avoid: Ken said that he was wrong, and that he wished to apologize.
Use: Ken said that he was wrong and that he wished to apologize.

29·B
Semicolon (;) The semicolon is used for a break that is often the equivalent of a period; in fact, the semicolon is sometimes called a weak period. It usually separates items of equal grammatical rank.

SECTION 29 INTERNAL PUNCTUATION

29·B·1
Clauses of compound sentence

Both the comma (see p. 182) and the semicolon are used to punctuate the compound sentence. Use the semicolon to separate clauses of a compound sentence when:

    a. no conjunction is used to connect the independent clauses

    b. either or both of the clauses of the compound sentence contain internal punctuation

    c. a conjunctive adverb such as <u>however</u>, <u>namely</u>, or <u>therefore</u>—or a transitional phrase such as <u>in fact</u> or <u>that is</u>—is used to join the clauses (Use a comma after the conjunctive adverb only if the adverb is considered to be parenthetical.)

> **EXAMPLES:** Our company cannot continue without products; it must produce or go out of business. *no connecting conjunction*
> Although Daphne has worked hard on the report, she seems unable to finish it; but she does hope to submit a preliminary report by June 1. *internal punctuation*
> The company has increased its profits each year; therefore it has increased its dividends to stockholders as well. *clauses joined by conjunctive adverb*
> The tennis team won the playoff match; in fact, it has won all of its matches this season. *clauses joined by transitional phrase*

29·B·2
Items in series

The semicolon is used to separate items in a series if those items contain internal punctuation.

> **EXAMPLES:** He suggested selecting one of these dates for the meeting: Saturday, June 4; Friday, June 17; or Monday, June 27.
> The candidates for the president of the company were Mr. Taylor, the assistant vice president; Mr. Harper, the sales manager; and Mrs. Kelly, the head administrative assistant.

29·B·3
Before explanation or enumeration

The semicolon is used before words or phrases that introduce explanations and enumerations such as <u>for example</u>, <u>for instance</u>, and <u>namely</u>. Either a colon or a comma may also be used.

PUNCTUATION 188

> EXAMPLES: At the club meeting the president introduced both of the candidates; that is, Mrs. Hazlitt and Mr. Scott.
> Many of the tax deductions were to charities: that is, the Red Cross, the Cancer Society, and the Heart Association. *colon used because the main clause anticipates a listing*
> I could not complete the tax return by the due date, that is, April 15. *comma used because the explanation is an appositive*

If the enumeration or explanation occurs within the sentence, it may be set off by commas, dashes, or parentheses.

> EXAMPLES: Many European cities—for example, London, Paris, Brussels, and Rome—are experiencing great inflation.
> Relative pronouns (for example, who, which, and that) introduce dependent clauses.

29·C
Quotation marks

Quotation marks are used to enclose any direct quotation, whether from a speaker or from written material. A direct quotation must be exactly as it is spoken or written. The explanatory expressions that accompany direct quotations are not placed within the quotation marks but are set off by commas. Explanatory material can be placed at the beginning, within, or at the end of the quotation.

> EXAMPLES: Franklin Roosevelt once said in a speech, "I have seen war. . . . I hate war." *explanatory material at the beginning of the quotation; ellipsis shows omission in the direct quotation*
> "The new computer is," Mr. Ryan wrote, "exactly what I want." *explanatory material within the direct quotation*

29·C·1
Quotation within quotation

When a quotation contains a quotation within the quoted matter, enclose the internal quotation in single quotation marks and the whole quotation in double quotation marks. This is the only time single quotation marks are used.

> EXAMPLE: This statement was in a student's paper: "In a book written by Arthur M. Schlesinger, Jr., John Kennedy is quoted as saying, 'Washington is a city of southern efficiency and northern charm.'"

SECTION 29 INTERNAL PUNCTUATION

29·C·2
Special points Notice these special points about using quotation marks:

a. When a quotation consists of more than one paragraph, place quotation marks at the beginning of each paragraph and at the end of the last paragraph.

b. When *etc.* follows a quotation, it is not a part of the quotation and should not be enclosed in quotation marks.

29·C·3
With other marks of punctuation The period and the comma always go inside closing quotation marks.

EXAMPLES: "I paid the bill two months ago," the customer wrote.
Harvey said, "Mr. Lee took care of the matter immediately."

The colon and the semicolon always go outside closing quotation marks.

EXAMPLE: Dan calls his Mercedes "a set of wheels"; I think this is a slight understatement.

The dash, the question mark, and the exclamation point may be placed either inside or outside closing quotation marks depending upon whether the entire sentence or just the quotation is the question or the exclamation or includes the dash.

EXAMPLES: Did Sheila ask, "Where are the tickets"?
I heard Sheila say, "Where are the tickets?"

29·C·4
Other uses Quotation marks are also used to enclose:

a. Titles of short stories, poems, one-act plays, articles, reports, lectures, catalogs, essays, chapters of books, unpublished works, and other literary works that are less than book length

b. Songs and radio and television programs

c. Words used as words, unusual or technical terms, and words accompanied by their definitions (In print these are sometimes shown in italics.)

EXAMPLES: "Rain" is one of Somerset Maugham's well-known stories.
"Politics and the English Language" is an essay by Orwell.

PUNCTUATION   190

> "Upstairs, Downstairs" was shown for four years on television.
> "Capitol" refers to the legislative building.
> He used the word "viable" six times in three minutes.

SECTION 30 Other punctuation

These four marks of punctuation—the colon, the dash, parentheses, and brackets—have more limited uses than the other punctuation marks. Italics, although not a mark of punctuation but a kind of type, are also included.

30·A
Colon (:) The colon frequently introduces listings. It is often placed after or in place of *namely* or *as follows*.

Use colons:

a. Before listed items

b. Before long formal quotations

c. To separate two independent clauses when the second clause explains or illustrates the first

d. To introduce an explanation

e. After a salutation in mixed punctuation

f. To show hours, minutes, and seconds

g. To separate chapter and verse in biblical selections

h. To separate volume and page in bibliographical references

EXAMPLES: Please send these items:
   3 dozen No. 24L5 typewriter ribbons
   10 reams No. 8-11-16 paper
   2 dozen No. 426 pencils   *listing*
I am quoting from Aldous Huxley who wrote:
   "There is no substitute for talent. Industry and all the virtues are of no avail."   *formal quotation*
I had but one wish: to find the missing letter.   *explanation*
The manager put into effect a new policy: all mail must be in the mailroom by three o'clock.   *two clauses*

SECTION 30   OTHER PUNCTUATION   **191**

>   Dear Mrs. Ellis: *salutation*
>   I left at 4:30.   *hour; minutes*
>   Gourmet 37:6   *bibliographical listing*

30·B
Dash (—)   The dash has uses similar to those of the comma. However, it indicates more abruptness and is used for clarity when commas have already been used. Dashes can also set off parenthetical expressions to make them more emphatic.

> **EXAMPLES:** Two of our best secretaries—Janet Ross and Henry Lyons—are becoming administrative assistants.
>
> If you want—and I am not sure that you do—to accept the position, we should all be pleased.

30·C
Parentheses
(( ))   Parentheses are used to set off supplementary or explanatory material that is not essential to the sentence. Do not use them around any material that is essential. They can also be used mechanically in outlines or in numbered series to enclose numbers or letters.

> **EXAMPLES:** Read the explanation on parallel construction (see page 70).
>
> The old movie (filmed in 1939) is frequently shown on television.
>
> Follow these steps in taking the test: (1) read all of the directions, (2) fill in the information asked for on the first page, (3) answer as many items as you can, and (4) go back to the items that caused trouble.

30·D
Brackets
([ ])   Brackets are used around corrections or inserted material that is added to direct quotations by someone other than the original author.

The word *sic* (thus, so) is placed in brackets after an error in a direct quotation to show that the error was in the original quotation.

> **EXAMPLES:** The report contained this sentence: "The total sales [this was later adjusted] for the year amounted to over a billion dollars."
>
> Georgina wrote, "The principle [sic] export of the country is coffee."

30·E
Italics   In typing or handwriting, italic type is indicated by underlining.

Usage of italics varies, but these are some of the commonly given uses:

a. Titles of book-length literary works, periodicals, newspapers, pamphlets, musical works, plays, and movies

b. Names of ships, aircraft, and spacecraft

c. Foreign words, but not words of foreign origin that are now a part of the English language

d. Legal citations

e. Paintings and works of art

f. Words or phrases used as words or phrases and not for their meaning

g. Emphasis of words or statements

EXAMPLES: the San Francisco *Examiner*   *usually the city in newspaper names is not italicized*
Moby Dick   book
Mozart's *The Marriage of Figaro*   *musical composition*
the *Lusitania*   *ship*
tete-a-tete; quid pro quo but vice versa   *foreign phrases*
Brown v. Board of Education   *legal citation*
For is either a preposition or a conjunction.   *word used as word*
Do *not* turn the dial backwards!   *emphasis*

10

style

Style (or mechanics) has to do with abbreviations, capitalization, and expressing numbers as words or in figures. It also has to do with some punctuation and usage problems that are discussed elsewhere. Mechanical usage varies considerably, and business usage can vary from general usage.

SECTION 31 Abbreviations

Abbreviations should not be used if there is the slightest chance that they will cause confusion. Consult a dictionary when questions arise, for dictionaries contain definitions and correct forms of abbreviations.

31·A
Abbreviations to use

These abbreviations are accepted in most business as well as general writing. Follow these rules unless indicated otherwise.

Accepted business abbreviations include:

31·A·1
With personal names

a. These abbreviations that come before and after personal names.

Mr./Messrs.	St. (before a saint name)	Sr.
Mrs./Mmes.	Dr.	Esq.
Ms./Mses.	Jr.	

b. Earned or honorary degrees or special awards, such as B.A., M.A., M.S., Ph.D., D.D.S., D.S.C. (Distinguished Service Cross).

31·A·2
Within firm names

Abbreviations in firm names if the firms show such abbreviations—and *Ltd.* and *Inc.* following firm names. Use the ampersand (&) in place of *and* only if the firm uses it.

EXAMPLES: Lester Lumber Co.   R. O'Brien & Son
Stone Builders, Inc.   Helicopters, Ltd.

STYLE 194

31·A·3
With time elements

These abbreviations used to designate time:
    33 B.C. (before Christ)
    A.D. 1900 (anno Domini—in the year of our Lord)
    8 A.M. or 8 a.m.
    5:30 P.M. or 5:30 p.m.
    EST (Eastern Standard Time), CST (Central Standard Time), MST (Mountain Standard Time), and PST (Pacific Standard Time)
    DST (Daylight Saving Time), EDST (Eastern Daylight Saving Time), and so on

31·A·4
Organization names

Letters used in place of complete names of various well-known organizations, either government or private. They are often written without periods. Radio and television station letters are not abbreviations; they are call letters and are written in all capitals without periods.

EXAMPLES: UNICEF   Y.M.C.A.
                   CIO   KQED (television station)
                   UMW

31·A·5
Compass points

Compound compass points (southeast, northwest) as part of street addresses. The periods after the abbreviations are optional.

EXAMPLES: 2074 N.W. 15 Avenue
                   2074 Seventh Avenue NW

31·A·6
State and province names

States and Canadian provinces as part of addresses. Use the two-letter ZIP Code abbreviations for both states and provinces. See the listing in the Appendix (p. 213) for the correct abbreviations.

EXAMPLE: Mr. Roger T. Wellington
                  340 Hill Drive
                  Detroit, MI 48201

31·A·7
Latin terms

Latin words and phrases used in general and business writing; use English forms if possible.

EXAMPLES: etc.   i.e.   e.g.

31·A·8
Number

Number (No.) when followed by a number.

EXAMPLES: Social Security No. 333–18–4567
                 Order No. 24671

SECTION 31   ABBREVIATIONS

31·B Abbreviations to avoid

The following items generally are not abbreviated in business writing. These are guidelines only, for usage does vary.
Abbreviations to avoid include:

31·B·1 Titles

Titles (other than those listed in 31·A·1) when used with surnames only. When a title precedes a complete name, usage varies.

EXAMPLES: Colonel Dawson   Governor Brown
Professor Tyler

31·B·2 Compass points

Compass points—*north, south, east, west*. See 31·A·5 for abbreviation of compound compass points.

EXAMPLES: 262 East 55 Street   232 Tenth Avenue South

31·B·3 Personal names

Personal first names.

EXAMPLES: Avoid: Geo.   Wm.
Benj.   Jas.

31·B·4 Calendar divisions

Days, months, and seasons.

EXAMPLES: Avoid: The 31st of Jan. is a Fri.
Use: The 31st of January is a Friday.

31·B·5 Street addresses

Names of streets, avenues, boulevards, courts, and other such designations unless there are space limitations or they are used in computer addresses.

EXAMPLES: 614 Center Boulevard   computer address:
213 Spring Street   614 CENTER BLVD
                               213 SPRING ST

31·B·6 Foreign addresses

Foreign addresses, with the exception of U.S.S.R.

EXAMPLES: Brussels, Belgium
Birmingham, England

31·B·7 Weights and measurements

Weights and measurements.

EXAMPLES: Avoid: oz., min., lbs.
Use: ounces, minutes, pounds.

31·C
Special points

Here are some special points to observe about abbreviations:

31·C·1
Forming plurals

Plurals of abbreviations are formed in a number of ways:

    a. In most instances *s* is added to the singular form.

EXAMPLES: yr./yrs.   lb./lbs.   No./Nos.

    b. Some abbreviations are the same form for both singular and plural.

EXAMPLES: ft.—foot/feet   min.—minute/minutes

    c. If the abbreviation consists of letters with internal punctuation, the plural is formed by adding an apostrophe and -s.

EXAMPLES: M.D.'s   c.o.d.'s

    d. Some single-letter abbreviations double the letters for the plural form.

EXAMPLE: p.—page/pp.—pages

31·C·2
In tabulated material

Many abbreviations that would not ordinarily be accepted are used in tabulated material or in limited space. These include latitude and longitude, names of countries including the United States, weights and measurements, and measurements of time. In fact, any dictionary abbreviation could probably be used under such conditions.

SECTION 32 Capitalization

Practices in capitalization vary. Proper nouns and adjectives are generally capitalized; so are the first words of units such as sentences, lines of poetry, and items in an outline.

32·A
Capitalization rules

These are general rules for capitalization in business writing. Like other rules covering mechanical style, actual usage may vary.

    Capitalize:

32·A·1
Proper nouns and adjectives

Personal names as the bearer of the name does; geographic names as they are officially presented; proper adjectives that are derived from proper nouns (some proper nouns and adjectives are commonly spelled with lower case letters). An atlas or a dictionary can be helpful when questions arise.

EXAMPLES: Proper nouns: McMillan or Macmillan
Vondermahlen or Von der Mahlen
Proper adjectives: Victorian novels
Arabian horses
But: italic type
chinaware
aspirin

32·A·2
Organizations

Names of private and governmental organizations as well as *Government, Administration, Federal, Union, Nation,* and *Constitution* when used to refer to a specific country or to a part of an official name.

EXAMPLES: the Press Club   State Department
Kiwanis International   United States Supreme
General Motors, Inc.   Court
                        Democratic Party
Nation's economy **but:** national security

32·A·3
Religious terms

All references to the Deity (God)—but not deities—in recognized religions, all religions, religious sects, books, holy days, and adjectives derived from these terms.

EXAMPLES: Christ   Jewish
Mohammed   Catholic
Bible   Protestant
Koran   Christmas

Do not capitalize <u>who</u>, <u>whose</u>, and <u>whom</u> when these words refer to the Deity.

32·A·4
Calendar divisions and holidays

Names of calendar divisions and holidays.

EXAMPLES: Tuesday   Fourth of July
July   New Year's Day

Do not capitalize the names of seasons.

EXAMPLES: winter ski trips   spring sales

32·A·5
Geographic localities

Names of geographic localities—nations, states, provinces, continents, bodies of water, mountains, cities, parks, and specific geographic regions—and points of the compass that refer to definite regions.

EXAMPLES:	Great Britain	Indian Ocean	Central Park
	British Columbia	Columbia River	the Pacific Northwest
	Africa	Mount Ranier	
	Kentucky	New Orleans	the Middle East

But: I live north of the campus.

Do not capitalize geographic terms that are not a part of the name, are placed before the name, or are made plural.

EXAMPLES: the city of Buffalo
the valley of San Fernando
the American and Sacramento rivers

32·A·6
Trade names

Trade names of products but not the name of the product.

EXAMPLES: a Buick car   Kleenex tissue
Droste's Cocoa   Shell gasoline

32·A·7
Personal titles

Professional, business, civic, military, religious, and family titles immediately preceding personal names.

EXAMPLES: General George Marshall   Rabbi Horowitz
Dr. William Norris   Grandfather Mobley

Do not capitalize titles that follow names unless the title is part of an inside address, the title of a high governmental official, or a member of Congress.

EXAMPLES: Mrs. Hale, our personnel director, is ill.
Mr. Jones is the new president of our company.

32·A·8
Course titles

Specific names of educational courses and general names of such courses if the name is formed from a proper noun.

EXAMPLES: Intermediate Shorthand   a course in shorthand
Introduction to Chemistry   a course in English

32·A·9
Titles of literary works and art

All beginning and principal words in titles of books, magazines, newspapers, plays, poems, reports, pictures, and works of art.

SECTION 32   CAPITALIZATION   199

>   **EXAMPLES:** This War without an   Man and Superman
>   Enemy   Madonna and Child
>   American Heritage   The New York Times

32·A·10
I and   The pronoun I and exclamations such as *oh, help,* and *ouch*
exclamations   when these words stand alone.

32·A·11
Nouns with   Nouns followed by numbers or letters unless the noun refers to
numbers   a minor item such as page, paragraph, line, or verse.
or letters

>   **EXAMPLES:** Requisition No. 245   Room 421
>   page 60, line 10

32·A·12
Abbreviations Abbreviations only if they would be capitalized when written
                   in full. Some abbreviations such as *f.o.b., c.o.d., a.m.,* and *p.m.*
                   may or may not be capitalized. The two-letter state abbreviations are written in all capitals and without periods.

>   **EXAMPLES:** U.S.A.   e.g.   CA

32·A·13
Initial words The initial words of the following:

>   a. Any sentence
>
>   b. A direct quotation
>
>   c. Every line of poetry
>
>   d. The salutation as well as any nouns in the salutation
>
>   e. The complimentary close of a letter
>
>   f. Items in an outline
>
>   g. Items following a colon in tabulated material

>   **EXAMPLES:** My job is time-consuming.
>   He said, "Finish the work next week."
>
>   Candy
>   Is dandy
>   But liquor
>   Is quicker.
>   —OGDEN NASH
>
>   Dear Mr. Hill
>   Very sincerely yours

STYLE 200

      I. Parts of the letter
        A. Date
        B. Inside address
        C. Salutation
        D. Body
        E. Complimentary close
        F. Signature

32·B
Lower case rules

The name for using small letters is lower case.
Do not capitalize:

32·B·1
Common names

Common names of persons, places, or things, such as food, animals, plants, general geographic terms, and musical instruments.

EXAMPLES:
baby	city	gardenia
playground	desk	lake
ball park	poodle	forest
table	oak	violin

32·B·2
Job titles

Names of job titles or occupations.

EXAMPLES: dentist   lawyer   professor
              dental assistant

32·B·3
Diseases

Names of diseases unless a proper name is part of the name of the disease.

EXAMPLES: chicken pox   Parkinson's disease
              measles

SECTION **33**   **Numerals**

In business writing numbers below ten are written as words; in general usage, however, numbers below 100 are written as words. There are obvious differences in the writing of numerals. Follow the style preference of the company or person for whom you are working. The important consideration is that you use a uniform style—do not write an amount of money, for example, in two different ways—and that the numbers can be read as easily as possible.

33·A
Numbers as words

Unless otherwise indicated, follow these rules for writing numbers.
Write these numbers as words:

SECTION 33 NUMERALS

33·A·1
Below ten   Numbers below and including ten when such numbers are used individually.

> **EXAMPLES:** Julia called at least six times about the shipment.
> I read three or four of the letters about the lost shipment.

Large round numbers over a million are spelled out: $20 million, 6 billion.

33·A·2
Beginning a sentence   Any number beginning a sentence. If the number is large, rewrite the sentence so that the number no longer comes at the beginning.

> **EXAMPLES:** Avoid: Two thousand four hundred and fifty signatures were on the petition.
> Use: The petition contained 2,450 signatures.

33·A·3
Round or indefinite numbers   Round or indefinite numbers.

> **EXAMPLES:** A hundred files were lost in the fire.
> I thought that there were several thousand people at the rally.

33·A·4
Fractions   Fractions standing alone.

> **EXAMPLE:** Prices will be cut one third to one half of the regular prices.

33·A·5
Ages   A person's age when given in number of years.

> **EXAMPLE:** At age thirty Greg will inherit the entire estate.

33·A·6
Periods of time   Periods of time unless such figures are used in credit terms or interest rates.

> **EXAMPLES:** Ms. Howard finished the work in twelve hours.
> Mr. Collins worked for the company for twenty-five years.
> **But:** The loan is due in 90 days.

33·A·7
With o'clock   Time of day when used with o'clock or when o'clock is understood.

> **EXAMPLES:** eleven o'clock   four o'clock
> We arrived at four.

STYLE   202

33·A·8
Centuries and decades

Names of centuries and decades.

EXAMPLES: the nineteenth century
the roaring twenties (but the 1920's)

33·A·9
Days of month

Days of the month—first through tenth—when written *before* the month.

EXAMPLES: ninth of August
first of May

33·B
Numbers as figures

Write these numbers as figures:

33·B·1
Over ten

Exact numbers over ten.

EXAMPLES: There were 14 typing errors on the page.
He interviewed 27 applicants for the job.

33·B·2
More than one number

Two or more numbers in a sentence. If two numbers immediately follow one another, the smaller number is usually spelled out and the larger one is written in figures. If the numbers are unrelated, they can be separated by commas. All numbers in a series of three or more are written as figures.

EXAMPLES: 30 thirteen-cent stamps
In 1977, 429 fires were started by carelessness.
We received separate orders for 2, 8, and 12 of the calculators.

33·B·3
Days of the month

Days of the month when they come after the month. Do not use ordinal endings (12th, 22d).

EXAMPLES: July 10   February 1   March 12

33·B·4
House and street numbers

All house numbers (except *One*) and street numbers over ten. Numbered streets below ten use ordinal endings—*First, Tenth*—but numbered streets over ten can be written without the ordinal endings.

EXAMPLES: One Fifth Avenue
1600 Tenth Street
1600 West 109 Street
1600–109 Street

SECTION 33   NUMERALS

33·B·5
Time   Exact time or when A.M. or P.M. is used.

EXAMPLES: 10:30   8 P.M.

33·B·6
Amounts of money   Amounts of money. Use the dollar sign when over $1; spell out the word *cents* when less than $1. Do not add decimal point and ciphers when amount of money consists of dollars alone.

EXAMPLES: $10   25 cents   3 cents
              $10,000 $55.45

33·B·7
Weights and measurements   Percentages; weights; measures; dimensions; distances; degrees; capacities; page numbers; person's age in months, days, and years; and bond and financial quotations. Note that the words with these figures are spelled out. Symbols (%, #) are not used unless there are space limitations.

EXAMPLES: 70 percent   50 pounds   60 miles
              90 degrees   40 feet   page 75
              25 years, 6 months, 22 days

appendix

Reference Sources

Dictionaries and word sources
1. *The American Heritage Dictionary of the English Language* (New College Ed.). Boston: Houghton Mifflin, 1976.
2. Leslie, Louis A. *20,000 Words* (5th Ed.). New York: McGraw-Hill, 1972. (Pocket-sized book for spelling and word division.)
3. *Roget's International Thesaurus* (3d Ed.). New York: Thomas Y. Crowell, 1974.
4. *Webster's Eighth New Collegiate Dictionary* (Rev. Ed.). Springfield, MA: G. and C. Merriam, 1975. (Desk-sized.)
5. *Webster's Collegiate Thesaurus.* Springfield, MA: G. and C. Merriam, 1976.
6. *Webster's Third New International Dictionary of the English Language.* Springfield, MA: G. and C. Merriam, 1971.
7. Wentworth, Harold, and Stuart Flexner. *Dictionary of American Slang.* New York: Thomas Y. Crowell, 1975.
8. *The Word Book.* Boston: Houghton Mifflin, 1976.

Directories
1. Business and professional directories, such as *Thomas' Register of American Manufacturers, American Banking Directory,* and *American Medical Directory.*
2. City directories (Primarily listings of names and addresses of residents of a city or area. Usually published annually by commercial firms but no longer published in some large cities—New York and Los Angeles, for example.)
3. *Official Congressional Directory.* Washington: United States Government Printing Office. (Published annually.)
4. Telephone directories. (Both local and out-of-town.)

General sources
1. Bartlett, John. *Familiar Quotations* (14th Ed.). Boston: Little, Brown, 1968.
2. *Encyclopaedia Britannica* (14th Ed.). Chicago: Encyclopaedia Britannica, 1975.
3. McWhirter, Norris and Ross. *Guinness Book of World Records.* New York: Sterling Publishing Company. (Published annually.)
4. *The New Columbia Encyclopedia* (4th Ed.). New York: Columbia University Press, 1975. (One volume.)
5. *The New York Times Index.* New York: The New York Times. (Published semimonthly.)
6. Post, Elizabeth. *Emily Post's Etiquette* (12th Ed.). New York: Funk & Wagnalls, 1975.
7. *Reader's Guide to Periodical Literature.* New York: H. W. Wilson. (Published semimonthly September to June; monthly July and August.)
8. *Statistical Abstract of the United States.* Washington: United States Bureau of the Census. (Published annually.)
9. Wallechinsky, David, and Irving Wallace. *The People's Almanac.* Garden City, NY: Doubleday, 1975.
10. *Who's Who.* London: A. & C. Black. (Published annually.)

APPENDIX 207

11. *Who's Who in America.* Chicago: Marquis. (Published biennially.)
12. *The World Almanac and Book of Facts.* New York: Newspaper Enterprise Association. (Published annually.)

Grammar, writing, and style books

1. Himstreet, William C., and Wayne M. Baty. *Business Communications* (5th Ed.). Belmont, CA: Wadsworth, 1977.
2. Hodges, John C., and Mary E. Whitten. *Harbrace College Handbook* (8th Ed.). New York: Harcourt Brace Jovanovich, 1977.
3. Krey, Isabelle, and Bernadette Metzler. *Principles and Techniques of Effective Business Communication.* New York: Harcourt Brace Jovanovich, 1976.
4. *A Manual of Style* (12th Ed.). Chicago: University of Chicago Press, 1969.
5. Menning, J. H., C. W. Wilkinson, and Peter B. Clarke. *Communicating Through Letters and Reports.* Homewood, IL: Irwin, 1976.
6. Perrin, Porter G., and Wilma R. Ebbitt. *Writer's Guide and Index to English* (5th Ed.). Glenview, IL: Scott, Foresman, 1972.
7. Sigband, Norman B. *Communication for Management and Business* (2d Ed.). Glenview, IL: Scott, Foresman, 1976.
8. Skillin, Marjorie E., and Robert M. Gay. *Words into Type* (3d Ed.). Englewood Cliffs, NJ: Prentice-Hall, 1974.

Postal, shipping, travel, and geographical sources

1. *Bullinger's Postal and Shippers Guide for the United States and Canada.* New York: Bullinger's Monitor Guide. (Published annually, with a supplement six months after publication.)
2. *National ZIP Code Directory.* Washington: United States Government Printing Office, 1970.
3. *Official Hotel Red Book.* New York: American Hotel Association Directory Corporation. (Published annually.)
4. *The Postal Manual.* Washington: United States Government Printing Office. (Kept up-to-date by supplements.)
5. *Rand McNally New Cosmopolitan World Atlas.* Chicago: Rand McNally, 1975.

Financial information sources

1. *Manual of Investments, American and Foreign.* New York: Moody's Investors Service. (Published annually with semiweekly supplements.)
2. *Reference Book.* New York: Dun & Bradstreet. (By subscription.)
3. *Standard Corporation Records.* New York: Standard & Poor's Corporation Services. (Published currently in loose-leaf form.)

Secretarial handbooks

1. Hanna, J. Marshall, Estelle L. Popham, and Rita S. Tilton. *Secretarial Procedures and Administration* (7th Ed.). Cincinnati: South-Western, 1978.
2. Janis, J. Harold, and Margaret Thompson. *New Standard Reference for Secretaries and Administrative Assistants.* New York: Macmillan, 1972.
3. Nanassy, Louis C., William Selden, and Jo Ann Lee. *Reference Manual for Office Workers.* Beverly Hills: Glencoe Press, 1977.

4. Sabin, William A. *The Gregg Reference Manual* (5th Ed.). New York: Gregg Division/McGraw-Hill, 1977.
5. *Webster's Secretarial Handbook.* Springfield, MA: G. and C. Merriam, 1976.
6. Whalen, Doris H. *The Secretary's Handbook* (3d Ed.). New York: Harcourt Brace Jovanovich, 1978.

Usage
1. Bernstein, Theodore M. *The Careful Writer.* New York: Atheneum, 1973.
2. Follett, Wilson. *Modern American Usage.* New York: Hill and Wang, 1966.
3. Fowler, H. W. *A Dictionary of Modern English Usage* (2d Ed.), revised by Sir Ernest Gowers. London: Oxford University Press, 1965.
4. Newman, Edwin. *A Civil Tongue.* New York: Bobbs-Merrill, 1974.
5. Newman, Edwin. *Strictly Speaking.* New York: Bobbs-Merrill, 1975.
6. Morris, William and Mary. *Harper Dictionary of Contemporary Usage.* New York: Harper & Row, 1975.
7. O'Haure, John. *Gobbledygook Has Gotta Go.* Washington: United States Government Printing Office, 1966.
8. Partridge, Eric. *The Concise Usage and Abusage.* London: Greenwood, 1954.
9. Strunk, William, and E. B. White. *The Elements of Style* (2d Ed.). New York: Macmillan, 1972.
10. Zizzner, William. *On Writing Well.* New York: Harper & Row, 1976.

Suggestions for Dictating

Dictating, particularly for the person who is inexperienced or unaccustomed to organizing business writing orally, may be difficult and time-consuming. Here are some suggestions to help either in dictating to a secretary or in dictating to a machine.

For all dictation:
1. Collect all of the information that you need to include (perhaps your secretary could do a great deal of this) and plan the dictation. You may need to make notes and to outline. Resist writing everything in longhand before you begin dictating. This is a repetition of what has already been discussed, but it is a most important step.
2. Have all of the information and files with each piece of correspondence that you are answering. Be sure that enclosures are readily available. Make any telephone calls and collect all information before you begin dictating.
3. Arrange material in the order in which you wish to dictate. It may be necessary to number items.

For dictation to a secretary:
1. Try to do all of your dictating in one session. If possible, schedule a regular time when you will be free from interruptions—callers, telephone calls, and the like. Schedule a time that is convenient for your secretary as well, probably early enough so that the rush dictation can be finished before the end of the day. Do not try to do too much at one time; both you and your secretary will have trouble concentrating if the dictation session is long.
2. Organize the dictation so that related letters are dictated consecutively.
3. Adjust the speed of your dictation to your secretary. Speak evenly and clearly. Encourage the secretary to ask questions after the dictation is completed. Slow down your speaking if your secretary is having difficulty in keeping up with the dictation. This is not necessarily a reflection upon the ability of the secretary; the average rate of speaking is 135–150 words per minute, and secretaries are employable at 100 words per minute.
4. Try to keep the dictation moving. Constant dictation that is given at a slower speaking rate is actually faster than rapid spurts of dictation that have to be changed, read back, added to, and revised.
5. Provide your secretary with a place where it is easy to write. Contrary to movies and television, secretaries write more easily at desks than when they are standing or writing notes on their laps.
6. Give the secretary the letters or items that you are answering when you have finished dictating. The material is then available for reference as transcription is being done. The item can also be filed along with any related material when it has been answered.
7. Give the secretary any special instructions that are needed. A routine for transcribing should be established, and any unusual requests should be explained. If you want a certain letter to go by registered mail or you want extra copies made, tell your secretary.

APPENDIX 210

Be sure, too, that work standards are set; usually if you demand high standards, that is what you will get. However, the secretary needs to know what your standards are.

8. If you often mark or change transcribed letters before you sign them, try doing some of these things: Give your secretary permission to change awkward or incorrect spots in the transcript—or ask that such spots be questioned before transcribing. Have the secretary do a rough draft before the transcript is typed in final form. Try to listen to yourself as you are dictating. (You know what you want to say but do your sentences convey that meaning?) And don't mail letters with crossed-out words or penned changes; these corrected letters are badly groomed messengers from any office.

For machine dictation:

1. Understand how to use the equipment; study the manual accompanying the machine. You may be dictating over telephone lines; by using a portable dictating unit when you are traveling or at home; or, as in most instances, by using a desk unit in your office.
2. Before you begin the actual dictation, give the transcriber any necessary instructions: a) identify yourself—it may be necessary to include your title and the location of your office; b) tell the transcriber what the message is—memo, letter, report, and so on; c) if there are special instructions such as extra copies, special typing form, directions that the work is confidential (and therefore should be erased immediately after transcribing), or the item is to be sent by special mail service, tell the transcriber what you want.
3. During the dictation enunciate clearly. Your tone of voice should be natural. Eliminate the *ah's, uhh's,* and *you know's*. Try, too, to control outside noises so that the secretary is not confused by them when transcribing. Spell out names and difficult or technical words. Indicate paragraphing, capitalization, and unusual punctuation. Dictate figures very carefully. Give them one by one; that is, *four, zero, two, nine*. Indicate the end of each item and whether there is more dictation to follow. List and describe enclosures that will accompany the transcript. If you have made corrections, indicate where and what they are.

PROOFREADERS' MARKS

INSTRUCTION:	MARK IN MARGIN:	MARK IN TYPE:	CORRECTED TO READ:
Align	‖	Find all errors. ‖Find all errors.	Find all errors. Find all errors.
Capitalize	cap	find all errors.	Find all errors.
Close up space	⌒	Fi nd all errors.	Find all errors.
Delete	ℓ	Find all errors.	Find errors.
Delete and close up space	ℓ⌒	Find all errors.	Find all errors.
Insert apostrophe	⩔	Find Kays errors.	Find Kay's errors.
Insert colon	⊙	Find these errors	Find these errors:
Insert comma	⩓	I found errors errors errors.	I found errors, errors, errors.
Insert em dash	1/M / 1/M	Find and correct all errors.	Find—and correct—all errors.
Insert en dash	1/N	Find 10 15 errors.	Find 10–15 errors.
Insert hyphen	=	error free copy	error-free copy
Insert parentheses	(/)	Find errors page 1.	Find errors (page 1).
Insert period	⊙	Find all errors	Find all errors.
Insert quotation marks	⌄⌄ / ⌄⌄	Find the error fo.	Find the error "fo."
Insert semicolon	⩕;	Find all errors correct all errors.	Find all errors; correct all errors.
Insert space	#	Findall errors.	Find all errors.
Insert indicated material	all	Find errors.	Find all errors.
Let it stand	stet	Find all errors.	Find all errors.
Make lower case	lc	Find All errors.	Find all errors.
Move left	⊏	⊏Find all errors.	Find all errors.
Move right	⊐	Find all errors.	Find all errors.
Run in (no new paragraph)	run in	Find all errors. Correct all errors.	Find all errors. Correct all errors.
Spell out	sp	4 errors	four errors
Start paragraph	¶	Find errors; correct errors.	Find errors; correct errors.
Transpose	tr	Find errors all.	Find all errors.

Frequently Used Abbreviations

This is a list of some commonly used abbreviations. Many of them are found in bibliographies and footnotes.

abbr.	abbreviation	i.e.	id est (that is)
A.D.	anno Domini	id.	idem (the same)
a.k.a.	also known as	Inc.	Incorporated
a.m.	ante meridiem (before noon)	l.c.	lower case (no capitals)
bcc	blind carbon copy	loc. cit.	loco citato (in the place cited)
B.C.	before Christ	Ltd.	Limited
cc	carbon copy	m.	meridiem (noon)
ch.	chapter	ms., mss.	manuscript, manuscripts
c.o.d.	cash on delivery	MDT	Mountain Daylight Time
col.	column	MST	Mountain Standard Time
CDT	Central Daylight Time	OCR	Optical Character Reader
CST	Central Standard Time	op. cit.	opere citato (in the work cited)
EDT	Eastern Daylight Time	p., pp.	page, pages
EST	Eastern Standard Time	par.	paragraph
e.g.	exemplia gratia (for example)	p.m.	post meridiem (afternoon)
et al.	et alii (and others)	PDT	Pacific Daylight Time
et seq.	et sequens (and the following)	PST	Pacific Standard Time
etc.	et cetera (and so forth)	viz.	videlicet (namely)
f., ff.	and following page (pages)	vol.	volume
fig.	figure	ZIP Code	Zoning Improvement Program Code
f.o.b.	free on board		
ibid.	ibidem (in the same place)		

United States Postal Abbreviations

Alabama	AL	Kentucky	KY	Ohio	OH
Alaska	AK	Louisiana	LA	Oklahoma	OK
Arizona	AZ	Maine	ME	Oregon	OR
Arkansas	AR	Maryland	MD	Pennsylvania	PA
California	CA	Massachusetts	MA	Puerto Rico	PR
Colorado	CO	Michigan	MI	Rhode Island	RI
Connecticut	CT	Minnesota	MN	South Carolina	SC
Delaware	DE	Mississippi	MS	South Dakota	SD
District of Columbia	DC	Missouri	MO	Tennessee	TN
Florida	FL	Montana	MT	Texas	TX
Georgia	GA	Nebraska	NE	Utah	UT
Hawaii	HI	Nevada	NV	Vermont	VT
Idaho	ID	New Hampshire	NH	Virginia	VA
Illinois	IL	New Jersey	NJ	Washington	WA
Indiana	IN	New Mexico	NM	West Virginia	WV
Iowa	IA	New York	NY	Wisconsin	WI
Kansas	KS	North Carolina	NC	Wyoming	WY
		North Dakota	ND		

Canadian Postal Abbreviations

Alberta	AB		Nova Scotia	NS
British Columbia	BC		Ontario	ON
Labrador	LB		Prince Edward Island	PE
Manitoba	MB		Quebec	PQ
New Brunswick	NB		Saskatchewan	SK
Newfoundland	NF		Yukon Territory	YT
Northwest Territories	NT			

glossary

GLOSSARY

abbreviation A shortened form of a word or phrase used in writing to represent the complete form.

absolute adjective An adjective that cannot be compared as it represents the highest degree of a quality.

absolute phrase A phrase modifying a sentence or clause as a whole but not joined by a connective to the sentence.

abstract A term that names a quality, state, or idea; necessary to discuss ideas but may not be exact or forceful when writing about specifics.

active voice A verb form that has a direct object and is used to show that the subject is acting.

adjective A part of speech that describes, restricts, or limits a noun or pronoun.

agreement Correspondence in form (number, gender, person) of certain parts of speech with other parts (for example, a subject with its verb or a pronoun with its antecedent).

ambiguity Writing that can be interpreted in more than one way.

antecedent A word or a group of words to which a pronoun refers.

anticipatory subject (expletive) The word *it* or *there* used as a sentence beginning that anticipates the true subject which follows.

antonym A word with a meaning approximately the opposite of another word.

apostrophe (') A mark of punctuation used to show possessive case in nouns and indefinite pronouns, to indicate omission of letters in contractions, and to form plurals of nouns in some instances (figures, letters of the alphabet, and words used as words).

application form A printed business form containing questions that when answered give information enabling businesses to make decisions regarding such matters as credit and hiring.

appositive The placing of a noun or pronoun next to another noun or pronoun so that the second completes or supplements the first.

archaic A word formerly used that has now disappeared from the language.

article A word used before a noun to signal that a certain noun is to follow. There are three articles: *a*, *an* (indefinite) and *the* (definite). Articles are classified as adjectives.

attention line A part of the inside address of a letter that directs the letter to the attention of a specific person or department within an organization.

auxiliary verb A verb helper in a verb phrase. It is always placed before the main verb and indicates such things as voice or tense.

bibliography A list of reference sources (for instance, books, periodicals, newspapers, films, television programs) consulted or quoted in writing.

body The part of the letter containing the message.

brackets ([ ]) A pair of symbols used to enclose a correction or an insert of something other than the writer's own words.

carbon-copy notation The initials *cc* or the words *copy(ies) to* placed below the identification initials on a business letter to show that a carbon copy of that letter is being sent to a person or persons listed after the *cc* notation.

case The change in form of a noun or pronoun to indicate relationship to other words in the sentence. There are three cases: *nominative, objective,* and *possessive*.

clause A group of words that are made up of a subject and a predicate. There are two types of clauses: *independent* and *dependent*.

cliché A word or expression that is overused or out of date.

closing The ending paragraph of a business letter that embodies a courteous goodbye.

collective noun A noun made up of a group or collection of persons or things.

colloquialism Language appropriate in

GLOSSARY

speaking or in informal usage but inappropriate in formal writing.

colon (:) A mark of punctuation used to introduce something that follows, such as listed items or a direct quotation.

comma (,) A mark of punctuation used (1) to separate a single word or group of words from the rest of the sentence or (2) to set off parts of the sentence.

comparison of adjectives and adverbs Changes in the simple form of adjectives or adverbs to show a greater or lesser degree of the characteristic than the adjective or adverb expresses.

comparative degree An adjective and adverb form change used to compare two items. It is formed by adding -er to the positive form, by changing the positive form to another word, or by adding *more* or *less* to the positive form.

complement A noun or adjective completing the meaning of a linking verb and either modifying or renaming the subject. It is also the noun or pronoun that completes the infinitive *to be*.

complex sentence A sentence with one independent clause and one or more dependent clauses.

complimentary close A short courteous phrase used to end a letter.

compound adjective An adjective made up of two or more descriptive words serving as a single adjective and usually connected by hyphens.

compound-complex sentence A sentence with two or more independent clauses plus one or more dependent clauses.

compound noun A noun consisting of two or more words, usually a noun plus qualifying words. It can be written as one or two words, or it can be hyphenated.

compound sentence A sentence made up of two or more independent clauses.

concrete A term naming a person or thing that can be sensed—seen, touched, smelled, heard, or tasted.

conjunction A connecting word that introduces or connects clauses or joins series of words, phrases, or clauses.

conjunctive adverb A conjunction that connects independent clauses and shows a relationship between them.

contraction A word or words shortened by omitting or combining some of the letters or sounds.

coordinate conjunction A conjunction that connects elements of equal grammatical rank, such as dependent clause to dependent clause or infinitive phrase to infinitive phrase. The five principal coordinate conjunctions are *and, but, or, nor, for*.

correlative conjunction A pair of words that connect elements of equal grammatical rank, for example, *either/or* and *neither/nor*.

dangling modifier A modifier that is placed in the sentence so that it cannot reasonably apply to the word it is intended to modify, or there is nothing in the sentence that it can modify.

dash (—) A mark of punctuation used to indicate abruptness either in thought or in setting off parenthetical elements.

data sheet (résumé) A summary of personal qualifications for employment.

deductive A term derived from logic and applied to business writing to mean that the point or conclusion of the letter or report is presented first, followed by the supporting facts or details.

dependent clause A clause that cannot stand by itself and is dependent for its meaning on some other part of the sentence. There are three types: *adjective, adverb,* and *noun*.

direct address (nominative of address) A noun or pronoun used to address a person (or object) in speaking or writing.

direct mail A form of promotional advertising, usually consisting of a packet containing a sales letter, a brochure, and a reply form. The packet is sent in large quantities, usually by third-class mail.

direct object (object of a transitive verb) A noun or pronoun that receives the action of a verb; it answers the question *whom* or *what* about the verb.

direct quotation A passage taken from a written work or from direct speech and that must appear exactly as it was written or spoken.

double negative Two negative statements in the same sentence or clause but used to express a single negative.

dysphemism Substitution of a disparaging word or expression for an agreeable or ordinary term.

ellipsis (. . .) A clearly understood omission of words from a sentence. Spaced periods are used to show an elliptical omission in direct quotations.

enclosure notation A notation placed at the end of a letter to indicate that something is enclosed in the envelope with the letter.

equivocation Language that is intentionally ambiguous or evasive.

euphemism Substitution of an inoffensive word or expression for one that might be considered offensive.

exclamation point (!) A mark of punctuation used after sentences or expressions to show strong emotion.

expletive See *anticipatory subject*.

footnote A note placed at the bottom of a page of manuscript to add a comment or to give a reference to a source.

full-block letter A business-letter style in which every line of writing is begun at the left margin.

future tense A verb form used to express action that will take place in the future. The future tense uses *shall* or *will* as an auxiliary.

gender A form of a noun or pronoun that indicates sex or the absence of sex.

gerund A verb form ending in *-ing* that functions as a noun, never as a verb.

gobbledegook Language that is wordy and therefore unclear, usually used to describe bureaucratic writing.

homonym One of two or more words with the same sound and spelling but different meanings.

hyphen (-) A mark of punctuation between parts of a hyphenated compound word or between syllables of a word divided at the end of a line.

identification initials A notation placed at the end of a business letter to indicate who dictated the letter and who typed it.

idiom An expression that is grammatically acceptable even though it cannot be translated literally or may violate established rules of grammar.

illiterate A word or expression corrupted into an incorrect form.

imperative (mood) The form of a verb that gives a command or makes a request.

indefinite pronoun (adjective pronoun) A pronoun that does not name any particular individual or thing.

indefinite reference Use of a pronoun that does not clearly refer to its antecedent.

independent (main) clause A group of related words containing both a subject and a predicate and able to stand by itself as a simple sentence.

indicative (mood) The form of a verb that states a fact or asks a question.

inductive A term derived from logic and applied to business writing to mean that supporting facts or details of a letter or report are presented first, followed by the conclusion.

infinitive A verb form consisting of *to* plus the present tense and functioning as an adjective, an adverb, or a noun—never as a verb.

inside address A part of a business letter that indicates the name and address of the addressee.

intensive (reflexive) pronoun A pronoun formed by adding the suffix *-self* (singular) or *-selves* (plural) to a personal pronoun in order to express emphasis.

interjection A part of speech that expresses strong emotion in the form of an exclamation.

interoffice memorandum A business form used for messages within a company.

intransitive verb A verb that does not require an object to complete its meaning. It describes the subject or expresses a condition or state of being.

irregular verb A verb that does not follow standard rules for forming its past tense and past participle—that is, by adding *-d* or *-ed* to the present tense.

italics A style of printing type used to set off a word or passage distinctively within a text. In typing italics are indicated by underscoring.

jargon Specialized terms of those in the same trade, profession, industry, or organization.

letterhead Stationery printed with a person's or firm's name and address, and—sometimes—the telephone number and cable address.

linking (copulative) verb An intransitive verb that needs a predicate nominative or predicate adjective to complete it; it relates the subject to the subject complement.

mailing notation A notation on a letter and its envelope indicating that the letter is being sent by special postal service.

malaprop (malapropism) Humorous misuse of a word.

manuscript A typewritten version of a report, book, article, etc., usually typed according to specifications and often intended for publication.

mixed punctuation A business-letter style of punctuation that places a colon after the salutation and a comma after the complimentary close.

modified-block letter A business-letter style in which the date and the closing lines are placed at the right margin or are centered; paragraphs may be blocked or indented.

modifier Any word or word group functioning as an adjective or an adverb.

mood The form of a verb that indicates the manner of action expressed by that verb. There are three moods: *indicative*, *imperative*, and *subjunctive*.

nominative (subjective) case The case form of a noun or pronoun showing it as the subject of a sentence or a clause or as a word identified with the subject (such as a predicate nominative).

nonrestrictive modifier A modifying phrase or clause not essential to the meaning of a sentence. The modifier is usually set off by commas.

noun A part of speech that names a thing, person, animal, place, quality, idea, or action.

noun clause A dependent or subordinate clause used as a noun.

number The form of a noun, pronoun, demonstrative adjective, or verb that indicates whether the word is singular or plural.

object of a preposition A noun or pronoun joined to the sentence by a preposition.

objective (accusative) case The case form of a noun or pronoun indicating that it is the direct object of a verb, the subject of any infinitive, or the object of a preposition.

obsolete A word or expression no longer used.

open punctuation A business-letter style

of punctuation in which no punctuation is placed after the salutation or complimentary close.

opening (introduction) The first paragraph of a business letter, usually indicating the purpose of the letter.

outline A plan for writing; an outline may be short, consisting of only three or four points, or it may run several pages long and consist of several levels of subordination.

parallelism In a sentence, the use of two or more identical grammatical units, usually connected by coordinate conjunctions, to express contrasted or similar ideas.

parentheses (( )) A pair of punctuation marks used to mark off explanatory or qualifying remarks within a sentence.

part of speech Classification of any word by its function in the sentence.

participle A verb form that ends either in -*ing* (present participle) or in -*ed* (past participle) and that functions as an adjective—never as a verb.

passive voice A verb characteristic used to show that the subject is receiving the action of the verb. It consists of a form of the verb *be* plus the past participle.

past tense A verb form indicating that action has already taken place.

perfect tense A verb form that combines a form of *have* with the past participle to indicate action or state of being that is completed at the time of speaking or at a time spoken of.

period (.) A mark of punctuation indicating a full stop. It is placed at the end of declarative sentences, indirect questions, abbreviations, and other statements considered to be complete.

person The form of a verb or a pronoun that indicates whether a person is speaking (first person), spoken to (second person), or spoken about (third person).

personal pronoun A pronoun that refers to persons (or animals) and that indicates by form whether the person is speaking, spoken to, or spoken about.

phrasal preposition Two or more words used as a preposition.

phrase A sequence of two or more related words not having a subject and a predicate but functioning as a single part of speech.

plural A form of a noun, pronoun, or verb indicating more than one.

poetic A shortened word or term found in poetry but not in other writing.

positive degree The simple form of an adjective or an adverb.

possessive (genitive) case The form of nouns and pronouns that shows ownership.

postscript A message added at the end of a letter below the signature.

predicate The part of a sentence or clause that expresses something about the subject; it consists of the verb plus any complements, objects, or modifiers.

predicate adjective An adjective that comes after a linking verb and describes the subject.

predicate nominative (predicate noun, subject complement) A noun or pronoun that comes after a form of the verb *be* and renames the subject.

prefix A syllable or two placed at the beginning of a word in order to change the meaning of the word.

preposition A single word or a group of words used to connect a noun or pronoun to some other word in the sentence.

prepositional phrase A phrase consisting of a preposition, its object, and any modifiers.

present tense A verb form indicating action that is taking place now. It also indicates general or permanent truths, or habitual action.

principal parts of a verb The forms of any verb from which the various tenses are derived. The principal parts are *present*, *past*, and *past participle*.

progressive verb A verb phrase made up of the auxiliary—a form of *be*—and the present participle. It expresses continuous action or state of being.

pronoun A word used for or in place of a noun.

proofreaders' marks Marks made on manuscripts or printed proof indicating changes, deletions, or additions made in the text.

proper adjective An adjective derived from a proper noun and usually capitalized.

proper noun A noun that designates a particular person, place, or thing. A proper noun is always capitalized.

question mark (?) A punctuation mark that asks a direct question when placed at the end of a sentence or that shows doubt or approximation when placed in parentheses.

quotation marks (" ") Punctuation marks used to enclose written or spoken quotations.

rare A word not commonly used and for which there are better synonyms.

redundancy Writing that is wordy and therefore unclear.

reflexive (intensive) pronoun A pronoun formed by adding the suffix *-self* (singular) or *-selves* (plural) to a personal pronoun and used to reflect verb action toward a noun or pronoun already used.

regional (local) A word or expression used in one area or region of the country rather than throughout the country.

relative clause A dependent adjective clause introduced by a relative pronoun—*that, which, what,* or a form of *who*—that refers to the antecedent of the relative pronoun.

relative pronoun A pronoun used to join a dependent adjective (relative) clause to the antecedent of that relative pronoun. The relative pronouns are *who* (*whom* or *whose*), *which, that, what, whoever, whomever, whatever*.

restrictive modifier A modifying phrase or clause that is essential to the meaning of the sentence.

run-on (fused) sentence A sentence in which two sentences are connected without punctuation and with the result that the meaning is obscure.

salutation A part of a letter that serves as the greeting, as "Dear Mr. Lee."

semicolon (;) A mark of punctuation used to separate clauses of a compound sentence, items in a series containing internal punctuation, explanations, and enumerations from the rest of the sentence.

sentence A group of related words that constitute a complete thought, which may be a statement, a question, a command, or an exclamation.

shifted (mixed) construction A sentence that begins with one kind of grammatical construction and incorrectly shifts to a different kind.

signature A part of a letter that includes the penwritten signature of the person writing the letter and, in a business letter, the typed name and title of the signer.

Simplified letter A business-letter style in which every line is blocked at the left margin, and the salutation and complimentary close are omitted.

singular A form of a noun, pronoun, or verb showing that the word is single.

slang A word or expression that has not been accepted as standard usage. It may be peculiar to a group and of temporary usage, and often appears spontaneously.

subject The person or object about which something in the sentence is said or asked.

subject line A part of the body of a business letter that tells what the letter is about.

subjunctive (mood) The verb form indicating wish, possibility, or doubt. It changes for certain forms of the verb *be* and in the first and third person singular.

subordinate (dependent) clause A clause that cannot stand by itself and is dependent for its meaning upon some other part of the sentence. There are three kinds: *adjective, adverb,* and *noun.*

subordinate conjunction A conjunction that connects a dependent clause to an independent clause.

suffix A syllable added at the end of a word and that alters the meaning or function of that word.

superlative degree An adjective or adverb form that compares three or more items. It is formed by adding *-est* to the positive, by changing the positive to another word, or by placing *most* or *least* before the positive.

synonym A word with a meaning similar to that of another word.

syntax The grammatical arrangement of words into phrases, clauses, and sentences.

technical (field) A word or expression that is specialized and has to do with technical, industrial, professional, or scientific areas.

tense A verb form that expresses distinctions of time.

transitive verb A verb requiring an object to complete its meaning.

trite Quality of a word or expression that is overused or out of date.

verb A part of speech that makes a statement, asks a question, or gives a command.

verb phrase A phrase consisting of a main verb and one or more auxiliaries. The auxiliary verb or verbs are always first, followed by the main verb.

verbal A verb form used as one of three parts of speech—adjective, noun, or adverb.

voice The verb characteristic used to show whether the subject is acting or receiving an action. The two voices are *active* and *passive.*

exercises

EXERCISES

EXERCISE 1 KINDS OF SENTENCES

1. Identify the parts of these sentences by drawing one line under the simple subject and two lines under the verbs in all clauses.
2. Label the sentences as *simple, complex, compound,* or *compound-complex* in the blank to the right.

Example: <u>I</u> <u>have read</u> the report many times, but <u>I</u> still <u>do</u> not <u>understand</u> it.   _compound_

1. Mr. Jones and Mr. Scott are out of the office for the rest of the week. _____
2. Do you think that the new computer will help us? _____
3. I cannot find the Jackson or Davis files, but I think that they are only mislaid and not lost. _____
4. Many of the secretaries who work in the word-processing center have received promotions. _____
5. The new system for ordering equipment seems to be a big improvement over the old one. _____
6. By using electronic equipment, the company was able to do more work, to complete it more quickly, and to cut operating costs considerably. _____
7. My employer reported that both sales and profits for our company rose 15 percent in the last quarter. _____
8. Although the windows of the office building were shattered by the explosion, no one was hurt in the accident. _____
9. The windows of the office building were shattered by the explosion; however, no one was hurt in the accident. _____
10. Can you complete the letters and mail them by this afternoon? _____

EXERCISE 2 SYNTAX: WORD ORDER

Each sentence below contains all of the necessary elements, but some of the information is placed so that the sentence does not convey a precise or intended meaning, or else the emphasis is on the wrong part of the sentence. Rewrite the sentences as necessary so that the meaning is precise and the emphasis is on the important part of the sentence.

Example: Return the enclosed card immediately if you wish to receive a free sample of Soapo Shampoo in the postage-paid envelope.

<u>A free sample of Soapo Shampoo will be sent you imme-</u>

diately when you return the enclosed card in the postage-paid envelope.

1. When we receive your check, your order for woolen fabrics in the amount of $275 will be shipped.

2. Because our factory was severely damaged by fire and has not been in operation for three weeks, we are unable to ship your order for auto parts; and it will be three months before we can do so.

3. If you need the order for auto parts that you placed recently, we suggest that you order from Jones Supply Company as we had a severe fire recently in our factory and are unable to fill any orders for three months.

4. We have received your order and are shipping by Mountain Auto Freight the paint in the amount of $279.60 next Friday, August 9.

5. We do not know what has happened to your recent order, which you inquired about in your letter of March 12 and which we shipped on March 5; but we are duplicating the order and shipping it by air express tomorrow, March 18.

EXERCISE 3 **TRANSITIVE/INTRANSITIVE VERBS**

1. Draw one line under the verbs and two lines under any direct objects in these sentences.
2. Label each sentence *transitive* or *intransitive*.

Example: Read the letter carefully before signing it.   transitive

1. The soprano sang off-key throughout the entire performance.
2. The soprano sang three songs before the intermission.

EXERCISES **226**

3. Eric put his coffee cup in the desk drawer. _____
4. The coffee cup has been in the desk drawer for more than a week. _____
5. Do you believe the story about the energy crisis? _____
6. The door of the vault has been open all day. _____
7. The driver was able to steer the bus off the freeway. _____
8. It seems difficult to type on a manual typewriter. _____
9. Work in our office begins at nine o'clock. _____
10. I begin work each day at nine o'clock. _____
11. The traffic light has not been working properly all day. _____
12. We are sorry about the error. _____
13. The children played hide-and-seek on the playground. _____
14. The children played from eight in the morning until two in the afternoon. _____
15. The small boat remained upright throughout the storm. _____

EXERCISE 4 **ACTION/BE VERBS**

1. Underline all be verbs in these sentences.
2. Substitute action verbs for the be verbs and write the new sentences in the blanks.

Example: It is my opinion that the typewriter has been repaired.

I think that the typewriter has been repaired.

1. He is someone who can accomplish a great deal in a short period of time.

   _____

2. There were several pages in Mr. Lee's report on letter writing skills.

   _____

3. It is important to read the instructions before using the machine.

   _____

4. We have been in business manufacturing fine fabrics for over a hundred years.

   _____

5. General Motors is the largest producer of automobiles in the United States.

   _____

6. It is our plan to open a new branch store in Denver.

   _____

EXERCISES

7. It is our expectation that the store will sell both men's and women's clothing.

8. There are several methods of handling the computer transaction.

9. It is hoped that the new typewriters will help the secretaries in their work.

10. Here is our check for $500 in payment of your statement.

EXERCISE 5 **ACTIVE/PASSIVE VOICE**

1. Underline the passive-voice verbs in these sentences.
2. Change those verbs to active voice and write the new sentences in the blanks.

Example: Your order for office supplies has been received, and it will be shipped immediately.

We are shipping your order for office supplies immediately.

1. Our suggestions were made to the Board of Directors, but no action has been taken.

2. Your statement for July has been checked; a copy of it is enclosed.

3. The error in addition is called to your attention.

4. A complete check of all of the figures was made by Mr. Fisher, our accountant.

5. These wool suits have been made by Superior Clothiers for over fifty years.

6. Mr. Wilson's report was sent to the president for his approval.

7. Your attention is called to the many advantages of using the EZ Typewriter.

8. The plans for your new building will be carefully studied by Mr.

EXERCISES 228

Allen, one of our architects; and any needed corrections will be made by him.

9. Mr. Carson's resignation was submitted to the Personnel Division last Friday.

10. Judy was asked by the president to type the report.

EXERCISE 6 VERB SHIFTS: TENSE, VOICE, MOOD

Find any verb shifts in these sentences; then rewrite the sentences to eliminate the shifts.

Example: The men's clothing department is on the third floor of the store, and the women's was on the fifth.

<u>The men's clothing department is on the third floor of the store, and the women's is on the fifth.</u>

1. During the drive Mr. Jay talked about the problems of traffic safety as the driver of the car breaks the speed limit.

2. If I were you and if I was offered the job, I should accept it immediately.

3. The mystery story tells how the detective finds the body, discovers the motive for the crime, and exposed the killer.

4. After the job interview, Linda called me and asks for a letter of recommendation.

5. If this information concerning inflation be true and if prices continue to rise, salaries will not be adequate.

6. Open the shutters and then you can see the parade in the street.

EXERCISES   **229**

   7. Susan unlocked the office at eight, but the doors were locked at five by the office supervisor.

   _____

   _____

   8. The members of the union signed the contract, but it was not approved by many of the members.

   _____

   _____

   9. Mrs. Terry said that she needed my typewriter and she asked that I should use another.

   _____

   _____

   10. I do not understand the instructions, and I wanted to get further clarification.

   _____

   _____

EXERCISE 7 **SINGULAR/PLURAL: NOUNS/PRONOUNS**

   Indicate in the first blank whether the following nouns and pronouns are singular or plural; then give the singular form if the word is plural or the plural form if the word is singular. If there is no singular or plural form, write the word <u>none</u> in the second blank.

	Singular/Plural	Other Form
Example: I	singular	we
1. hunch		
2. restaurant		
3. choices		
4. you		
5. body		
6. synopses		
7. everyone		
8. hoof		
9. I.O.U.		
10. teeth		
11. ratio		
12. zoo		
13. losses		
14. comedies		
15. proviso		
16. children		

EXERCISES

17. M.D.'s _____ _____
18. staff _____ _____
19. commander in chief _____ _____
20. shelf _____ _____

EXERCISE 8 **POSSESSIVES: NOUNS/PRONOUNS**

Fill in the blanks with the singular possessive and the plural possessive of the following nouns and pronouns. If there is no singular or plural form for the word, write <u>none</u> in the appropriate blank.

	Singular Possessive	Plural Possessive
Example: woman	woman's	women's
1. week		
2. child		
3. you		
4. someone else		
5. attorney		
6. sheriff		
7. nurse		
8. hero		
9. lady		
10. railroad		
11. day		
12. me		
13. watchmaker		
14. traveler		
15. nobody		
16. girl		
17. man		
18. dentist		
19. stockholder		
20. Indian		

EXERCISE 9 **AGREEMENT: RELATIVE/INDEFINITE PRONOUNS**

Underline the correct word in each set of parentheses.

Example: One of the girls left (<u>her</u>, their) pen(s) on my desk.

1. All of the items on the agenda (is, are) to be discussed at the next board meeting; (it, they) must be voted on at this meeting.
2. Either Jane or Linda will lend you (her, their) car.
3. I read one of the books that (is, are) on reserve in the library.
4. Each of the men on the swimming team (has, have) a locker for (his, their) clothing.
5. Bill asked for one of the new typewriters that (is, are) available.

EXERCISES   231

6. Did anyone forget to sign (his or her, their) check?
7. We watched one of the television programs that (is, are) new this fall.
8. Our company is building (its, their) reputation on quality products.
9. If any one of the women in our office needs help, (she, they) can ask Miss Jones, the supervisor, for assistance.
10. Rogers and Company recently started a retirement program for (its, their) employees.

EXERCISE 10 **AGREEMENT: SUBJECT/VERB**

Underline the correct word in each set of parentheses.

Example: One of my friends (has, have) a new job in New York.

1. A good secretary along with a good dictionary (is, are) an unbeatable combination.
2. A number of errors (has, have) been found.
3. The town council (meets, meet) every Thursday evening.
4. Either the secretary or one of the typists (is, are) handling all telephone calls.
5. Over half of the files (was, were) lost in the fire.
6. Neither Mr. Lewis nor the salesmen (is, are) in the office today.
7. My employer, as well as the president and general manager, (seems, seem) pleased with the results of the sale.
8. Not one of the books (has, have) information about word processing.
9. The analyses of the urban problems (is, are) many and varied.
10. Many a man and woman (votes, vote) in each election.

EXERCISE 11 **INDEFINITE REFERENCE**

1. Underline any pronouns that do not have easily recognizable antecedents.
2. Write the correct sentence in the blank.

Example: I do not want to take the course at eight from Mr. Smith. This makes it difficult to plan my program.

Because I do not want to take the course at eight from Mr. Smith, I am having difficulty in planning my program.

1. Mr. Williams told Mr. Davis that he could not do the job.

2. The main problem with most people who grow African violets is that they stop blooming.

EXERCISES 232

3. The library is not open on Saturdays or Sundays. This causes many problems.

4. They predict that next winter will be cold.

5. Mr. Roberts asked for the report from the sales manager, who did not know where he could find it.

6. Mary told Janet that her typing was full of errors.

7. The Second National Bank does not open until ten and has no night deposit facilities. This makes it difficult for the restaurant to deposit the night's receipts.

8. The president asked the members of the organization to meet Monday afternoon to consider all of the items on the agenda. This is impossible.

9. To keep lettuce fresh, put your head in a plastic bag and store it in the refrigerator.

10. After reading David's proposal for increasing sales and hearing Bill's objections to the plan, I agreed with him.

EXERCISE 12 **NOUN/PRONOUN SHIFTS: SUBJECT/PERSON**

Find any noun or pronoun shifts in these sentences; then rewrite the sentences to eliminate the shifts.

Example: All employees receive ten days of sick leave each year; you are entitled to full pay when you are absent for any illness.

All employees receive ten days of sick leave each year; they are entitled to full pay when they are absent for any illness.

EXERCISES 233

1. Our sales representatives call on companies in many California cities; companies in Nevada and Arizona are also called upon.

2. Mr. Perry said that he was leaving and would I sign the letter and mail it.

3. One cannot be sensitive to criticism when you are running for public office.

4. To set off parenthetical expressions, you should use a pair of commas.

5. Full-time students must attend all credit classes regularly; but non-credit classes may be attended irregularly by auditing students.

EXERCISE 13 **PLACEMENT OF MODIFIERS**

1. Underline any misplaced or dangling modifiers in these sentences.
2. Rewrite the sentences so that modifiers are correctly placed.

Example: The city's fountain of health, hailed for its curative powers for generations, was declared polluted yesterday by the city government.

Yesterday the city government declared the fountain of health, hailed for its curative powers for generations, to be polluted.

1. The defendant, who was wearing Levis and a red-checked shirt, sat flanked by three attorneys with a pipe cleaner throughout most of the hearing.

2. Some twenty groups are asking for pieces of George Moneybag's multimillion-dollar fortune left in a vaguely written will that he penned after his death on April 7.

EXERCISES

3. Davis doesn't feel self-conscious about wearing the big black hat on his city walks given him by friends as a joke.

4. The golf course is beautiful where the match is being held.

5. The child only ate the dessert.

6. Rusted by the rain, the man was unable to unlock the door.

7. Not being able to eat all of my dinner, the dog received an extra meal.

8. The long plane trip passed quickly, reading a book and watching a movie.

9. While waiting for the light to change, the fast-moving truck splashed water on me.

10. The notice attracted his attention on the bulletin board.

EXERCISE 14 PREPOSITIONS

A. Substitute one-word prepositions for the phrasal prepositions.

Example: in the matter of   <u>in, about</u>

1. prior to _____
2. in the event of _____
3. subsequent to _____
4. with regard to _____
5. inasmuch as _____
6. in the course of _____
7. after the conclusion of _____
8. on the part of _____

B. Underline the correct word or phrase in each set of parentheses.

Example: We wrote you recently (on the part of, <u>for</u>) our client, John Day.

1. I did not differ (with, from) his proposed plan, only (with, from) his procedures.

EXERCISES 235

2. He found that he was equal (to, for) the emergency.
3. She said that she is in search (for, of) the perfect job!
4. The defense attorneys agreed (to, with) a settlement, but they could not agree (to, with) the plaintiff concerning the amount.
5. Now that Mr. Ray is retired, he is free (from, of) all responsibility.

C. Cross out any unnecessary prepositions in the sentences.

Example: Would you type ~~up~~ a copy for the files?

1. When will you begin on the work?
2. Call me up when the work is finished.
3. Where is your car at?
4. The roof blew off of the house during the hurricane.
5. Where did Mr. King go to?

EXERCISE 15 PARALLEL CONSTRUCTION

1. Underline the coordinate and correlative conjunctions in these sentences.
2. Correct any errors in parallelism by rewriting the sentences.

Example: Margaret is a pretty girl with an attractive smile <u>and</u> she has blue eyes.
Margaret is a pretty girl with an attractive smile and blue eyes.

1. Mr. Wilson asked me where the meeting would be held and would I plan to attend.

2. Raise your hand when you have finished the assignment and then you should bring your paper to the instructor.

3. I want him either to take care of the matter or I suggest that it be transferred to another sales representative.

4. I should like to remind you that your insurance premium which covers both your automobile and your home, is now due and suggesting that you send your check for $375 immediately.

EXERCISES   **236**

5. The news reporter spent months with the presidential candidate, in densely populated urban areas, in sparsely populated rural communities, and where there were many people in the suburbs.

   _____
   _____

6. Our hotel can give you attractive rooms, low daily rates, and our dining room is excellent.

   _____

7. I finished the report by working both in the office and while staying at home.

   _____

8. Mrs. Martin said that either she would pay the bill or return the merchandise.

   _____

9. The CPA examinations were given on Thursday afternoon, Friday morning and afternoon, and on Saturday morning.

   _____

10. No carrying charges will be added to your account if:
    1. You pay each monthly statement within 15 days of the billing date.
    2. There is no unpaid balance from the previous billing period.
    3. Any items about which you have questions are reported to our Credit Department within 15 days of the billing date.

    _____
    _____
    _____
    _____

EXERCISE 16   READER/<u>YOU</u> EMPHASIS

1. Underline all first-person pronouns in these sentences.
2. Rewrite any sentences that are not reader-oriented.

   Example: <u>We</u> are pleased to open one of <u>our</u> revolving credit accounts for you.
   A revolving credit account has been opened for you.

   1. I hope that my application for the position of secretary will be considered by your company.

   _____

EXERCISES 237

2. We are happy to enclose our check for $25, which represents an overpayment on your account.

_____

3. I'd appreciate your sending me this information so that I can include it in our next report.

_____

4. I know that you will enjoy shopping in our store.

_____

5. We are sure that our service and products are superior to any others on the market.

_____

6. We are so convinced that our new Soapo Shampoo is the best on the market that we are enclosing a coupon good for 25 cents on the purchase of any size of Soapo Shampoo.

_____

_____

7. We want to thank you for buying the all-new Speedo Bicycle.

_____

8. I know that our service is the best in the area. Drive in to our new gasoline station and let us service your car and fill its tank with gasoline.

_____

_____

9. I am sure that I can fill the position of accountant with your firm.

_____

10. We want to tell you about our new real estate office. We have been in business for twenty-five years; we have six branch offices; we are open seven days a week; we can show you property in any part of the city. Now we have an office in your neighborhood.

_____

_____

_____

EXERCISE 17   GETTING TO THE POINT IMMEDIATELY

Rewrite these openings so that they get to the point immediately.

Example: Thank you for writing us for information about our new delivery service. We have been in business for six months, and already our customers are finding the service is de-

EXERCISES 238

pendable and economical. A brochure giving complete details about our service is enclosed. Please call us at 123-4567 should you have additional questions.

A brochure giving complete details of our new delivery service is enclosed. Thank you for requesting this information. Should you have additional questions, please call us at 123-4567.

1. In regard to your letter of March 25, we cannot find a record of your order for rug shampoo. We are very sorry. We have searched all of our files to no avail. Would you please send us a copy of your original order; and when we receive it, we'll rush it to you by special delivery. Again, we regret this error.

2. Thank you for requesting a copy of our brochure, *Converting to the Metric System*. We are glad to comply with your request and will see that a copy is mailed to you within the week.

3. This is in reply to your letter of April 15 in which you inquired about the dealer in your area who handles Acme Clock Radios. We are happy to supply this information. At the present time, the dealer who handles our products exclusively in your area is J. Rogers & Son, 211 Main Street, Greenfield, ID 83700.

4. We are sorry that you have not received your order for an X-L Pocket Calculator. The order was sent two weeks ago by parcel post, but mails seem to be slow lately—perhaps it is because of seasonal delivery problems. If the calculator has not arrived by the time you receive this letter, either call us collect or write us; and we will send you another calculator immediately.

5. We wonder if you still have available No. 876 Marking Pens. We placed an order for them two years ago, but we have now used all

of them. We liked them very much. If they are available, would you please send us 4 dozen and bill our company.

_____

_____

EXERCISE 18 **OVERUSED AND OUT-OF-DATE EXPRESSIONS**

Substitute acceptable expressions for the overused and out-of-date terms below. If there is no substitute, place a check mark in the blank.

Example: at the present writing   <u>now</u>

1. lion's share _____
2. as the crow flies _____
3. at the present time _____
4. face the music _____
5. among other things _____
6. leave no stone unturned _____
7. conspicuous by its absence _____
8. first and foremost _____
9. high and dry _____
10. in less than no time _____
11. spell out _____
12. one and the same _____
13. part and parcel _____
14. the likes of which _____
15. flesh and blood _____
16. the long and short of it _____
17. see how the land lies _____
18. every effort is being made _____
19. not worth the paper it's written on _____
20. the more the merrier _____

EXERCISE 19 **REDUNDANT AND REPETITIOUS EXPRESSIONS**

Substitute expressions that are less repetitious and redundant. If there is no substitute, place a check mark in the blank.

Example: final outcome   <u>outcome</u>

1. on a few occasions _____
2. in a majority of instances _____

EXERCISES   **240**

   3. in a number of cases _____
   4. advance warning _____
   5. any and all _____
   6. bring (put, come) to an end _____
   7. among other things _____
   8. null and void _____
   9. equally as _____
10. when and if _____
11. unless and until _____
12. in terms of _____
13. small in size _____
14. few (fewer) in number _____
15. still and all _____
16. quoted as saying _____
17. for the simple reason that _____
18. up until _____
19. joined together _____
20. repeat the same _____

EXERCISE 20   WORDS AND TERMS TO BE AVOIDED

These sentences contain euphemisms, insincere language, negative terms, and inaccurate or incorrectly used expressions. Underline any incorrect expressions; then write the correct sentences in the blanks. (There may be more than one error in a sentence.)

Example: Joe made a <u>colossal</u> mistake when he signed the letter without reading it.
             <u>Joe made a serious mistake when he signed the letter without reading it.</u>

1. The salesman told a little fib when he said that the ten-year-old car was a late model.

   _____

2. Because you handled the XY Camera carelessly, it is impossible for us to accept the return of it for credit.

   _____

3. Although job-wise it seemed to be a good opportunity, you never should of accepted the position.

   _____

EXERCISES 241

4. The receptionist and/or the secretary can't seem to handle all of the telephone calls.

   _____

5. We should finalize all of the plans for the fall sales campaign by July 1.

   _____

6. Only a good customer like you can appreciate the tremendous bargains in our October sale.

   _____

7. You neglected to make the September payment on your account.

   _____

8. You failed to return the warranty card when you purchased the television set; as you no doubt know, this failure on your part makes the warranty void.

   _____
   _____

9. His reason for not working is that he is temporarily between jobs.

   _____

10. We have stepped up production so that we can bring you these stunning dresses at absolutely sensational prices.

    _____
    _____

EXERCISE 21 CONFUSED AND INCORRECTLY USED WORDS

Select the correct word from those in the parentheses.

Example: Please (advise, tell) us where we can call you.

                    tell

1. The company asked for a(n) (disinterested, uninterested) person to be an arbiter in the labor dispute.   _____
2. Please (advise, tell) us when we can deliver your new range.   _____
3. He spent the (balance, rest) of the day finding the error in addition.   _____
4. I thought the forecast said that it is (apt, liable, likely) to rain today.   _____
5. Mrs. Lester (implied, inferred) that there had been some mishandling of the funds.   _____
6. I do not know the (party, person) who took the message.   _____

EXERCISES 242

7. Many familiar expressions are really (quotations, quotes) from Shakespeare. _____
8. We were not (conscience, conscious) that there had been an earthquake until we read about it in the newspaper. _____
9. Jones & Company cannot fill orders quickly (as, like) the Smith Company did. _____
10. The (continual, continuous) showing of the movie lasted throughout the night. _____
11. The latest (addition, edition) of the book will be a real (addition, edition) to any library. _____
12. This new ruling will not (affect, effect) our firm in any way. _____
13. The job is more difficult (than, then) I had expected. _____
14. Mr. Thompson is an (eminent, imminent) authority on contracts. _____
15. I did not (choose, chose) this typewriter; it was in the office when I began working for the company. _____

EXERCISE 22 OPENING SENTENCES

Rewrite these opening sentences so that they get to the point quickly and say only what is necessary.

Example: As you requested in your letter of January 13, we are sending you a brochure describing our all-new ABC Typewriter.
Here is the brochure that you requested and that describes our all-new ABC Typewriter.

1. In regard to your letter of March 5, we do not have any secretarial openings in our firm at the present time. If you are still interested, we suggest that you write us again in two months.

_____

_____

2. Thank you for placing an order for Excellent Typewriter Ribbons with us. We will ship them within the week.

_____

3. This is in reply to your letter of January 15 in which you inquired about the price of our X-L Calculator. At the present time the price including shipping charges is $49.50; this does not include sales tax.

_____

_____

EXERCISES 243

4. The booklet, *Care of the Typewriter,* that you requested in your letter of June 4 is, unfortunately, temporarily out of print; but we will see that you get a copy just as soon as we receive a new printing.

5. We are happy to send you a refund for the amount of the overcharge on your account. Enclosed is our check for $35.

EXERCISE 23   CLOSING SENTENCES

Rewrite these closing sentences.

Example: So pleased that you could accept our invitation to speak to our group.
<u>We are happy that you will be our guest speaker on January 7, for we think that you will have many interesting things to tell us.</u>

1. With best wishes for the holiday season, I am . . . Sincerely yours,

2. We hope that we will receive an order from you soon.

3. We look forward to hearing from you.

4. Glad you can attend the meeting.

5. It was good to receive your order, and we hope we'll receive future orders from you as well.

EXERCISE 24   APPLICATION LETTER WRITING

Rewrite these opening and closing sentences from application letters.

Example: I should like to be considered for a position with your company. I can do almost any kind of office work.
<u>Would you please consider my application for the position of secretary that was advertised in Friday's News.</u>

EXERCISES **244**

1. I am answering your advertisement in last night's paper for a clerk-typist. When may I come for an interview?

   _____

2. Do you have any vacancies for a secretary? I am a top-notch secretary and am presently available to begin work immediately.

   _____

3. Call me anytime for an interview so that I can prove to you in person that I am the one for your company.

   _____

4. Please send me an application blank; then when you have looked over my qualifications, I'm sure you'll realize what a valuable employee I would be.

   _____
   _____

5. Just call me or drop me a line when you would like to see me to talk about my working for your company.

   _____
   _____

EXERCISE 25   **PUNCTUATION: END OF THE SENTENCE**

Supply any periods, exclamation points, and question marks needed by the following sentences. Circle any punctuation marks not needed. (Some of the sentences may be correct.)

Example: I wonder whether he heard my question(?).

1. That is the correct form, isn't it
2. I don't know the answer to that question
3. Do you know where Mr. Lacey is
4. Congratulations   You have won first prize in the national contest
5. Bill asked whether I was taking my vacation in July or August
6. Lock the door when you leave the office
7. Are you planning to leave before I return
8. The call came at 8 p.m..
9. I think the typewriter cost $700 (?)
10. Open the safe at nine o'clock!
11. Won't you drop the card in the mail today
12. Don't you think it would be a good idea to call Mrs. Taylor
13. You called Mr. Little yesterday, didn't you
14. How large will the ad be   one page   a half page   two pages
15. I doubt that he can answer your question

EXERCISES   **245**

EXERCISE 26   **PUNCTUATION: COMMAS**

Insert any missing commas in these sentences. Circle any commas that are not needed.

Example: Mary read the notice⊙and decided to ignore it.

1. I saw table lamps and floor lamps at the home furnishings exhibit.
2. By 1985 air pollution laws will be very strict.
3. I heard Mr. Lee close the door but I did not hear him open it.
4. We thought that we would receive the contract by July 31 and that we would complete the building by December 1.
5. David wanted to finish the work before five o'clock but he could not do so because of the power failure.
6. Because he has worked late every day this week he is determined to finish early on Friday.
7. Mr. Scott selected either Friday July 10 or Friday July 17 for the sales meeting.
8. She talked with Mrs. James Miss Evans and Mr. Ball before she made a decision.
9. It is a dependable foolproof method.
10. Yes I think I would like a new green car like that one.
11. My cousin who graduated from the university last year has an exciting new job in Washington.
12. Anyone who could pass that test deserves an A!
13. I think that your answer is wrong.
14. It was Jane's father not her mother who visited her recently.
15. The letter was returned because it was addressed to Springfield Ohio instead of Springfield Illinois.
16. We hope Mrs. Bell that you will continue to be one of our satisfied customers.
17. The report that Mrs. Leslie submitted, has been lost.
18. The beautiful, valuable, antique, ring was on display in the shop.
19. Frank Stanley, III, will replace his grandfather Frank Stanley Sr. as president of the company on June 1 1980.
20. When I receive the statement I will pay for the shipment.

EXERCISE 27   **PUNCTUATION: SEMICOLONS, COMMAS**

Insert any missing commas and semicolons in these sentences. Circle any commas or semicolons that are not needed.

Example: The secretary read the letter quickly; therefore, she did not find all of the errors.

1. When I saw the advertisement for the sale in the paper I planned to attend for I thought there were many bargains advertised.
2. Many of the national parks are closed because of the drought; as a matter of fact more parks are closed than are open.

EXERCISES 246

3. Friday July 1 Friday July 8 and Friday July 15—are all possible dates for conducting the balloting.
4. No conjunction is used in this sentence to connect independent clauses therefore a semicolon is used to separate the clauses.
5. Our company produces many fine products it has, in fact, a reputation for quality merchandise.
6. Mr. Scott paid his license fees before the due date that is August 1.
7. I cannot wait any longer for your answer I assume that you are not interested in the job.
8. We were told that the company was considering Seattle Washington Boise Idaho Denver Colorado or Phoenix Arizona as a possible site for the plant.
9. At the next meeting the president plans to introduce a new motion to raise dues by 10 percent.
10. In the first quarter prices rose 5 percent in the second quarter 3 percent and in the third quarter 7 percent.

EXERCISE 28 OTHER PUNCTUATION

Insert the missing quotation marks, dashes, colons, parentheses, brackets, and italics in these sentences.

Example: The quotation, " 'Tis an ill cook that cannot lick his own fingers," comes from Shakespeare's <u>Romeo and Juliet.</u>

1. Mr. Daw dictated, Dear Mr. Dun; but his secretary transcribed, Dear Mr. Fun.
2. Many of the dividends came from large corporations that is, General Motors, Exxon, and International Business Machines.
3. Many large corporations for example, General Motors, Exxon, and International Business Machines have paid dividends for many years.
4. I heard him ask, Is Mrs. Hanna in?
5. Please enter one-year subscriptions to each of these magazines <u>Harper's,</u> <u>The New Yorker,</u> <u>The New York Review of Books,</u> and <u>American Heritage.</u>
6. The letter said, The affect sic was devastating.
7. The directions for assembling the toy read 1 read all of the directions before you begin putting the toy together, 2 check to see that the carton contains all of the parts, and 3 fit the numbered parts together.
8. I do not think, Mrs. Steele dictated, that you want your policy to lapse. Therefore, I suggest that you send us your check immediately.
9. I read in the Los Angeles Times that the decision in the case was based on Williams v. United States.
10. I began typing the well-known quotation from Dicken's A Tale of Two Cities It is a far, far better thing I do, than I have ever done, etc.

EXERCISES   247

EXERCISE 29 **ALL PUNCTUATION**

Insert any needed punctuation in these sentences.

Example: Mrs. Gray listed three qualifications for the job: (1) typing speed of 75 words per minute, (2) shorthand speed of 100 words per minute, and (3) transcription speed of 35 words per minute.

1. There were chalk erasers pencils etc on the desk in the classroom
2. My sister Linda who works for a large bank is visiting me in August
3. Miss Allen said that she would finish the letter quickly and that it would be mailed by five o'clock
4. The new advertising campaign which was started last spring is proving very successful
5. I can type the letter right away and when I finish it I will bring it to you for signature
6. Two of our customers Johnson & Smith Inc. and Thomas Martin Ltd did not receive copies of our price list
7. If you cannot finish the billing you should tell Mr Evans so that he can get someone to help you
8. The bonds will mature in January 1998
9. Although I did not want to work on Saturday I knew that it would be necessary if the typing was not finished on Friday
10. To serve our customers is the purpose of our company

EXERCISE 30 **MECHANICS: ABBREVIATIONS, CAPITALIZATION, NUMBERS**

In the following sentences underline any words that should be capitalized, that are incorrectly capitalized, or that contain errors in the writing of numbers or abbreviations.

Example: 75 People were hurt in the apartment house fire at 8 o'clock on Feb. seventh.

1. On Mar. first Mr. horton left on American airlines for Calif. for a 2-wk. vacation.
2. My Check #475 for 27 dollars was issued Aug. 1 in payment of the monthly statement.
3. After Aug. 31st John's address will change from 634 S. W. 12 Street to 4101 2d St.
4. Mr. Jas. Norman, Junior, will replace his father, Mr. Jas. Norman, Senior, as pres. of the co. on 7/1/80.
5. Judy has worked as a Computer Analyst for Standard Mfg. Co. for 7 yrs.
6. Our neighborhood Grocery Store is open 7 days a wk. and has been in business since the Fall of nineteen seventy.

EXERCISES   **248**

7. I think Saint Thos. is an island in the Carribean.
8. The cost of the new Smith Bldg. on 5th Ave. will be twenty million dollars, and it will not be finished before the Spring of '85.
9. The savings and loan co. lent Mr. Jones twenty thousand dollars for 3 yrs. at eight percent interest.
10. Bill's Summer cottage is one hundred miles North of the city in the Blue Mts.

key to exercises

KEY TO EXERCISES 250

Note: Some of the exercises require that sentences be rewritten. Suggested answers for these exercises are given below. There are, of course, other satisfactory answers.

EXERCISE 1 KINDS OF SENTENCES

1. simple
2. complex
3. compound-complex
4. complex
5. simple
6. simple
7. complex
8. complex
9. compound
10. simple

Underline: Mr. Jones, Mr. Scott, are
you, do think; computer, will help
I, cannot find; I, think; they, are
Many, have received; who, work
system, seems
company, was
employer, reported; sales, profits, rose
windows, were shattered; no one, was hurt
windows, were shattered; no one, was hurt
you, can complete, mail

EXERCISE 2 SYNTAX: WORD ORDER

1. Your order for woolen fabrics will be shipped as soon as we receive your check for $275.
2. We are sorry that we cannot ship your order for auto parts. Because of a fire in our factory, no orders can be shipped for three months.
3. We are sorry that, because of a fire in our factory, we are unable to fill your order for auto parts. We suggest that you order from Jones Supply Company until we are able to resume production.
4. Your order for paint will be shipped Friday, August 9, by Mountain Auto Freight.
5. We are shipping a duplicate of your March 3 order for fabrics by air express on March 18. In the meantime, we shall continue to trace the original order that was shipped on March 5.

EXERCISE 3 TRANSITIVE/INTRANSITIVE VERBS

1. sang — Intransitive
2. sang, songs — Transitive
3. put, cup — Transitive
4. has been — Intransitive
5. do believe, story — Transitive
6. has been — Intransitive
7. was — Intransitive
8. seems — Intransitive
9. begins — Intransitive
10. begin, work — Transitive
11. has been working — Intransitive
12. are — Intransitive
13. played, hide-and-seek — Transitive
14. played — Intransitive
15. remained — Intransitive

EXERCISE 4 ACTION/BE VERBS

1. is   He can accomplish a great deal in a short period of time.
2. were   Mr. Lee's report on letter writing skills contains several pages.
3. is   Read the instructions before using the machine.
4. have been   We have manufactured fine fabrics for over a hundred years.

KEY TO EXERCISES   251

5. is   General Motors produces more automobiles than any other car manufacturer in the United States.
6. is   We plan to open a new branch store in Denver.
7. is   We expect that the store will sell both men's and women's clothing.
8. are   You can use one of several methods for handling the computer transaction.
9. is   We hope that the new typewriters will help the secretaries in their work.
10. is   We enclose our check for $500 in payment of your statement.

EXERCISE 5   ACTIVE/PASSIVE VOICE

1. were made, has been taken   We made suggestions to the Board of Directors, but it has taken no action on them.
2. has been checked, is enclosed   We are enclosing a copy of your July statement, which our accounting office checked.
3. is called   We should like to call your attention to an error in addition.
4. was made   Mr. Fisher, our accountant, made a complete check of all of the figures.
5. have been made   Superior Clothiers has made wool suits for over fifty years.
6. was sent   We sent a copy of Mr. Wilson's report to the president for his approval.
7. is called   May we call your attention to the many advantages of using the EZ Typewriter.
8. will be studied, will be made   Mr. Allen, one of our architects, will study the plans for your new building and will make any needed corrections.
9. was submitted   Mr. Carson submitted his resignation to the Personnel Division last Friday.
10. was asked   The president asked Judy to type the report.

EXERCISE 6   VERB SHIFTS: TENSE, VOICE, MOOD

1. During the drive Mr. Jay talked about the problems of traffic safety as the driver of the car broke the speed limit.
2. If I were you and if I were offered the job, I should accept it immediately.
3. The mystery story tells how the detective finds the body, discovers the motive for the crime, and exposes the killer.
4. After the job interview, Linda called me and asked for a letter of recommendation.
5. If this information concerning inflation is true and if prices continue to rise, salaries will not be adequate.
6. Open the shutters and watch the parade in the street.
7. Susan unlocked the office at eight, but the supervisor locked the doors at five.
8. Although the members of the union signed the contract, it was not approved by many of the members.
9. Mrs. Terry said that she needed my typewriter and asked that I use another.
10. I do not understand the instructions, and I want to get further clarification.

KEY TO EXERCISES

EXERCISE 7   SINGULAR/PLURAL: NOUNS/PRONOUNS

1. singular   hunches
2. singular   restaurants
3. plural   choice
4. either   none
5. singular   bodies
6. plural   synopsis
7. singular   none
8. singular   hoofs (or hooves)
9. singular   I.O.U.'s
10. plural   tooth
11. singular   ratios
12. singular   zoos
13. plural   loss
14. plural   comedy
15. singular   provisos (or provisoes)
16. plural   child
17. plural   M.D.
18. singular   staffs (or staves)
19. singular   commanders in chief
20. singular   shelves

EXERCISE 8   POSSESSIVES: NOUNS/PRONOUNS

1. week's   weeks'
2. child's   children's
3. your   your
4. someone else's   none
5. attorney's   attorneys'
6. sheriff's   sheriffs'
7. nurse's   nurses'
8. hero's   heroes'
9. lady's   ladies'
10. railroad's   railroads'
11. day's   days'
12. my (or mine)   our (or ours)
13. watchmaker's   watchmakers'
14. traveler's   travelers'
15. nobody's   none
16. girl's   girls'
17. man's   men's
18. dentist's   dentists'
19. stockholder's   stockholders'
20. Indian's   Indians'

EXERCISE 9   AGREEMENT: RELATIVE/INDEFINITE PRONOUNS

1. are, they
2. her
3. are
4. has, his
5. are
6. his or her
7. are
8. its
9. she
10. its

EXERCISE 10   AGREEMENT: SUBJECT/VERB

1. is
2. have
3. meets
4. is
5. were
6. are
7. seems
8. has
9. are
10. votes

EXERCISE 11   INDEFINITE REFERENCE

1. <u>he</u>   Mr. Williams told Mr. Davis, "I cannot do the job." or Mr. Williams said that Mr. Davis could not do the job.
2. <u>they</u>   The main problem with growing African violets is that they stop blooming.
3. <u>This</u>   Many problems are caused because the library is not open on Saturdays or Sundays.
4. <u>They</u>   The meteorologists predict that next winter will be cold.
5. <u>he</u>   Because Mr. Roberts did not know where to find the report, he asked the sales manager to find it.
6. <u>her</u>   Mary said that Janet's typing was full of errors.

7. <u>This</u> Because the Second National Bank does not open until ten and has no night deposit facilities, the restaurant is having difficulties in depositing its night's receipts.
8. <u>This</u> It is not possible to comply with the president's request to meet Monday afternoon to consider all of the items on the agenda.
9. <u>your</u> To keep lettuce fresh, put it in a plastic bag and store it in the refrigerator.
10. <u>him</u> After reading David's proposal for increasing sales and hearing Bill's objections to the plan, I agree with Bill.

EXERCISE **12** **NOUN/PRONOUN SHIFTS: SUBJECT/PERSON**

1. Our sales representatives call on companies in many California, Nevada, and Arizona cities.
2. Mr. Perry said that he was leaving and asked that I sign the letter and mail it.
3. One cannot be sensitive to criticism when one is running for public office.
4. To set off parenthetical expressions, use a pair of commas.
5. Full-time students must attend all credit classes regularly; auditing students may attend non-credit classes irregularly.

EXERCISE **13** **PLACEMENT OF MODIFIERS**

1. <u>with a pipe cleaner</u> The defendant, who was wearing Levis and a red-checked shirt and holding a pipe cleaner, sat flanked by three attorneys throughout most of the hearing.
2. <u>after his death on April 7</u> Following George Moneybag's death on April 7, some twenty groups are asking for pieces of his multimillion-dollar fortune that was left in a vaguely written will.
3. <u>given him by friends as a joke</u> On his city walks, Davis doesn't feel self-conscious about wearing the big black hat given him by friends as a joke.
4. <u>where the match is being held</u> The golf course where the match is being held is beautiful.
5. <u>only</u> The child ate only the dessert.
6. <u>Rusted by the rain</u> The man was unable to unlock the door that was rusted by the rain.
7. <u>Not being able to eat all of my dinner</u> Because I could not eat all of my dinner, the dog received an extra meal.
8. <u>reading a book and watching a movie</u> By reading a book and watching a movie, I made the long plane trip pass quickly.
9. <u>While waiting for the light to change</u> While I waited for the light to change, the fast-moving truck splashed water on me.
10. <u>on the bulletin board</u> The notice on the bulletin board attracted his attention.

EXERCISE **14** **PREPOSITIONS**

A. 1. before   3. after   5. because   7. after
   2. if   4. about, concerning 6. when   8. for
B. 1. with, with   2. to   3. of   4. to, with   5. from
C. 1. on   2. up   3. at   4. of   5. to

KEY TO EXERCISES 254

EXERCISE 15 **PARALLEL CONSTRUCTION**

1. and   Mr. Wilson asked me where the meeting would be held and whether I planned to attend.
2. and   Raise your hand when you have finished the assignment and then bring your paper to the instructor.
3. either . . . or   I want him either to take care of the matter or to transfer the account to another sales representative.
4. and   I should like to remind you that your insurance premium, which covers both your automobile and your home, is now due and to suggest that you send your check for $375 immediately.
5. and   The news reporter spent months with the presidential candidate in densely populated urban areas, in sparsely populated rural communities, and in heavily populated suburbs.
6. and   Our hotel can give you attractive rooms, low daily rates, and excellent dining facilities.
7. both . . . and   I finished the report by working both in the office and at home.
8. either . . . or   Mrs. Martin said that she would either pay the bill or return the merchandise.
9. and   The CPA examinations were given on Thursday afternoon, on Friday morning, on Friday afternoon, and on Saturday morning.
10. No carrying charges will be added to your account if:
    1. Each monthly statement is paid within 15 days of the billing date.
    2. No unpaid balance is left from the previous billing period.
    3. Any questioned items are reported within 15 days of the billing period.

EXERCISE 16 **READER/YOU EMPHASIS**

1. I, my   Would you please consider my application for the position of secretary with your company.
2. We, our   A check for $25, which represents an overpayment on your account, is enclosed.
3. I'd, me, I   Will you please send this information quickly so that it can be included in our next report.
4. I, our   You will enjoy shopping in our store.
5. We, our   You will find that our service and products are superior to those of other dealers in the area.
6. We, our, we   You can use the enclosed 25-cent coupon toward the purchase of any size of Soapo Shampoo.
7. We   Thank you for buying the all-new Speedo Bicycle.
8. I, our, our, us   Drive your car into our new gasoline station and let us service your car and fill its tank with gasoline.
9. I, I   Will you consider my qualifications for the position of accountant with your firm.
10. We, our, We, we, we, we, we   You can now have in your own neighborhood the services of our established real estate office. Salespeople in our new office, which is one of six branches, can show you property in any part of the city.

KEY TO EXERCISES 255

EXERCISE 17 GETTING TO THE POINT IMMEDIATELY

1. As we are unable to find a record of your order for rug shampoo, would you please send us a copy of your original order. As soon as we receive it, we will rush the order to you by special delivery. We hope that this will be satisfactory.
2. Our brochure, Converting to the Metric System, is enclosed.
3. The Acme dealer who handles our clock radios in your area is J. Rogers & Son, 211 Main Street, Greenfield, ID 83700. We are sure that he can help you.
4. Your X-L Pocket Calculator was shipped by parcel post on February 1. If you have not yet received the calculator, let us know by calling collect or by writing us. Another will then be sent immediately.
5. We should like to order 4 dozen No. 876 Marking Pens. If this product is not available or has been replaced by another pen, would you please let us know.

EXERCISE 18 OVERUSED AND OUT-OF-DATE EXPRESSIONS

1. larger share
2. direct, straight
3. now
4. √
5. √
6. do everything possible
7. √
8. first
9. alone
10. quickly
11. explain in detail
12. the same
13. √
14. √
15. relative
16. all of it
17. √
18. doing everything possible
19. worthless
20. √

EXERCISE 19 REDUNDANT AND REPETITIOUS EXPRESSIONS

1. occasionally
2. usually
3. often
4. warning
5. all
6. conclude
7. √
8. void
9. equally
10. (use one or the other; they have different meanings)
11. (use one or the other; they have different meanings)
12. about, concerning
13. small
14. few (fewer)
15. √
16. quoted
17. because
18. until
19. merge
20. tell

EXERCISE 20 WORDS AND TERMS TO BE AVOIDED

1. <u>a little fib</u> The salesman did not tell the truth when he said that the ten-year-old car was a late model.

KEY TO EXERCISES   **256**

2. <u>carelessly</u>, <u>impossible</u>   We found that the XY Camera that you returned for credit has been dropped; we are, therefore, returning the camera to you, for dropping it voids the warranty.
3. <u>job-wise</u>, <u>never</u>, <u>of</u>   Although the job seemed to be a good opportunity, you should not have accepted the position.
4. <u>and/or</u>, <u>can't seem</u>   The receptionist and the secretary cannot handle all of the telephone calls.
5. <u>finalize</u>   We should finish all of the plans for the fall sales campaign by July 1.
6. <u>Only a good customer like you</u>, <u>appreciate</u>, <u>tremendous</u>   We think you, as one of our good customers, will recognize the outstanding bargains in our October sale.
7. <u>neglected</u>   Did you forget to make the September payment on your account?
8. <u>failed</u>, <u>as you no doubt know</u>, <u>failure</u>   Did you return the warranty card when you purchased your Keno Television? We must have the warranty card on file in order for the warranty to be in effect.
9. <u>temporarily between jobs</u>   His reason for not working is that he is unemployed.
10. <u>stepped up</u>, <u>stunning</u>, <u>absolutely sensational</u>   We have increased production of our new fall dresses so that we can offer you a large selection of these dresses at unusually low prices.

EXERCISE 21   CONFUSED AND INCORRECTLY USED WORDS

1. disinterested
2. tell
3. rest
4. likely
5. implied
6. person
7. quotations
8. conscious
9. as
10. continual
11. edition, addition
12. affect
13. than
14. eminent
15. choose

EXERCISE 22   OPENING SENTENCES

1. Thank you for applying for a secretarial position with our firm. We do not have any openings at this time, but we shall keep your application on file for two months.
2. Your order for Excellent Typewriter Ribbons will be shipped on Friday, February 20.
3. The price of our new X-L Calculator is $49.50, including shipping charges. State sales tax is extra for New Jersey residents.
4. As soon as we receive copies of the booklet, *Care of the Typewriter*, we shall send you one. We do not have this booklet now, but we expect additional copies within ten days.
5. A check for $35, representing a refund of any overcharge on your account, is enclosed.

EXERCISE 23   CLOSING SENTENCES

1. I hope that your holiday season is enjoyable.

2. We think that you would be pleased with the many fine office supplies that we manufacture. May we expect an order from you soon?
  3. We should like to know if you are interested in Goodline Auto Supplies.
  4. We are glad that you can attend the annual sales meeting on July 31.
  5. Thank you for your order; we hope that we can fill future orders for you, too.

EXERCISE 24   APPLICATION LETTER WRITING

  1. Would you please consider my application for the position of clerk-typist that was advertised in last night's <u>Post Dispatch</u>.
  2. Would you tell me if Jones Construction has any vacancies for secretaries? I should like very much to be considered for a secretarial position with your company.
  3. I should like to come for an interview to discuss the accounting position that is open with your company. You can call me at 123-4567 between one and five any weekday.
  4. Would you please send me an application blank. I should like to submit my application for a position as computer programmer.
  5. May I come for an interview? I can be reached by telephone at 123-4567 daily after one o'clock or by mail at the address given below.

EXERCISE 25   PUNCTUATION: END OF THE SENTENCE

  1. That is the correct form, isn't it?
  2. I don't know the answer to that question.
  3. Do you know where Mr. Lacey is?
  4. Congratulations! You have won first prize in the national contest.
  5. Bill asked whether I was taking my vacation in July or August.
  6. Lock the door when you leave the office.
  7. Are you planning to leave before I return?
  8. The call came at 8 p.m.
  9. I think the typewriter cost $700 (?).
  10. Open the safe at nine o'clock.
  11. Won't you drop the card in the mail today.
  12. Don't you think it would be a good idea to call Mrs. Taylor?
  13. You called Mr. Little yesterday, didn't you?
  14. How large will the ad be? one page? a half page? two pages?
  15. I doubt that he can answer your question.

EXERCISE 26   PUNCTUATION: COMMAS

  1. I saw table lamps and floor lamps at the home furnishings exhibit.
  2. By 1985 air pollution laws will be very strict.
  3. I heard Mr. Lee close the door, but I did not hear him open it.
  4. We thought that we would receive the contract by July 31 and that we would complete the building by December 1.
  5. David wanted to finish the work before five o'clock, but he could not do so because of the power failure.

KEY TO EXERCISES 258

6. Because he has worked late every day this week, he is determined to finish early on Friday.
7. Mr. Scott selected either Friday, July 10, or Friday, July 17, for the sales meeting.
8. She talked with Mrs. James, Miss Evans,* and Mr. Ball before she made a decision.
9. It is a dependable, foolproof method.
10. Yes, I think I would like a new green car like that one.
11. My cousin, who graduated from the university last year, has an exciting new job in Washington.
12. Anyone who could pass that test deserves an A!
13. I think that your answer is wrong.
14. It was Jane's father, not her mother, who visited her recently.
15. The letter was returned because it was addressed to Springfield, Ohio, instead of Springfield, Illinois.
16. We hope, Mrs. Bell, that you will continue to be one of our satisfied customers.
17. The report that Mrs. Leslie submitted⊙ has been lost.
18. The beautiful, valuable, antique⊙ ring was on display in the shop.
19. Frank Stanley⊙ III⊙ will replace his grandfather, Frank Stanley, Sr., as president of the company on June 1, 1980.
20. When I receive the statement⊙ I will pay for the shipment.

* optional comma

EXERCISE 27   PUNCTUATION: SEMICOLONS, COMMAS

1. When I saw the advertisement for the sale in the paper, I planned to attend; for I thought there were many bargains advertised.
2. Many of the national parks are closed because of the drought; as a matter of fact, more parks are closed than are open.
3. Friday, July 1; Friday, July 8; and Friday, July 15—are all possible dates for conducting the balloting.
4. No conjunction is used in this sentence to connect independent clauses; therefore, a semicolon is used to separate the clauses.
5. Our company produces many fine products; it has, in fact, a reputation for quality merchandise.
6. Mr. Scott paid his license fees before the due date, that is, August 1.
7. I cannot wait any longer for your answer; I assume that you are not interested in the job.
8. We were told that the company was considering Seattle, Washington; Boise, Idaho; Denver, Colorado; or Phoenix, Arizona, as a possible site for the plant.
9. At the next meeting the president plans to introduce a new motion to raise dues by 10 percent.
10. In the first quarter prices rose 5 percent; in the second quarter, 3 percent; and in the third quarter, 7 percent.

KEY TO EXERCISES 259

EXERCISE 28 **OTHER PUNCTUATION**

1. Mr. Daw dictated, "Dear Mr. Dun"; but his secretary transcribed, "Dear Mr. Fun."
2. Many of the dividends came from large corporations: that is, General Motors, Exxon, and International Business Machines.
3. Many large corporations—(or ,) for example, General Motors, Exxon, and International Business Machines—(or ,) have paid dividends for many years.
4. I heard him ask, "Is Mrs. Hanna in?"
5. Please enter one-year subscriptions to each of these magazines: <u>Harper's</u>, <u>The New Yorker</u>, <u>The New York Review of Books</u>, and <u>American Heritage</u>.
6. The letter said, "The affect [sic] was devastating."
7. The directions for assembling the toy read: (1) read all of the directions before you begin putting the toy together, (2) check to see that the carton contains all of the parts, and (3) fit the numbered parts together.
8. "I do not think," Mrs. Steele dictated, "that you want your policy to lapse. Therefore, I suggest that you send us your check immediately."
9. I read in the Los Angeles <u>Times</u> that the decision in the case was based on <u>Williams v. United States</u>.
10. I began typing the well-known quotation from Dickens' <u>A Tale of Two Cities</u>: "It is a far, far better thing I do, than I have ever done," etc.

EXERCISE 29 **ALL PUNCTUATION**

1. There were chalk, erasers, pencils, etc., on the desk in the classroom.
2. My sister Linda, who works for a large bank, is visiting me in August.
3. Miss Allen said that she would finish the letter quickly and that it would be mailed by five o'clock.
4. The new advertising campaign, which was started last spring, is proving very successful.
5. I can type the letter right away; and when I finish it, I will bring it to you for signature.
6. Two of our customers, Johnson & Smith, Inc., and Thomas Martin, Ltd., did not receive copies of our price list.
7. If you cannot finish the billing, you should tell Mr. Evans so that he can get someone to help you.
8. The bonds will mature in January,* 1998.
9. Although I did not want to work on Saturday, I knew that it would be necessary if the typing was not finished on Friday.
10. To serve our customers is the purpose of our company.

* optional comma

EXERCISE 30 **MECHANICS: ABBREVIATIONS, CAPITALIZATION, NUMBERS**

These words should be underlined:
1. Mar., first, horton, airlines, Calif., 2, wk.
2. #, 27 dollars, Aug.

KEY TO EXERCISES

3. 31st, 2d, St.
4. Jas., Junior, Jas., Senior, pres., co., 7/1/80
5. Computer Analyst, Mfg., 7, yrs.
6. Grocery Store, 7, wk., Fall, nineteen seventy
7. Saint Thos.
8. Bldg., 5th Ave., twenty million dollars, Spring, '85
9. co., twenty thousand dollars, 3 yrs., eight
10. Summer, North, Mts.

index

Abbreviation, 193–196
  of calendar divisions, 195
  Canadian postal, 194, 213
  of compass points, 194
  defined, 216
  in firm names, 193
  in foreign addresses, 195
  in forming plurals, 196
  frequently used, 212
  in Latin terms, 194
  No. as, 194
  in organization names, 194
  in personal names, 193, 195
  in state names, 194, 213
  in street addresses, 195
  in tabulated material, 196
  in time elements, 194
  in titles, 193
  in weights and measurements, 195
  United States postal, 194, 213
Absolute adjective, defined, 216
Abstract language, 79
  defined, 79, 216
Accede/exceed, 75
Accept/except, 75
Acceptance of employment, letter of, 144
  sample, 144
Access/excess, 75
Action/be verbs, 20
Active voice, 23
  defined, 23, 216
  use of, 23
Adapt/adept/adopt, 76
Addition/edition, 76
Address, inside, 3
  defined, 3, 219
  sample, 2
Adjective, 38
  clauses, 40
  comparison of, defined, 217
  compound, defined, 217
  defined, 216
  form changes, 38

  phrases, 39
  placement of, 39
  predicate, 39
Adjustment or claim letters, 104–113
  sample, 108
Admission/admittance, 71
Adverb, 38
  clauses, 42
  comparison of, defined, 217
  form changes, 38
  placement of, 39
  phrases, 42
Advice/advise, 76
Advise/inform, 71
Affect/effect, 76
Agreement, 31
  of compound subjects, 34
  of collective nouns, 34
  defined, 31, 216
  of foreign nouns, 33
  of indefinite pronouns, 32
  of relative pronouns, 31
  of subject and verb, 33
  of subject as part of something, 33
Allude/refer, 71
Ambiguous statements, 66
  defined, 216
Antecedent, 31
  defined, 31, 216
Anticipatory subject, 13
  defined, 13, 216
Anxious/eager, 71
Antonym, defined, 216
Apostrophe, defined, 216
Application forms, 130–131, 142–143, 179
  credit, 179
  defined, 216
  employment, 130, 142
Application, letters of, 138
  sample, 141
Appositive, defined, 216
  punctuation of, 184

INDEX   262

Apt/liable/likely, 71
Archaic words, 59
   defined, 59, 216
Article, defined, 216
As/like, 71
Attention line, 3
   defined, 3, 216
   sample, 2

Balance/remainder/rest, 72
Be, conjugation of, 21
Biannual/biennial, 76
Bibliography, 167
   defined, 167, 216
   sample, 168
Body of letter, 5, 87, 216
   defined, 5, 87
   sample, 2
Brackets, 191
   defined, 191, 216
Bring/take, 72

Can/may, 72
Capitalization, 196–200
   of abbreviations, 199
   of calendar divisions, 197
   of course titles, 198
   of exclamations, 199
   of geographic localities, 197
   of holidays, 197
   of *I,* 199
   of initial words, 199
   of nouns with numbers, 199
   of organizations, 197
   of personal titles, 198
   of proper adjectives, 196
   of proper nouns, 196
   of religious terms, 197
   of titles of literary words and art, 198
   of trade names, 198
Carbon-copy notation, 7
   defined, 7, 216
   sample, 2
Case, 29
   defined, 29, 216
Choose/chose, 76
Claim or adjustment letters. See Adjustment letters.

Clauses, 14
   adjective, 40
   adverb, 42
   defined, 14, 216
   dependent, 15
   independent, 14
   noun, defined, 219
   relative, defined, 221
Cliché, 62
   defined, 216
Closing, 87
   defined, 87, 216
Collection letters, 113
   sample, 115, 116
Collective nouns, agreement of, 33
Colloquialism, defined, 217
Colon, 190
   defined, 190, 217
   use of, 190
Coma/comma, 76
Commas, 182–186
   defined, 182, 217
   miscellaneous uses, 185
   to separate clauses of compound sentence, 182
   to separate items in series, 182
   to separate coordinated adjectives, 183
   to set off explanatory elements, 185
   to set off introductory elements, 183
   to set off nonrestrictive modifiers, 184
Comparative degree, 38
   defined, 38, 217
Complement, defined, 217
Complex sentence, 15
   defined, 15, 217
Compound adjectives, 43
   defined, 43, 217
Compound-complex sentence, 16
   defined, 16, 217
Compound noun, defined, 217
Complimentary close, 5
   defined, 5, 217
   sample, 2

INDEX

Compound sentence, 15
  defined, 15, 217
Compose/comprise, 76
Concrete language, 79
  defined, 217
Consul/council/counsel, 76
Conjunctions, 48–50
  conjunctive adverb, 49
  coordinate, 48
  correlative, 48
  defined, 217
  subordinate, 49
Conjunctive adverb, 49
  defined, 49, 217
Connectors, 44–50
Conscience/conscious, 72
Consumer complaints, 176
Continual/continuous, 72
Contractions, defined, 217
Coordinate conjunction, 48
  defined, 48, 217
Correlative conjunction, 48
  defined, 48, 217
Credit application forms, 179
Credit letters, 117–120
  sample, 118, 119, 120

Dangling modifier, 40
  defined, 217
Dash, 191
  defined, 191, 217
Data sheet, 136–139
  defined, 136, 217
  sample, 139
Date of letter, 3
Deductive, 85
  defined, 85, 217
Dependent clause, 14
  defined, 217
Dictating, suggestions for, 209–210
Dictionaries, as reference, 206
Direct/directly, 73
Direct address, defined, 218
Direct mail, 176
  defined, 218
Direct object, defined, 218
Direct quotation, 188
  defined, 188, 218

Directories, as reference, 206
Double negatives, 43
  defined, 43, 218
Dysphemism, 67
  defined, 67, 218

Eager/anxious, 71
Edition/addition, 76
Effect/affect, 76
Ellipsis, 35–36
  defined, 35, 218
  faulty, 35
  as punctuation, 181
Eminent/imminent, 76
Employment application forms. See Application forms.
Employment writing, 130–145
  for employees, 136–145
  for employers, 130–136
Enclosure notation, 7
  defined, 7, 218
  sample, 2
Envelopes, 8
  samples, 9
Equivocal statements, 66
  defined, 66, 218
Eraser/erasure, 76
Euphemism, 66
  defined, 218
Evaluation, of employees, 135–136
Exceed/accede, 75
Except/accept, 75
Excess/access, 75
Exclamation point, 181
  defined, 218
Expletive, 13
  defined, 13, 218

Favor or assistance letters, 97
  samples, 98, 99
Footnote, 166
  defined, 166, 218
Foreign language words, 60
Form letters, 128
Formal report, 155
  parts of, 160
Formally/former/formerly, 73
Former/first, 73

Fragments, sentence, 17
Full-block letter, defined, 218
Future tense, 22, 23
   defined, 22, 218

Gender, defined, 218
General sources, as reference, 206
Geographical sources, as reference, 207
Gerund, defined, 218
Gobbledegook, 64
   defined, 65, 218
Goodwill letters, 122
   sample, 122
Grammars, as reference, 207
Graphic aids, 169–173
   bar graph, 171
      sample, 170
   circle graph, 171
      sample, 172
   line graph, 171
      sample, 172
   pictograph, 171
      sample, 173
   table, 171
      sample, 173

Homonym, 75
   defined, 75, 218
Homophone, 75
   defined, 75
Hopefully, 73
Hyphen, defined, 218

Identification initials, 7
   defined, 7, 218
   sample, 2
Idiom, 77
   defined, 77, 218
   prepositional, 45
Illiterate words, 59
   defined, 59, 218
Imminent/eminent, 76
Imperative mood, 25
   defined, 25, 218
Imply/infer, 73
Incorrect expressions, 69
   illiterate usage, 69
   made-up words, 70
   malaprops, 69
   words with similar meanings, 71
   wrong prefixes, 69
Indefinite pronouns, 32
   defined, 32, 218
Indefinite reference, 34
   defined, 34, 218
Indicative mood, 25
   defined, 25, 218
Independent clause, 14
   defined, 14, 218
Inductive, 85
   defined, 85, 219
Infer/imply, 73
Infinitive, defined, 219
Inform/advise, 71
Informal report, 155
   sample, 158–160
Inside address. See Address, inside.
Insincere language, 67–69
   gross flattery, 67
   overhumility, 68
   superlatives, 68
   sweeping generalities, 68
Intensive pronoun, defined, 219
Interjection, defined, 219
Interoffice memorandum, 123
   defined, 123, 219
   sample, 124
Intransitive verb, 19
   defined, 19, 219
Irregular verb, 21
   defined, 21, 219
Italics, 191–192
   defined, 191, 219

Jargon, 62
   defined, 62, 219

Language to avoid, 62–74
Last/latest/latter, 74
Leave/let, 74
Length, of sentences, 18
Letter report, 155
   sample, 156–157
Letterhead, defined, 219

INDEX

Letters, business, 1–11
  answering of, 81
  beginning to write, 80
  body of, 5, 87
  closing of, 87
  initiating writing of, 83
  opening of, 85
  organization of, 84–91
  parts of, 3–8
  purposes of, 83–84
  sample, 2, 9, 82, 89, 91, 108, 121, 124, 156, 178
  shortcuts for writing, 123–129
Liable/apt/likely, 71
Like/as, 71
Linking verbs, 20
  defined, 219
Loose/lose/loss, 76

Made-up words, 70
Mailing notation, 3
  defined, 3, 219
Malaprops (malapropisms), 69
  defined, 69, 219
Manuscript, defined, 219
May/can, 72
Memorandum report, 153
  sample, 154
Message of letter. *See* Body.
Mixed punctuation, defined, 219
Modified-block letter, 2
  defined, 219
  sample, 2
Modifiers, 38–44
  adjective, 39
  adverb, 41
  defined, 38, 219
  nonrestrictive, 41
  placement of, 39
  prepositional phrases as, 46
  restrictive, 41
  usage of, 38
Mood, 25–26
  defined, 25, 219
  imperative, 25
  indicative, 25
  shifts in, 26
  subjunctive, 25

Multicopy memorandum forms, 127

Negative terms, 78–79
Nominative case, defined, 219
Nonrestrictive modifiers, 41
  defined, 41, 219
  placement of, 41
  punctuation of, 184
Notations, 3, 7
  mailing, 3
  samples, 2
  after signature, 7
Nouns, 27–37
  agreement of, 31
  case of, 29
  defined, 27, 219
  plural forms of, 27–28
  possessive forms of, 28–29
Number, 27–28
  defined, 219
  as property of nouns and pronouns, 27
Numerals, expression of, 200–203
  in ages, 201
  beginning a sentence, 201
  below ten, 201
  for centuries, 202
  for days of month, 202
  for decades, 202
  as fractions, 201
  in house numbers, 202
  indefinite, 201
  as money, 203
  with more than one number, 202
  with o'clock, 201
  for periods of time, 201
  round, 201
  of streets, 202
  over ten, 202
  as weights and measures, 203

Object of preposition, defined, 219
Objective case, defined, 219
Obsolete words, 59
  defined, 59, 220

INDEX

Open punctuation, defined, 220
Opening, 85
  defined, 85
Order letter, 92–96
  samples, 93, 95
Outline, 164–165
  defined, 220
  kinds of, 164–165
Overhumility, 68
Overused expressions, 62–64

Parallel construction, 50–53
  with articles and prepositions, 51
  with correlative conjunctions, 51
  defined, 50, 220
  in listing points, 52
  in writing units, 52
Parentheses, 191
  defined, 191, 220
  use of, 191
Participle, defined, 220
Parts of speech, 19
  chart of, 20
  defined, 19, 220
  functions of, 19
Party/person, 74
Passive voice, 23
  defined, 23, 220
  use of, 23
Past tense, 22
  defined, 22, 220
Perfect tense, 22
  defined, 22, 220
  use of, 22
Periods, 180–181
  defined, 180, 220
  as ellipsis, 181
  at end of sentence, 180
  special uses, 180
Person, 30
  choice of, 30
  defined, 30, 220
  nouns and pronouns as, 30
  shifts in, 36
Person/party, 74
Personal business writing, 174–179
  pointers for, 175
  sample, 178
  situations requiring, 176–179
Personal pronouns, 29
  chart of, 29
  defined, 220
Phrasal preposition, 44–45
  defined, 44, 220
Phrase, 14
  absolute, defined, 216
  adjective, 39
  adverb, 42
  defined, 14, 220
  prepositional, 44
  verb, 19
Plurals, 27–29
  of compound nouns, 28
  defined, 220
  of nouns ending in *f* or *fe*, 28
  of nouns ending in *ch*, *sh*, *s*, or *z*, 27
  of nouns ending in *o*, 28
  of nouns ending in *y*, 27
  of numbers, 28
  of pronouns, 29
  of signs and symbols, 28
Poetic words, 59
  defined, 59, 220
Positive degree, 38
  defined, 38, 220
Positive terms, 78–79
Possessive case, 28–29
  with compound nouns, 28
  defined, 220
  in expression of amounts, 29
  in expression of personification, 29
  in expression of time, 29
  with nouns ending in *s*, 28
  with nouns not ending in *s*, 28
  with names of organizations, 29
  with personal pronouns, 29
  to show joint ownership, 29
  use of, 28
Postal card, 125
  sample, 127
Postal sources, as reference, 207
Postscript, 7, 103

INDEX

defined, 7, 220
sample, 2, 8
Predicate, 13
   defined, 13, 220
Predicate adjective, 39
   defined, 39, 220
Predicate nominative, defined, 220
Prefix, defined, 220
Prepositional phrase, 44
   defined, 44, 220
Prepositions, 44–48
   defined, 44, 220
   ending a sentence, 47
   idiomatic use of, 45
   phrasal, 44
   in phrases, 44
   nine most used, 45
   as modifiers, 46
   unneeded, 47
Present tense, 22
   defined, 220
Primary tenses, 22
Principal parts of verbs, 21
Progressive verb, defined, 221
Pronouns, 27–37
   agreement of, 31
   case of, 29
   chart of personal, 29
   defined, 221
   indefinite, 32
   person of, 29
   plural forms of, 29
   possessive, 29
   relative, 31
Proofreaders' marks, 211
   defined, 221
Proper adjective, defined, 221
Proper noun, defined, 221
Punctuation, 180–192
   brackets as, 191
   colon as, 190
   comma as, 182–186
   dash as, 191
   exclamation point as, 181
   italics as, 191
   parentheses as, 191
   period as, 180
   question mark as, 181

   quotation marks as, 188–190
   semicolon as, 186–188

Question mark, 181
   defined, 181, 221
   use of, 181
Quotation marks, 188–190
   defined, 221
   with direct quotation, 188
   omission of words in quotation, 188
   with other marks of punctuation, 189
   other uses of, 189
   as single quotation marks, 188
   special uses of, 189
Quotation/quote, 74

Rare words, 59
   defined, 59, 221
Reader-oriented writing, 53–56
   addressed to person, 53
   getting to point immediately, 54
   unknown writer, 54
   use of *I* or *we*, 54
   answering promptly, 55
Reality/realty, 76
Recommendation, letters of, 133–135
Redundant expressions, 64–65
   defined, 64, 221
Reflexive pronoun, defined, 221
Refer/allude, 71
Reference sources, 206–208
Refusal, letter of (Employment), 144
   sample, 144
Regional words, defined, 221
Relative clause, defined, 221
Relative pronoun, defined, 221
Remainder/balance/rest, 72
Repetitious expressions, 64
Reports, 146–173
   documentation of, 166
   format of, 166
   forms of, 153
   graphic aids for, 169
   outline for, 164

samples, 154, 156, 158
steps in writing, 164
Request for information, 96–97
   sample, 97
Resignation, letter of, 145
   sample, 145
Respectfully/respectively, 74
Restrictive modifiers, 41
   defined, 41, 221
   placement of, 41
   punctuation of, 184
Résumé. *See* Data sheet.
Routine letters, 120–122
   sample, 121
Run-on sentence, 17
   defined, 17, 221

Sales letter, 100–104
   sample, 103
Salutation, 4
   defined, 4, 221
   sample, 2
Secretarial handbooks, as reference, 207–208
Semicolons, 186–188
   defined, 221
   to separate clauses of compound sentences, 187
   to separate items in series, 187
   to separate explanations and enumerations, 187
Sentence fragment. *See* Fragment, sentence.
Sentences, 12–18
   complex, 15
   compound, 15
   compound-complex, 16
   defined, 15, 221
   kinds of, 15
   length, 18
   parts of, 12
   simple, 15
   order of, 16
   fragment, 17
   run-on, 17
Shifts, 25, 36
   defined, 25, 221
   in mood, 26

in person, 36
in subjects, 36
in tense, 25
in voice, 26
Shipping sources, as reference, 207
Shortcuts, letter-writing, 123–129
Signature, 6
   defined, 6, 221
   sample, 2
Simplified letter style, 4
   defined, 221
   sample, 9
Singular, defined, 221
Slang, 60–62
   defined, 60, 221
Sound-alike words, 75–77
Speech, parts of. *See* Parts of speech.
Style, 193–203
   abbreviations, 193–196
   capitalization, 196–200
   numerals, use of, 200–203
Style books, as reference, 207
Subject line, 5
   defined, 5, 221
   sample, 2
Subject of sentence, 13
   defined, 13
   omission of, 37
   placement of, 13, 37
   shifts in, 36
Subjunctive mood, 25
   defined, 25, 222
Subordinate conjunctions, 49
   defined, 49, 222
Suffix, defined, 222
Superlative degree, 38–39
   defined, 39, 222
Superlatives, 42, 68
Sweeping generalities, 68–69
Synonym, defined, 222
Syntax, 16
   defined, 16

Take/bring, 72
Technical words, 59
   defined, 59, 222

INDEX

Telephone, use of in place of writing, 123
Tenses of verbs, 22–23
  defined, 22, 222
  perfect, 22
  primary, 22
  shifts in, 25
Than/then, 77
Thank-you letters, 143, 177
  employment, 143
  personal, 177
  sample, 143
Transitive/intransitive, 19
Transitive verbs, 19
  defined, 19, 222
Travel sources, as reference, 207
Trite expressions, 62
  defined, 222

Usage books, as reference, 208
Usage, nonstandard, 58–62
  archaic, 59
  foreign-language, 60
  jargon, 62
  illiterate, 59
  obsolete, 59
  poetic, 59
  rare, 59
  regional, 60
  slang, 60
  technical, 59

Verbals, 20
  defined, 20, 222
Verbs, 19–26
  action, 20
  auxiliary, 19
  be and conjugation of, 21
  defined, 19, 222
  linking, 20
  mood of, 25
  order of, 26
  principal parts, 21
  shifts in, 25
  tense, 22
  transitive/intransitive, 19
  voice of, 23
Visual aids. *See* Graphic aids.
Voice of verbs, 23–25
  active, 23
  defined, 23, 222
  passive, 23
  shifts in, 26
  use of, 23–25

Weather/whether, 77
Word sources, as reference, 206
Words that do not exist, 69
Words with similar meanings, 71–74
Writing books, as reference, 207
Wrong prefixes, 69

ZIP Code abbreviations, 213